EVERYTHING®

GUIDE TO STARTING AND RUNNING A RETAIL STORE

Dear Reader,

Ever wonder what it would be like to start your own retail store? Of course you have. Just about everyone has. The difference is that *you* picked up this book and are now considering whether your life would be better as a retail store owner. It *can* be—if you know what you're getting into and how to do it successfully.

We wondered, too. Dan has an extensive business background and has owned various service businesses. Judy worked in retail before moving on to education. Together, we set up an independent retail store in Northern California and successfully ran it for nearly three years before selling it at a profit. Because we are writers, we researched and documented everything. What came out of it is proven experience as independent retailers. Yes, we made mistakes—and learned from them. In fact, we learned more from our mistakes than from our successes. Recently, we sat down and listed all the questions we had when starting, and then wrote this book to answer them for you.

This book is the result of our education, training, experience, successes, and mistakes in retailing. We cherish the days of being independent retailers in a receptive community, adding to the lives of customers and employees alike. We sincerely hope that our efforts and experience will benefit your life as you consider the opportunities of service as an independent retailer.

Best wishes,

Dan Ramsey and Judy Ramsey

WELCOME TO THE

EVERYTHING
CAREER GUIDES

These handy, accessible books give you all you need to tackle a difficult project, gain a new hobby, or even brush up on something you learned back in school but have since forgotten. You can choose to read from cover to cover or just pick out information from our four useful boxes.

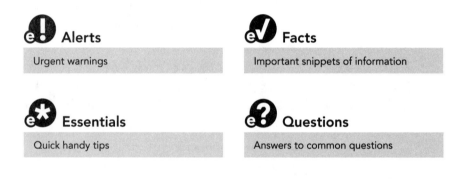

Alerts

Urgent warnings

Facts

Important snippets of information

Essentials

Quick handy tips

Questions

Answers to common questions

When you're done reading, you can finally say you know **EVERYTHING**®!

PUBLISHER Karen Cooper

DIRECTOR OF ACQUISITIONS AND INNOVATION Paula Munier

MANAGING EDITOR, EVERYTHING® SERIES Lisa Laing

COPY CHIEF Casey Ebert

ACQUISITIONS EDITOR Lisa Laing

SENIOR DEVELOPMENT EDITOR Brett Palana-Shanahan

EDITORIAL ASSISTANT Hillary Thompson

EVERYTHING® SERIES COVER DESIGNER Erin Alexander

LAYOUT DESIGNERS Colleen Cunningham, Elisabeth Lariviere, Ashley Vierra, Denise Wallace

Visit the entire Everything® series at *www.everything.com*

THE

EVERYTHING®

GUIDE TO STARTING AND RUNNING A RETAIL STORE

All you need to get started and
succeed in your own retail adventure

Dan Ramsey and Judy Ramsey

Avon, Massachusetts

To the success of our readers in finding and
enjoying a lifestyle retail business.

An Everything® Series Book.
Everything® and everything.com® are registered trademarks of F+W Media, Inc.

Published by Adams Media, a division of F+W Media, Inc.
57 Littlefield Street, Avon, MA 02322 U.S.A.
www.adamsmedia.com

ISBN 10: 1-59869-783-8
ISBN 13: 978-1-59869-783-4
eISBN 10: 1-60550-767-9
eISBN 13: 978-1-60550-767-5

Printed in the United States of America.

10 9 8 7 6 5 4 3 2

Library of Congress Cataloging-in-Publication Data
is available from the publisher.

This publication is designed to provide accurate and authoritative information with
regard to the subject matter covered. It is sold with the understanding that the publisher is not engaged in rendering legal, accounting, or other professional advice.
If legal advice or other expert assistance is required, the services of a competent
professional person should be sought.

—From a *Declaration of Principles* jointly adopted by a Committee of the
American Bar Association and a Committee of Publishers and Associations

Many of the designations used by manufacturers and sellers to distinguish their
products are claimed as trademarks. Where those designations appear in this book
and Adams Media was aware of a trademark claim, the designations have been
printed with initial capital letters.

This book is available at quantity discounts for bulk purchases.
For information, please call 1-800-289-0963.

Acknowledgments

The list of people and businesses who have contributed to our retailing education is quite long, and probably boring to anyone but the authors. Thanks to Eastern Oregon University, Evergreen College, and Iowa State University for offering their best efforts to educate us. Thanks, especially, to Clark College of Vancouver, Washington, for bringing us together.

For this book, the authors thank editor Lisa Laing and agent Bob Diforio, two consummate professionals who also make writing fun. Thanks also go to Brett Palana-Shanahan and Kate Petrella for helping make this book more valuable to readers. Especially, we thank our many thousands of customers who taught us how to help them for fun and profit.

Top Ten Things Every
Successful Retailer Must Know

1. Who your customers are

2. What your customers want

3. How your customers perceive your business and employees

4. Who your competitors are

5. What your competitors are doing right now

6. What your inventory level is for all merchandise in your store

7. What your turnover is for all merchandise

8. What your profitability is for all merchandise

9. Where your losses are going

10. How to continue to enjoy what you are doing

Contents

Introduction

Retailing is big business. That is, if *$4 trillion a year* impresses you. Big-box and franchise stores get a chunk of that, but a significant—and growing—percentage is done by small, independent retail stores that sell everything from abaci to zithers. The owners, typically one or two people who love what they sell, make a good living and enjoy their lives. Independent retail stores are lifestyle businesses. Maybe it's a lifestyle for *you*.

The problem is that so many business books are written for folks with loads of cash or credit, and they focus primarily on the profit side of business. Financial profit is vital to staying in business, but it isn't the *only* reason to open a store. There are many types of retailing rewards, and not all of them have a price tag. Most small business books don't cover the other reasons for retailing. They don't see the other side of owning your store: helping customers fulfill their needs, giving employees a living wage, and building your community.

The Everything® Guide to Starting and Running a Retail Store is written by lifestyle retailers for readers who are considering their own stores. Candidates have lots of questions. What can they profitably sell? What are the start-up costs? How much will their store make? How can it serve both the customers and the owner(s)? Should they sell online? How can a small retailer ever compete with the big-box stores like Wal-Mart, Target, and all the others that seemingly have everything in the world at low prices? These and hundreds of other questions are answered for you in this book.

There are many types of independent retail stores. All face about the same problems as they set up and operate. Chapters 1 through 4 will help you plan for retail success. Chapters 5 through 13 tell you what you need to know about starting your retail store. Chapters 14 through 17 offer specifics on running your store day-to-day. Chapters 18 through 22 show you how to build and, if you desire, eventually sell your store. Along the way you'll learn how to use technology to compete with big stores and how to increase profits with online sales. The appendices include retailing resources and a comprehensive glossary of retailing terms. The authors suggest that you read through the entire book before making a full commitment to retailing, then read it again once your store has begun and is growing.

To clarify basic business principles, the authors use Bob's Widgets as an example retailer. You'll see Bob's business plan and watch him start and run his store with practical tips and advice. In addition, sidebars offer additional information that you can put to work right now as you plan your own store. The sidebars include E-Fact (facts and statistics), E-Alert (cautions), E-ssential (tips), and E-Question (questions and answers), written to clarify and expand retailing basics.

Maybe lifestyle retailing is exactly what you're looking for. Maybe not. This book will help you make that decision based on real-world information and advice developed by experienced lifestyle retailers.

Please invite us to your store's Grand Opening! E-mail us at *retail@danramsey.com*.

CHAPTER 1

How the Retail Business Works

People love to shop. They buy at mega-malls, strip malls, big-box stores, downtown stores, corner shops, kiosks, booths, and online. And they shop for everything under the sun, from air conditioners to zippers. Besides filling a physical need, shopping, for many, fulfills an emotional need. You're a shopper who is now thinking about turning your time, money, and skills into a retail store. This chapter outlines the basic principles and practices of retail and will help you decide whether starting and running a retail store is the right decision for you.

What You Already Know about Retail

You already know something about retail sales and how they operate—at least from the customer side of the counter. Maybe you've even worked behind a counter or two. You'll need to know more than that, of course, but it's a good place to start your journey.

The journey begins by summarizing your shopping experiences, your retail background, and your retail friends, and then adding a healthy dash of common sense.

Your Shopping Experiences

Chances are that you first considered opening a retail store because you are an experienced shopper. You may have been in a gift shop and said to yourself, "I could do this" or "If I had this store I'd make things easier to find." Or maybe your first thought as a potential retailer was "This community really needs a friendly jewelry store."

So you already know that retailing can be fulfilling for the shop owner, helpful to the customer, and a service to your community. Those aren't adequate reasons to go out and rent a building, but they illustrate an understanding of the needs that retailers and customers have. For now, use a notebook to note your shopping experience and how you, as a customer, like to be treated. One of the greatest assets in retailing is being a store owner who thinks like a customer.

✹ Essential

Organizing your thoughts is an excellent way to begin planning your success as a retailer. Start by picking up a notebook or opening a new word-processor file to document your journey. Make notes on retailing basics, resources, store ideas, and further research. Writing it down can help you retain information and develop creative ideas. Keep your retail notebook with you as you shop.

Your Retail Background

More than half of the people in the work force have held a retailing job during their career. For some it was as a retail clerk. Others didn't directly interact with customers, but provided a secondary service such as stocking shelves or delivering merchandise. This retail experience can be a beginning point for your plans to start and run your own successful retail store. If you do have this experience, jot down what you liked and didn't like about your job. How would you, as a retail employee, like to be treated?

Your Retail Friends

Some of your close friends may be in the retail sales business right now. If you don't have friends in retailing, ask a friendly clerk or even a store owner with whom you trade. Ask about their experiences, their training, and their suggestions on how to run a profitable retail store. You may not use all of their ideas, but it will give you a different perspective on the retail trade. Take notes.

Your Common Sense

As a retailer you will need to solve dozens of problems every day. The best tool for making smart decisions is the skill of problem analysis and resolution, also known as common sense. It's a skill you will develop even further as you build your retail store. For now, apply your inherent problem analysis and resolution skills to begin your retail journey. Start gathering a deeper analysis of retailing (with this book and your retailing notebook) until you are ready to make the best resolution.

Retailing 101

With that little warm-up exercise out of the way, it's time to define exactly what retailing is. You have been a retail customer and maybe even worked in the trade, but may not have developed a definition. Retail is, by definition, the sale of small quantities of goods directly to the user. The word *retail* comes from the French word *retaillier,* meaning cut up or divided up. Thus a merchant who bought a large quantity of one or more products, then divided it up into smaller quantities for resale to consumers, was called a *retailer.*

Buying Wholesale

Wholesale is the resale of large quantities of goods to a retailer. In most cases, the wholesaler purchases these large quantities directly from the manufacturer, though there may be other sellers—distributors, consolidators, importers, and others—in the process. The manufacturer makes a thousand widgets, selling a hundred to each of ten wholesalers, who then sell five to each of twenty retailers, who sell one to each of five customers. It's not quite that simple, but you get the idea. Chapters 11 and 12 will give you more information about selecting initial stock and replacing sold stock through wholesalers.

Pricing

A *price* is the monetary value placed on a product or service. Of course, there's much more to it than that, but that's the bottom line. The craft of pricing has greatly changed since the early days of *keystone* pricing, when a retailer simply set the retail price at twice of what was paid to the wholesaler for the product. Modern pricing is much more complex. Chapter 11 will help you determine pricing for your retail merchandise.

Selling Retail

A *retail transaction* occurs when a customer agrees to pay the retailer's price for a product or service. By doing so, the customer agrees that the perceived value of the product is worth the value of the monetary price. In most cases, the customer is also buying convenience. The customer doesn't have to buy a five-year supply of widgets, but can expect to come back and purchase another widget when this one is used up or broken. The customer also can pay by cash, check, credit, or debit—all more convenient than trading an hour's labor for a widget. Buying small quantities of products at a value price in a convenient location and monetary transaction is called *retail shopping*.

The Merchandising Process

Wouldn't it be great if all a retailer had to do was place the products on a table and let the customers pick up what they wanted and pay for it? Maybe the first retailers got away with that, but competition among retailers has made simple retailing a thing of the past. That's because customers wouldn't long put up with sloppy retailing: "Bob's Widgets has a much better selection in all sizes, and the clerks are so helpful." Bob's business grows and the sloppy retailer is soon looking for another trade. Obviously, there's more to the merchandising process than just placing products on a table. There's selection, presentation, and transaction.

Product Selection

Customers want choices. They don't want just shoes; they want a wide variety of shoes for men, women, and children in a variety of sizes. A single customer wants just one pair of shoes in his size. Your shoe store sells to more than just one customer, so you must stock a wide selection. And the selection must meet the current and anticipated needs of a diverse group of people that you've previously defined as "your customers."

Product Presentation

Products that you have put away in a forgotten location won't sell, because the customer doesn't know about them. A product that is placed in a logical location within a well-designed store has a better chance of being purchased. And if the product's packaging illustrates its use or explains the value or application of the product, that product—if value priced—may soon be part of a sales transaction.

Sales Transaction

A *sales transaction* occurs when a seller and a buyer agree to trade ownership of a product (or service) for money. That's the goal of your retail store: sales transactions. Lots of *profitable* sales transactions. These transactions occur because the products that you have selected and presented sufficiently meet the needs of your customers that they are willing to purchase them for your price.

All of this may sound like a simplification of the retail process. It is. However, most retailers fail because they forget the basics of meeting customer needs at a profit. There's certainly much more to retailing than this, but all retail success is built upon the foundation of offering value to customers.

The Back Room

The side of retailing that customers typically don't see is called the back room. The back room contains the supporting materials and services that make the sales transaction successful. It's the inventory of products standing by to be moved to the sales floor, the supplies used in the retail process but not sold to the customer, and the things that managers and employees need to do their jobs. Managing the back room is an important task in retailing. It can be critical to profitability.

Inventory

Your goal as a retailer is to reduce or eliminate unique back room inventory. That's because if the inventory isn't out on the main floor—the *sales floor*—it has much less chance of selling. Customers can't buy what they don't know about.

 **Question**

Do I need a degree in business or in retailing to manage a store?
No, but everything you learn about business and retailing will help you succeed. Many retail candidates start with evening classes or books on financial management, banking, and sales and marketing, and then take a job in retail to apply what they've learned.

Successful retail stores make sure that they have at least a few of every product they sell out on the floor; the back room only holds redundant stock. Some types of retail stores require extensive redundant stock due to fast sales or slow restocking time. If it takes six months to fill an order for your stock of imported products, your back room should have more than you will sell in six months. However, keeping back-room stock also means that you must frequently check the sales floor and replenish it with stock from the back room. Inventory will be discussed further in Chapters 11 and 12.

Supplies

No matter what type of retail operation you run, you will need supplies. These may include cash register tape, shopping bags in which to put customer purchases, and printer paper, as well as a variety of specialty supplies needed by specific types of retailers. Supplies must be tracked and ordered just like inventory, so they must be easily found when needed. Chapter 9 covers planning your retail store layout, including the back room.

Support

Where will your office be? Where will employees take a break or eat lunch? Where will you store holiday decorations and sale signs during the off-seasons? Where do the phone lines come in? Is a bathroom required? Are sinks and plumbing required? All these elements of retailing require room and take away from the space available for sales. However, they are necessary to productivity and profitability, so you'll need to plan for them—once you determine what type of retail store you'll start and run (see Chapter 2).

How Independent Retailers Beat Big Stores

You may be wondering whether the little retail store you're thinking about can ever go up against the big retailers and make any kind of a profit. Aren't small retailers going out of business all the time? If your store does become successful, won't the big-box stores simply squash you? Why should you even consider starting and running a retail store in today's marketplace?

Good questions! They've probably occurred to you many times as you've pondered whether retailing is a business for you. The truth is that thousands of small independent retailers and specialty stores *are* competing in the same marketplace as Wal-Mart, Target, Costco, and all the other big-box stores that many shoppers shop. How do independent retailers profitably compete with the big stores? They learn how to compete on price, selection, and service.

Selling Against Price

Superduper Stores has a staff of hundreds of buyers at its corporate headquarters, each with the mandate of getting the lowest price on the products they buy for their department. Each department buys millions of dollars in wholesale goods each year, often cutting out the wholesaler and working directly with the manufacturer. In some cases, the super retailers *own* the manufacturer. How can your little independent store compete on price with the big stores?

 Fact

Annual retail sales in the United States now total approximately $4 trillion ($4,000,000,000,000), and that number is increasing by an average of about 5 percent a year, reports Plunkett Research. Retailing is the second largest U.S. industry; manufacturing is first.

It can't—and it shouldn't even try. Chances are that the superstore can sell products at a lower retail price than what you can get them for from your wholesaler. Your customers may love your store and appreciate that you are a locally owned business that employs their friends—but they're not going to pay much more than they have to.

Selling Against Selection

Whoever thought that there were 143 models of digital cameras? But there they are, lined up in the showcase at the big-box store. And the store's office supplies department has every office product you can think of. The same is true throughout the store. As a new independent retailer, you can't compete with the selection of major retailers. Focus, instead, on what they *don't* carry.

Selling Against Service

"Where's a clerk when you need one?" "Can you tell me the difference between these two models?" Good luck. Finding knowledgeable and friendly help in most big-box stores is frustrating. Yes, there are exceptions, but few.

That's how your independent retail store (whatever you choose it to be) can compete and actually profit against the big stores: by offering customer service. In other words, know what you offer and help your customers buy it. Certainly, there's more to successful independent retailing—like finding a specialty line that the big-boxes are ignoring (see Chapter 2)—but customer service is the key to your success. Based on your own experiences as a shopper, you know that you are more willing to shop at a helpful store even if it doesn't have the lowest price or the widest selection. Who needs 143 digital cameras? You just want some help finding the one that's best for your requirements.

Retailing in the Computer Age

Another advantage that big-box stores had—until recently—is close control of inventory, the sales process, employees, and other retail components, all through computers. They could, at any time, tell you exactly how many green widgets were on the sales floor, how many in the back room, how many were in the next shipment, and when it would arrive. They knew that green widgets outsold blue ones by two-to-one on Thursdays and three-to-one on Saturdays. They had control.

Fortunately, small retailers now can have nearly as much control because the costs of computers and software has been dramatically reduced. For a few thousand dollars, your independent retail store can be nearly as informed as the nearby big-box store. Chapters 8, 10, and 15 will give you the specifics. Here's an overview of how small retailers use computers.

Inventory Control

Even small retail stores have thousands of inventory items. Fortunately, each of the products found in most stores is manufactured with a Universal Product Code (UPC) that uniquely identifies the product. Even the book you're holding has a unique UPC on the back cover. Using a scanner at the checkout counter (and some software), the business computer reads the code, looks up the product and price, and, once the item is sold, removes one unit of the product from the computer's inventory database.

As products are delivered to the store, the shipping boxes are scanned and the inventory program adds the specified number of products to the inventory database. Even the shipping box has a unique shipping code label that helps the shipper and the store track the box's location. Ordering replacement inventory from most wholesalers also can be done using computer programs.

Point of Sale

At the checkout counter in most stores, the sale is automated using point-of-sale (POS) software. Depending on the complexity (and cost) of the program, the price and quantity are entered (for inventory control), discounts are issued, subtotals and totals are made, and a receipt is printed. The receipt may include the store information, the transaction date and time, the clerk's name and location, and maybe an advertisement or discount coupon for the customer's next visit.

When it's time to pay, the clerk scans a debit or credit card or passes a check through a reader, and the computer finishes the transaction. The system makes a data call to a banking service that verifies the card information and then takes the money out of your customer's account (or charges their credit account) and puts it in yours. Even if the customer pays cash, the computer will calculate change and notify the clerk.

⊛ Essential

Generic POS software for small retail stores can be purchased for less than $1,000. Free trial versions are available at *www.download.com* and other freeware sites. Search for "POS" or "point of sale." Read the reviews of these products. Try out a few before you buy any of them.

Financials

Computers don't finish their work after the sale. Depending on the software you use, the POS system can automatically update your financial records as appropriate. In real time and at any time you'll be able to see your exact inventory level on any UPC product; what sales levels have been; how the product was purchased, and when; which of your clerks sold it; and even what else the customer bought in the transaction. Chapter 15 will explain more about computerizing your financial records.

Banking

As previously mentioned, POS systems can automate transaction payment as well. Thanks to merchant accounts (see Chapter 8), banking can be securely transacted over telephone data lines. Once the transaction is verified against potential fraud and approved by the merchant card service (in seconds), the customer's bank account is reduced and the store's bank account is increased by the transaction amount.

Deposits of checks and cash are usually done in the old-fashioned way (dropping them off at the bank), but everything else (debit and credit cards) is done electronically. Even your bank statements are fully automated, with images of checks you've written appearing on the statement.

As a shopper, you've seen the phenomenon of computerized retailing. As a retailer you will truly appreciate it. It gives you many of the tools used by big-box stores to help you compete against them.

Is Retailing Right for You?

Even with all these tools at their disposal, many retailers still close up the store within the first few years. Why? There are a variety of reasons. Most retailers who fail can identify what went wrong, and maybe even why. In most cases, the failure was avoidable. Here are the primary reasons why small retailers fail:

- **Grandiose ideas.** Retailers expected that they were going to take over the business world without first investing time and money in it.
- **Lack of experience.** Retailers started a business in which they weren't knowledgeable.
- **Lack of information.** Retailers didn't do sufficient research to know what they were getting into.
- **Limited market.** Retailers tried to make a living selling something that not enough people needed.
- **Bad location.** Retailers thought that they could locate their business where *they* wanted to be rather than where *their customers* were.
- **Poor planning.** Retailers didn't understand what they were doing, and why.
- **Insufficient capital.** Retailers thought they could start on a shoestring and let the business build itself.

Does that mean you shouldn't try to start and run a retail store? Not at all. It means that you should first make sure that you have the experience, information, market, location, planning, and capital to make it a success. Most important, though, you should make sure that you really *want* to make it a success. In other words, does retailing fit your lifestyle, personal plans, and individual goals? Can you see yourself as a retailer for the next five years? If so, do you see yourself happy about it?

ⓔ Alert

Want to benefit from the experiences and advice of other small retailers in your area? Join the local chamber of commerce or local merchants association right now and attend its meeting. The topics will be helpful, but the networking you will do as you meet other local retailers will be invaluable.

To help you answer these subjective questions, here's a realistic overview of what it will take to be a successful retailer: time, money, stamina, and emotions.

Time

Depending on how you set up your store, it probably will require at least sixty hours of your time each week. You eventually should be able to reduce this with trustworthy employees, but plan on giving your business that much time for the first year. That's typical.

If you really don't think that you can give your new business sixty hours a week, consider a partner who can share the workload, or consider an online retail business instead (Chapter 19). Fortunately, not all of those sixty hours must be worked at your retail store. Thanks to portable computers, you may be able to work some of those hours (such as those spent on recordkeeping) from home or even on a business trip. However, thinking that you can operate your store successfully on just twenty hours of work a week is irrational.

Money

To set up and operate the typical small retail store requires an initial investment of up to $100,000 (see Chapter 3). A minimum is $25,000. Buying a franchise or an existing store (see Chapter 4) will cost more, in most cases. You can reduce initial costs by working without pay, but you'll need a way to pay your ongoing living expenses. An online retail business can be started for less, but you will be competing with retailers who have more capital, so you may stay unprofitable longer.

Physical Requirements

Long hours can reduce your stamina and may even lead to injuries. Make sure that you have the physical requirements to successfully start and run your retail store before you begin. Don't decide to build your own store fixtures unless you have the skills, experience, and health to do so. If you have any adverse health issues—asthma or a bad back, for instance—be certain that the retail business you select doesn't exacerbate them. Who's going to mind the store while you're recuperating?

The physical requirements of operating a retail store include lifting, storing, unpacking, and shelving inventory as well as assisting customers who need help with merchandise and purchases. In addition, you may be on your feet all day long. Are you physically ready for that?

Emotional Requirements

If, for whatever reason, your retail store must close after just a year of operation, can you handle it emotionally? What will you do next? How will others in your life treat it? Retail success is not assured—if it were, everyone would be doing it. Use your retailing notebook to identify and resolve the emotional issues that you and your life partners may have if your store doesn't succeed.

CHAPTER 2

Deciding What Retail Store Fits You

If you're thinking about opening up your own retail store you probably already have an idea of what type it is. That's good. However, before you make a full commitment, read this chapter and consider your options. It may confirm your decision, or it may help you find an opportunity that even better fits your needs and your marketplace. If nothing else, it can present you with some secondary opportunities that can make your retail store more profitable.

Your Personal Goals

Box-store retailers are started and run to make a profit. Period. However, small retail businesses and lifestyle businesses have additional goals. Make money, yes, but also contribute to the lives of the owners, employees, and customers. It's noble and it's doable. Many thousands of small retail businesses in the United States and Canada successfully combine personal and financial goals. Yours can, too.

How can you select a winning retail business that meets your needs and goals? You can do a little brainstorming, look at needs within your own lifestyle, and consider your financial and emotional needs and limitations. Here's how to start.

Brainstorming

Pull out that retailing notebook mentioned in Chapter 1 and plan on doing lots of writing. Write a short description of retail stores that you think might be successful—even those you're not yet sure you want to own. A good place to start is in your telephone book's yellow pages. If you live in a smaller community, get a phone book from a nearby metropolitan area. Go from A to Z, writing down retail business concepts. For example:

- Antiques Dealer
- Aquarium and Pet Supplies
- Baby Clothing
- Bicycles
- Clothing—Used
- Draperies
- Fabric and Sewing
- Fireplace Tools
- Garden Equipment
- Hobby and Model Supplies
- Jewelry

Include on your list anything that remotely interests you. You'll prioritize them later. For now, just get your brain thinking about the possibilities.

Lifestyle

Next, look to your own life for products that you often purchase from retailers. Add them to your list.

- School supplies
- New books
- Used books
- Woodworking materials
- Computer software

- CDs
- DVDs
- Bulk coffee and tea
- Garden tools

You're getting the idea. Fill a couple of pages in your retailing notebook with products that you have experience buying or know that others would buy. The more you list, the more opportunities you'll have to consider.

Question

What should I do if a store like the one I'm considering recently closed up?
First, do some research. Why did it close? Was it profitable? What were the owners' mistakes? Could you do better? If you find that the store closed for reasons you can remedy, contact the owners about buying the inventory and fixtures!

Financial

Okay, it's time to start trimming back your initial list of retail candidates. After reviewing your list you will see duplicates or product groups that can be combined. However, the most obvious removals will be those businesses that probably take more time, knowledge, or money to start than you have. For example, a retail garden equipment store can easily cost more than $100,000 to open, and maybe there's already a successful one nearby. Scratch it. Or, if it's something you'd like to do, consider whether there's a group of popular products within it that you could profitably sell, such as quality garden hand tools.

You don't want to eliminate all your retail candidates. You want to refine the list. Later you'll choose from among the best candidates.

Emotional

"Do what you love and the money will follow." Well, it doesn't quite work that way in retailing. It's more like "do what your *customers* love and the money will follow." Even so, you must have at least a modicum of passion for what you are selling. The more passion you have, the easier it will be to represent what you sell. For many people, operating an adult bookstore is totally out of the question, even if there is a market for it. But selling kids' books is a passion. That one stays on their lists.

As you build and refine your retail candidate list, review your past experiences with retail stores, positive and negative. Have you lived in other communities and fondly remember a favorite store? Did you visit a great store on a business trip or vacation and maybe even wonder if you'd like to run it? Do you have a friend or relative who has told you about a favorite retailer? Whatever type of store you decide to run, for whatever reason, just make sure that it is a *profitable* business.

The remainder of this chapter offers an inside look at the most popular types of independent retail businesses. They are offered to help you select the right business for you.

High-End Merchandise Retailers

Chapter 1 suggested that you should not attempt to compete against the big-box stores on price alone. Especially if you offer outstanding service, you can sell products that are higher in price than the big stores. If your local mall anchor stores are selling cosmetics at $5–$20, find a line of higher-quality cosmetics that retails for $40 and up.

Jewelry and gift stores are just two primary examples of small retail businesses that beat the big-store competition by offering products and services of a better quality, at a higher price. Here is a closer look at each.

Jewelry Retailer

Many big-box stores sell some jewelry and related items, typically of lower quality at discount prices. If jewelry is your interest, consider handling higher-priced jewelry and offering superlative service. Make minor jewelry repairs without charge. Design a store that says to customers that you know quality and you treat your customers well.

Though the retail value within a jewelry store can be high, you can work with wholesalers who will offer more expensive items to you on consignment. You can fill out the inventory with lower-priced jewelry that will be your primary sales.

Gifts

A very popular concept for independent retailers is gifts. These are gift items that aren't found at the area's major retailers. They are higher priced, of better quality, and tend to encourage collecting that will earn return customers. Gifts are often emotional or impulse buys, so the small retailer will train all employees in emotional salesmanship. For more on emotional salesmanship check out *The Everything® Sales Book*.

⬟ Essential

Gift stores require quality displays where the merchandise can best be presented. Fortunately, most gift items are small, so many gifts can be displayed in a single case. This is how you can differentiate your quality gift store from the stores that display multiple units of common gifts on shelves and racks. For more information, visit *www .giftshopmag.com* or subscribe to *Gift Shop Magazine*.

Gifts are even popular in locations where there are already many gift shops, such as in a historic or tourist town. Not everyone who visits wants a $6 trinket. Offering higher-priced gifts—and personal service—can minimize the competition.

Low-End Merchandise Retailers

In your local market, the stores may already be filled with high-priced inventory of all types. What is needed are stores that sell lower-priced products for the service employees and pensioners in your area who can't afford the expensive stores. In some more exclusive communities, the big-box stores aren't allowed, but a small, locally owned store may be welcomed.

Three popular concepts for low-end retailers include bargain stores, used books, and used clothing. One of them may meet your business goals and interests.

Bargain Store

A generation ago, these stores were called five-and-dimes. They offered low-cost merchandise that people frequently needed but didn't want to pay much for. Most items were sold for five or ten cents, with additional products available at up to twenty-five cents each. Today's version sells all or most of the merchandise at one dollar each. Inflation will soon increase the "dollar" price, so many are moving to "Bargain Store" and other concepts and offering inventory in dollar increments up to $5.

Inventory for bargain stores typically comes from wholesalers who specifically serve this field of retailing. Some sell in wholesale lots of popular items, which are shipped to you on pallets. Markup often is at least 100 percent. For $1,000 you get a pallet of popular inventory with a retail value of $2,000. If this is the type of small business you select, your relationship with one or more proven wholesalers can make or break your business.

Used Books

Used-book stores are a popular option for small retailers who love books but can't afford the high costs of setting up an independent new bookstore. A used-book store can be set up and stocked for as little as $25,000 and the owner's labor. Initial inventory can come from your own careful shopping at garage sales and library book sales or from a used-book wholesaler. Replacement inventory is largely derived from your customers, who will trade in their used books for store credit.

Because many of the books within a used-book store are no longer in print, your only competition is another store like yours. People who buy the latest novel at Target, for example, will come to you to trade in their used book and buy another by the same author. The markup on used books typically is 100 to 400 percent, though some labor is required to select and prepare the books for resale.

✅ Fact

Used-book stores that accept books as trade merchandise typically supplement their inventory with purchases from book scouts. Scouts are knowledgeable book buyers who shop garage sales, library sales, and other events and select books for resale to used-book stores. Because many book scouts don't advertise their services, you will probably need to be an employee of a bookstore to discover who its scouts are.

Used Clothing

Clothing often is tossed out before it wears out. Most modern clothing can be cleaned up and reused, especially in markets where there is a need for lower-priced clothing. The markup on used clothing is 100 to 500 percent; however, as with used books, the process requires labor, in this case to clean and prepare the clothing for resale. Used-clothing stores can be profitable near areas that sell high-priced clothing. One successful store purchased used clothing from residents of luxury homes (by appointment) and resold it at a store in a lower-middle-class neighborhood.

Used clothing and even baby items can be sold on consignment. Inventory is marked with the retail price and a code identifying the consignor. When the item sells, the consignor gets cash or credit for the purchase, typically between 25 and 40 percent of the sales price. There's more recordkeeping required for a consignment shop, but the store owner doesn't have to buy the inventory.

Specialty Merchandise Retailers

Most small retailers elect to specialize in products that aren't available at local big-box stores. In fact, some earn referrals from the big stores. "Sorry, we don't carry that item, but Bob's Widgets does."

The key to specialty merchandise retailing is selling products that customers need, but can't find elsewhere. The potential problem of specialty merchandising is that a local big-box store *could* pick up your line and customers and possibly run you out of business. It will be your job to select merchandise that makes this highly unlikely, to keep a close eye on your competitors' movements, and to develop a loyal customer base. Following are some suggestions.

Hobby Store

People love their hobbies. A consumer who will buy beans on sale may spend $500 or more on a radio-controlled airplane without blinking. And though many of the big-box stores offer some hobby merchandise, the inventory is limited and the clerks rarely know anything about it. A specialty hobby store with good customer service can successfully compete against larger and impersonal stores.

Some hobby stores focus on a specific hobby, such as RC models or model trains, while others stock a wide variety of hobby items. In most cases, the stock reflects the interests of the owner. Smart retailers will, instead, focus on the local marketplace and stock what customers will buy. Some hobby stores also choose to sell toys, at least as secondary merchandise.

The biggest competitor to hobby stores today is online retailers. In fact, it is difficult to compete with the price and selection available to the growing number of consumers who are comfortable buying online. For that reason, many brick-and-mortar (those with a physical location) hobby stores attempt to serve the two types of customers—the local buyer and the online buyer—with separate inventories. Because their business is at a retail location, they sometimes can get better deals on wholesale inventory than can their online-only competitors.

Craft Store

Craft stores used to be specialty stores. But today franchise craft stores sell a little of everything at competitive prices.

If you're considering opening up your own craft store, consider a specialty such as sewing, quilting, picture framing, woodworking, painting, and so on. Then make sure that your store is the first choice for anyone in your market who is even remotely interested in that craft. Of course, first make sure that your market will support your craft. An origami store won't succeed in most markets.

One way that successful craft stores differentiate from their competitors is by offering classes. In fact, many supplement their income with classes that relate to their specialty. If the class is after-hours, the store may stay open for class members to select merchandise.

Expert Store

Some products are more difficult for customers to select than others. For example, a new camera may take many hours to analyze and select, especially if the customer is not familiar with cameras or the newest photo technologies. If you're an expert (or can become one), your retail store could be an expert store.

The big-box stores sell cameras, so your specialty store would sell cameras to professional photographers, specialize in selecting appropriate lighting systems, or help customers select software to enhance their photos. These are expert services that customers just won't find in the big stores. You may decide to carry a brand of cameras that cannot be purchased at local big-box stores, such as Leica.

Expert stores include camera and photography, music and musical instruments, computers and software, televisions and home sound systems, car sound systems, and so on. If it is a higher-priced product or group that requires expert advice to buy, it is a candidate for your expert store.

Niche Store

Sometimes all of the major product lines and all of the major specialties are already offered in the local marketplace. What to do? Go for the niche—the specialty, specialty market.

For example, in a marketplace that already has enough sewing shops, consider a sewing machine center, which only sells and repairs machines. If the market is filled with hobby stores, consider one that offers model trains and layouts only, or one that focuses just on radio-controlled cars. If your town has enough gift shops, consider focusing on gifts for special events, such as weddings or anniversaries (there are more anniversaries than weddings!).

Use your imagination. If your marketplace is already filled in your specialty field, consider a specialty within it. Maybe the local market will support it.

Merchandise Sources

Most retailers sell new merchandise. A minority of small retailers sell merchandise that is used, but still in salable condition. The type of store that you select may dictate whether your merchandise is new or used. However, you should consider the advantages of both before you decide on your own store.

New Merchandise

The key to retailing new merchandise is selecting competitive wholesalers who not only offer what you want at a price that can make you a profit, but also dependably deliver the products.

Appendix A offers a wide variety of sources for finding appropriate wholesalers for your retail store. In addition, you can do some research by visiting stores similar to the type you've selected in other markets. You may find shipping boxes that identify the store's wholesalers. Sometimes prepriced merchandise has an identifier that can help you determine the sources. Also, watch for delivery trucks other than UPS. Larger wholesalers in metropolitan areas often have their own delivery trucks, which can be identified by their markings.

🅔✓ Fact

Retail Merchandiser is a monthly magazine for larger retailers, focusing on marketing and management issues. As a smaller retailer there is much you can learn from the big boys. If you qualify, Retail Merchandiser is free, and is available at www.retail-merchandiser.com. Or you can just visit the website, also at no charge, and get lots of information on mass retailing.

Used or Older Merchandise

Used, closeout, second-quality, and similar merchandise typically is more profitable to resell than is new merchandise. Consider selling used or remaindered (unsold older stock) merchandise, especially when you can significantly beat the prices of other stores and still make a good profit.

As pointed out in the earlier examples, used books and used clothing have a higher markup than do new items. Even though the total sale value is lower than it might be at new-merchandise stores, your total profit may be similar.

Buying and reselling closeout and remaindered merchandise can be profitable because the markup is higher than new merchandise yet there is little processing required, as there is for used books or used clothing.

Mixed Merchandise

Some stores profitably supplement their new merchandise with either used or remaindered merchandise. Why? Because customers shopping for price can get a bargain. In addition, some customers are looking for books, CDs, clothing, or other items that are no longer available as new.

The problem with selling both new and used or remaindered merchandise is keeping track of which is which. If someone buys a new blouse from you and returns it because it is defective, how do you determine whether you should credit the new or the used price? Some retailers put a cut on the clothing label to identify used merchandise. Bookstores may place an ink mark on the book spine. But if the customer says it's new, not used, and you want to keep the customer, what do you do?

The easiest solution is to sell either new *or* used merchandise. However, that may limit what you can sell and how you can compete against big-box retailers. So don't totally rule out a mixture of merchandise types. Down the road you may decide to mix—and profit.

CHAPTER 3

Analyzing Your Assets

Making the commitment to start and run a retail store is a big decision, financially and personally. It can impact you positively or negatively—or both—for many years. It can also impact relationships. Making the decision requires some analysis of your assets (financial and personal) as well as a definition of your personal goals. This chapter helps you in that analysis so that you can make the best decision about independent retailing. You'd like to get moving toward opening day, but take the time now to analyze your best route to success.

Defining Success in Independent Retailing

Every new retailer has at least one goal in common with all others: to make a profit. You can't serve your customers for years to come if you're no longer in business. But how much profit or income you need probably is different for you than for the store owner next door.

Even before you decide what retail products you'll sell, you need to analyze what "success" means to you. You don't want to get into the wrong business. Take some important time to define the three aspects of independent retail success as they relate to *you*: financial, personal, and community.

Financial Success

Yes, you want your new business to make a profit. How much profit? How soon? Are you looking for long-term financial success, or short-term? Here are a few scenarios to consider in defining financial success for your store.

- Harold needs his retail store to provide at least $4,000 a month in profit from Day One.
- Sharon has a second income source and doesn't need to draw from the profits for the first year of operation.
- Aisha can live off savings for part of the first year, but needs to begin drawing at least some from profits within three months of opening the door.
- Clyde hopes to operate his business for five years and sell it for enough capital to retire.
- Juan wants to build a long-term retail business that he can give to his children someday.

There are many ways of defining financial success. Use your retailing notebook (Chapter 1) to write your own realistic financial success goals based on your needs. Ask significant people in your life to make comments and suggestions.

Personal Success

As noted in Chapter 2, success in independent retailing isn't just about the money. Some new retailers simply want to make enough money to do what they love. Others are happy with doing something they just like to do if it will pay better. It's time to ask this question of yourself: how do you measure personal success in independent retailing? To help you answer the question, here are some examples from others:

- Frank has always wanted to be a shop owner.
- Valerie is tired of being a clerk in a retail store and wants to be the boss.

- Charles loves his business concept and would do it for free.
- Meredith enjoys helping customers, and it isn't important exactly what she is selling.
- Clarence prefers to set up a retail business where he can hire clerks to work with customers as he enjoys the back-room jobs.
- Elizabeth wants to find a business that she can operate on weekdays, leaving her weekends for family and travel.

Personal goals can dictate what you do and how you do it. Unfortunately, too many new retailers get stuck in a single concept because of passion or proximity and forget to consider their personal goals and definition of success. What is *your* definition?

Community Success

Big-box stores see community as demographics: who will buy, and why. Independent retailers see community as friends and neighbors. While demographics are vital to retail marketing, there are broader aspects of community that franchises and large stores don't consider because they are not a definable part of profit. Independent retailers can't ignore demographics—having enough customers for their chosen product line—but they can consider other aspects of merchandising, including multidimensional relationships called community.

Following are ways in which many community retailers see their roles:

- Manuel wants to share his knowledge and skills with his community through a retail store.
- Sallie plans to focus on her local specialty to build a retail business that benefits her family and her community.
- Curt wants to offer a local alternative to the nearby franchise stores.

- Ronda's retail goal is to bring additional employment opportunities to her community.
- Dave wants a business where young people can work other than at fast-food restaurants.

For most retailing candidates, community isn't the primary goal. However, for many it is a component of their decision to get into independent retailing as a lifestyle business.

Assess Your Personal Assets

Your customers will pay you for more than just the products you sell. They will pay you for your knowledge to select the products they want as well as your skills of managing a business well. You need these skills if you want your retail store to thrive. What knowledge and skills do you have now? Which do you need to succeed? Where can you learn skills you're missing?

Personal Asset Worksheet

Most people have extensive knowledge, skills, training, and experience in some area. You know how to do a thousand things and can remember a thousand facts. But the real question is this: what knowledge, skills, training, and experience do you have that are relevant to independent retailing?

Use the following Asset Worksheet to begin listing those personal assets. What should you list? Here are a few examples:

- Ability to help other people solve problems
- Knowledge of bookkeeping and banking
- Knowledge of the field of products you will sell in your store (be specific)
- Skill in successful event promotion
- Excellent communication skills (include examples)
- Strong people skills (patience, tolerance, humor)

- Business training (be specific, including coursework)
- Training relevant to your retail specialty
- Experience working in a retail store (be specific about where, and what you learned)

In addition, consider your physical health as an asset—or a liability. Retailing, especially when starting a new store, requires stamina to work the necessary long hours. In addition, make sure that you have the physical strength needed for the job. If you have back or leg problems, you probably don't want a store that will require you to move heavy boxes.

Take your time and consider the personal assets that you bring to your retail store. If you need help, ask a spouse, partner, or close friend to help you brainstorm. Look beyond your work experience for your assets. Valuable skills can come from experience in parenting, volunteering, leading a group or committee, and so on.

ASSET WORKSHEET

PERSONAL ASSET	EXAMPLE
Knowledge	
Skills	
Training	
Experience	
Financial assets	
Liquid assets	
Equity assets	
Credit assets	
Resources	
Partnership	
Business loan	
Supplier financing	
Employees	

Filling in the Blanks

It may soon become obvious which personal assets (knowledge, skills, training, experience) you *don't* yet have. For example, you may be an expert on the products that you will carry, but you don't have any retail experience. That's okay. Recognizing this, you may decide to take a part-time job in a related retail store for a while. Few retailers start their journey with a full set of these personal assets. Taking stock of your assets and your needs, and working on them, will help you reach your retailing goals.

Calculate Your Financial Assets

One of the primary personal assets you want to grow with your retail store is your financial assets. You'd like a financial return on your investment of money, time, and skills.

Before you select the appropriate retail concept for your needs, you need to analyze your current financial assets. Those assets include what you have in cash, what equity you can turn into cash, and what credit is available to you.

Liquid Assets

Liquid assets are any financial assets that are in ready-to-spend cash or in a form that you could quickly turn into cash, such as certificates of deposit. How quickly? By the time that you want to open your retail store.

Use the Asset Worksheet or your retail notebook to document these assets. Make sure you include all of them. If you need reminders, go through the last loan application you filled out. It will list your financial assets, including liquid assets (also known as short-term assets).

Equity Assets

Some of your assets may not be very liquid, especially if you own a home or other property. The difference between the property's current market value (less sales costs) and what you owe in mortgages is its *equity*. You can't immediately turn that equity into cash, so it is considered a long-term or non-liquid asset.

However, you've probably heard of home equity loans, also called second mortgages. These loans are increasingly popular, and are relatively easy to get, depending on the current equity in your home and your ability to repay what is borrowed. You could use this equity to help fund your retail store, but many financial advisers recommend against it. If the business doesn't succeed as planned, you could lose both your business and your home. Some retail candidates instead apply for a line of credit against their home equity that they can draw upon only in an emergency. Still, the risks are high and you should only consider an equity loan after talking with a qualified financial adviser and any co-owners of your property.

🛈 Alert

If you are considering a home equity loan to finance your small business or to serve as an emergency fund, do it now, before you quit your regular job. The loan's interest rate will depend on your perceived ability to repay the loan. Lenders want to see a stable employment history. Getting a loan once your primary income is from self-employment can be difficult—and expensive.

Credit Assets

A related financial asset you have is your credit, or your perceived ability to repay a loan based on your income. If you have a good job and you've paid your bills on time in the past, your credit rating probably is good. As you start and run your retail business you will need a good credit rating to lease or rent a store, get utilities and other services hooked up, buy wholesale merchandise on credit, and establish other accounts. If your credit is not so good, seriously consider holding off opening your retail store until you can repair your credit rating. Consult a reputable credit counselor to learn how to improve your credit rating.

Resources for Additional Assets

Take a close look at your Asset Worksheet, especially the financial part. Are you going to have the financial assets needed to start and run a retail store? You'll calculate your actual financial needs in Chapters 5 and 6, but you should know that a small independent retail store requires $25,000 to $100,000 in assets to get started on the right foot. If it's clear by your Asset Worksheet that you're not going to make it—or you know that your business will have higher start-up costs for required equipment—there still are things you can do to make it happen.

Modified Retail Concept

The first concession you may be able to make is modifying your retail concept. That is, cut your plans back a bit. For example, a candidate who wanted to open a flower shop determined that she didn't yet have the assets to succeed, so she decided to operate a floral kiosk in a busy mall for the first two years. If at the end of that time she had the assets she needed, she would use her good name and her customer base to open a full retail store with gifts and related items.

Another retail candidate decided to open a small bookstore online and operate it part-time until the business built enough to justify a retail store. The online component would be continued to help the fledgling brick-and-mortar store get off the ground.

If your finances don't quite meet your retail goals, don't hesitate to modify your goals. You still may reach them eventually.

Partnership

Taking in a partner to help fund the retail store is another popular way to increase assets. There are two types of partnerships (covered more fully in Chapter 8): general and limited. A general partner puts in money and time and gets to call the shots along with you. A limited partner puts in money only and may or may not (depending on your agreement) make management decisions.

The problem with partnerships is that you have to share. You not only share the costs, but also the profits. If your retail concept would barely support one person, how will it support two?

Business Loan

A business loan may be an option for realizing your retail goals. Your bank can advise you, or you can contact the Small Business Administration (*www.sba.gov*) for requirements and resources. In addition, some major credit card services offer business loans.

 Fact

The Small Business Administration (SBA) was founded in 1953 as an independent federal government body charged with helping small businesses successfully start up and run. Business loans through the SBA are made by commercial banks and other lenders and are insured by the SBA. Even if you don't need a business loan, contact the nearest SBA office to find out about its local training and counseling services.

Be aware that business loans, especially ones that are unsecured by fixed assets (such as real estate and equipment) are more expensive than many other types of loans. Shop around for the best rates available without tying up all of your equity or other assets.

Supplier Financing

Some retailers can get financing through their merchandise supplier. If your personal credit rating is good, the supplier may provide 90-day or even 120-day credit on a major portion of your initial inventory. You may need to sign an agreement making it your exclusive supplier, but this can help you start your business if you need some additional financial assistance.

Employees

Depending on the type of retail store you select, you may be able to get assets from your employees. As they will be an ongoing expense of labor, you may be able to find key employees who will participate in your business without pay in exchange for a percentage of the profits. The arrangement can be a little tricky to organize, but the results will be that you need less money to start than you otherwise would.

For example, Florence had a retired friend who agreed to clerk in her gift shop evenings and weekends for a commission on what was sold during those periods. Florence was the primary clerk during the weekdays. This arrangement helped build the store and make it more profitable by keeping it open longer hours (with no additional rent expense). When profits were adequate, Florence offered her friend a salary, but she preferred to work on commission.

Your Asset Worksheet: Liabilities

You're not done yet with your Asset Worksheet. To learn your total net worth you also need to document your liabilities. Liabilities are what you owe to others. If you buy something on credit, the something is an asset and the credit is the liability.

 Fact

The basic financial equation is Assets − Liabilities = Net Worth. Put another way: your financial worth is what you own less what you owe. You've used this formula if you've calculated home equity (Market Value − Mortgage = Equity). And you will use this formula many times as you build your business.

What are your personal liabilities?

- Home loans
- Car loans
- Personal loans
- Credit card balances
- Outstanding medical bills
- Alimony or child support

If you owe money to someone else, it is a liability whether or not you still own the asset purchased. These and other liabilities must be deducted from your assets to arrive at your net worth. Remember, these calculations are for you personally, not the business. You're trying to determine how much you can invest in a retail store. Completing this section of your Asset Worksheet will help you do that. The Asset Worksheet totals may or may not be adequate (you'll determine actual start-up and operating costs in Chapters 5 and 6), but it *will* give you a good idea of whether you have the financial and personal assets needed to invest in the retail store you've chosen. And it can help you identify which assets you need to build before you begin.

ASSETS WORKSHEET, CONTINUED

LIABILITIES

Home loans _____

Car loans _____

Personal loans _____

Credit card balances _____

Outstanding medical bills _____

Alimony or child support _____

Other _____

Your Point of No Return

At what point do you say, Yes, I'm going to open the store, or No, I'm not? Fortunately, you haven't reached it yet. Your planning is still on paper and you haven't spent any money. However, you need to be aware of your point of no return because you soon will be making decisions that require financial investment. Before that point, consider the following typical stages of commitment to a retail store.

Paper Planning

The first question you want to answer is, Will my store be profitable? You can answer the question on paper once you know how much you can invest in your business, what it will cost to start, what sales levels to realistically expect, and what your operating costs will be. Toward answering that question you can fill your retail notebook with facts, figures, calculations, and ideas without incurring much expense. Chapter 6 will guide you through developing a formal business plan.

The Decision Point

Once you've researched and compiled your investment costs and your expected profit return on that investment you can make one of these three choices:

- Go!
- Don't Go!
- Go Incrementally!

Most people who decide they want to open a retail store of their own opt to "Go!" However, prudence says the best plan is to "Go Incrementally!" even if it looks like a sure-fire plan. No plan is perfect, and you may discover a major hurdle after a few weeks of building. The smartest way to build your retail store is incrementally, implementing the least expensive requirements first. That is, don't yet sign a lease or buy fixtures for your store. Instead, develop your business plan (Chapter 6). Do all the market research you can to understand who your customers are and what they will buy.

CHAPTER 4

Franchises and Existing Stores

If you have the assets but lack retail management experience, setting up a franchise store may be a good option. You get to run a proven retail operation, get lots of professional advice, and have brand recognition from your potential customers. On the other hand, you'll have to sell what headquarters tells you to, buy from its suppliers, and only advertise through its programs. Another option you have is to buy an existing retail store and pay for someone having already set it up. Of course, it may not be exactly what you want, but you will have more latitude in changing it. This chapter offers you some insight into these store options.

Retail Franchises 101

Depending on where you live, at least half of all businesses in your area are franchises. What are franchises, and why are they a retail option? Following are some things you need to know about retail franchises, whether you buy one or compete with them.

Franchise Basics

A *franchise* is a right. In the case of retail franchises it is the right to use a brand and someone's knowledge. For example, Sears franchise stores are allowed to use the Sears and related names to sell merchandise supplied by Sears distribution centers within a geographic area. A franchise also comes with an operations manual that tells franchisees how to set up and run their business. The price of the franchise right ranges from thousands to hundreds of thousands of dollars, depending on market and store size. In addition, the franchisee (you) will pay an ongoing fee to cover corporate advertising as well as for consulting services. It can get expensive.

The upside is that a strong franchise brand will give you customer recognition before you open your door. Your initial and replacement inventory is standing by. Have a question? No problem—check the manual or call your franchise representative.

Fortunately, not all retail franchises are as expensive or as restrictive as large brands like Sears. The two most common types of franchises are business format and product distribution franchises.

Business Format Franchises

The most comprehensive type of franchise is the business format franchise. The franchisor, for a fee, will help you select a retail site, purchase and install fixtures, furnish signage, hire and train employees, provide computers and software to manage inventory and finances, assist in local marketing and advertising, and consult with you to solve business problems. Some of these franchises are turnkey, meaning that you write a check and they set up the business for you. If desired, some will hire a manager for you so you can be an absentee owner.

Product Distribution Franchises

An independent retailer who doesn't want others to have that level of control over their business can opt for a product distribution franchise. For example, a gift store can be a distribution franchisee for a specific line of gift items within its market. No one else in a specified area can sell that line of gifts. However, for that right the store may be limited in which competing lines it can carry. It also may or may not have to pay an initial fee, and it will have to adhere to marketing requirements.

Advantages and Disadvantages

There are a number of advantages to becoming a franchisee for a proven product or business, including these:

- Buying a well-established franchise can offer you a greater chance of success than starting the same business from scratch.
- You will have access to in-depth market analysis not easily available to non-franchise retailers.
- You will have access to the franchisor's expertise to help you solve the myriad problems that can hinder start-up and operation of a retail store.
- Your store will have the bulk-purchasing power of a big corporation to help you buy at the lowest price and pass it on to your customers.
- Start-up costs may be reduced because the franchisor can advise you on store planning and the appropriate initial inventory.
- Lenders will lend more to a franchise store than to an independent retail store.

So what is the downside? Here are some disadvantages to becoming a franchisee:

- The cost. The biggest negative to buying a franchise is the cost. The franchise fee alone can be $50,000 to $250,000 for smaller franchises, and the fees go up from there.
- The loss of control. Depending on what type of franchise opportunity you purchase, your retail business may no longer be independent.

Popular Retail Franchise Categories

What franchise opportunities are available to you? Some franchises are regional, and others may already be awarded in your market. Following is a list of common product retail franchise categories. Within these categories you can find both business format and product distribution franchises:

- Business supplies
- Clothing
- Convenience store
- Dollar (Bargain) store
- Electronics
- Flooring
- Footwear
- Furniture
- Gifts
- Gourmet foods
- Hardware
- Home improvement
- Homewares
- Party supplies
- Pets
- Toys
- Video

Unfortunately, many of the newer franchises will be out of business in five years. It seems that successful retailers often try to franchise their business before they open their own second store.

Should you consider a franchise? Remember, franchises are more profit-oriented than lifestyle-oriented. If you have sufficient capital or good credit, a franchise store can get you up and running faster than most independent retail stores. However, if you prefer the independence and already have or can develop the skills and knowledge needed, a franchise may be too costly in investment and control.

Finding a Franchise

How can you go about finding an appropriate franchise retail business? Because franchising is profitable—especially for the franchisor—be cautious when selecting and purchasing a franchise. There are helpful resources, but common sense is your best defense.

Following are proven resources for finding a franchise opportunity.

Publications

There are many magazines, newspapers, books, and printed guides to franchising. Some of the more popular franchise and business opportunity magazines are available at larger bookstores where magazines are sold. They include *Franchise Times* and *Franchise 500*. Refer to Appendix A for additional publications.

In addition, franchise opportunities are advertised in major metro newspapers and in national and regional business magazines. Be aware that just about anyone can set up a franchise and advertise it as such. It may be little more than an operations book and a list of suppliers. You will want to do some research on the legitimacy and financial strength of any franchise you select.

Trade Shows

Yes, even franchisors have their own trade show. One of the largest single shows is the International Franchise Expo (*www.ifeinfo.com*) held in Washington, D.C. The National Franchise & Business Opportunities Shows (*www.franchiseshowinfo.com*) are regional shows; fifteen in the United States and twelve in Canada. Both offer a venue to meet franchisors and business opportunity representatives large and small.

Associations

The International Franchise Association (*www.franchise.org*), founded in 1960, is a major trade association for franchise opportunities. It offers initial information about franchising as well as contact information for many major franchise systems.

The American Franchisee Association (*www.franchisee.org*) is a trade association for those who own or are considering buying a franchise. Larger franchises often have a separate association made up of those who own common franchises. The franchisees share their knowledge to help each other—and to help keep the franchisor honest.

Consultants

There are numerous franchise consultants who will help you find an appropriate franchise or business opportunity and represent you in signing up and getting things started. However, most franchise consultants only work with the major franchises, mostly in the fast-food business, and where the store will cost at least $500,000. If you decide to hire a franchise consult, make sure you get one who understands your budget and your business. You can find them at franchise trade shows and through ads in franchise publications.

Online

The Internet has made research for just about anything easier. In minutes you can learn about a franchise association or show, review the requirements of a specific franchisor, and even start an application.

The problem is that online resources don't tell you whether you found a legitimate and proven franchisor or a fly-by-night business opportunity. That takes some more research, talking with franchisees, and some phone calls. But you can use the Net to do your preliminary research and narrow the broad field.

If you're relatively certain that franchising isn't for you, the Internet can still be a powerful tool for discovering who your competitors will be and how you can differentiate your independent retail business. You might even pick up some key information to help you estimate start-up costs, demographics, and profitability.

Evaluating a Business Franchise

Found a franchisor that interests you and that you'd like to know more about? Following are some red flags that, if seen, should warn you that you are not dealing with a reputable franchisor or business opportunity:

- Promises extravagant returns for a modest investment
- Avoids answering your questions to your satisfaction
- Refuses to provide financial references to their franchisees
- Won't allow you to randomly select franchisor references to contact
- Attempts to pressure you into signing a contract before you have fully investigated the opportunity
- Refuses to cooperate with your accountant, business adviser, or attorney
- Seems more interested in selling you a franchise license than in helping you build a successful business

Before much of the franchise opportunity's confidential information is divulged to you, you probably will need to sign a confidentiality agreement. It simply says that you will not divulge the franchisor's secrets to others. Make sure that you show this agreement to an attorney before signing it. You, in turn, can ask the franchise representative to sign a confidentiality agreement about your financial information. Of course, before you sign such an agreement, be certain that you're not planning on opening a competitive store. Ask an attorney to help you understand limitations before you sign.

How can you verify the legitimacy of a franchisor? Here are some proven suggestions for making sure that the franchise opportunity you are offered is viable:

- Ask your business banker to check the franchisor's credit background with Dunn & Bradstreet or other credit rating services.
- Get a copy of and analyze the franchisor's most recent financial statements. Publicly traded stock companies must provide this information; nontraded franchise companies may or may not want to share this information with you.
- In analyzing financial statements, make sure that the franchisor's primary source of income is from royalties and sales rather than from initial franchise fees.
- Contact the attorney general's office in the state where the franchisor is headquartered and ask about current or pending litigation against the firm.
- If the franchisor is national, contact the Federal Trade Commission (*www.ftc.gov*) to determine whether the firm is reputable.
- Use the Internet to research the franchise opportunity. You may find comments from either satisfied or disgruntled franchisors in business blogs.
- Ask the franchisor about its future, what its three-, five- and ten-year plans are, and how the franchisor expects to accomplish them. Are the plans reasonable?
- Find out what the requirements are for transferring your franchise license if you decide to sell your business.

Evaluating a Product Franchise

If signing a full business franchise agreement is more than you want to tackle, consider a product franchise—the right to sell a product or line of products in a specified geographic area. You can retain much of your independence while getting name recognition built by a brand. For example, your store can become an exclusive reseller in your Zip Code for a line of herbal teas. Or you may be able to get exclusive rights to products within your county or province, or even within your state.

How can you find product franchises that fit your retail concept? By doing a little competitive research, analyzing the products, verifying the opportunity, and signing an agreement.

Competitive Research

As you do preliminary research for your retail store concept you'll be visiting competitive stores within your market as well as those in similar markets in other areas of your state or region. As you do so you may find a product that matches your needs. If the products are available for franchise (sometimes the label will tell you), you can contact the manufacturer or distributor about franchise opportunities in your location.

❓ Question

How can I determine whether a product is a franchised product? Most will say something about "exclusive" on the product itself or in store signage. You won't know what that actually means until you contact the franchisor, but it is a tip-off. In addition, retail trade publications often have ads for product franchises and products that can be rebranded (Bob's Widget Cleaner).

Product Analysis

Make sure that the products you consider fit your retail concept. Will the customers that you draw be interested in this product or line? Would they expect to see it in your store? Is it a product or line that will reflect the quality of merchandise that you will carry? Consider franchise products for your best line, using brand recognition to draw customers into your store.

Product Opportunity

If the product is of the quality you desire, contact the manufacturer or distributor to determine whether it is available to you. Even if it is not, you may be able to pre-apply for the opportunity if it again becomes available. Some product franchisors allow weaker franchisees to continue selling their product in a marketplace until they can find a better reseller. That may be you.

Agreement

There are many types of product franchise agreements. Most will describe the line, how it is to be marketed, where it can be marketed exclusively, and what fees are required. The fees typically help fund cooperative advertising (called "co-op") that promotes the product(s) nationally, regionally, and locally. Some product franchises require no up-front fees; the costs are built into the wholesale price of the merchandise. The franchise agreement is designed to keep the manufacturer's product in better stores at standardized—and more profitable—prices. You probably will need to maintain a specified level of inventory. Make sure that you fully understand the benefits, costs, and requirements of any product franchise agreement you sign. Hire an attorney with franchise experience to look over any agreements and advise you before you sign them.

Business Franchise Costs

Product franchises are relatively inexpensive. Business franchises, however, can be very expensive. How much? What do you get for your franchise fees? Here are some answers.

Turnkey Stores

A turnkey franchise fee is more common in restaurants than in retail stores, though more are being offered than in the past. A common turnkey store is what is called a dollar or budget store.

Investors in turnkey stores write a check and the franchisor does most of the work, selecting the site, stocking the store, hiring and training management and employees, advertising—the works. Turnkey franchise stores are expensive, with most ranging from $500,000 to $2,000,000 or more in cost. The franchisor typically makes a cash investment of 25 to 40 percent of the total cost as a down payment and signs a loan security agreement for the balance. The store also must have operating capital for a specified period, ranging from three to twelve months. Turnkey businesses are purchased primarily by individual and group investors who have little expertise in the chosen business; they purchase the franchise for the investment opportunity (and sometimes for the tax opportunities).

Before signing a turnkey franchise agreement, make sure an attorney with extensive franchise experience has reviewed it and advised you.

Franchise Fees

Whether you opt for a turnkey store or a franchise that you work cooperatively, you will be paying a franchise fee. Depending on the system, the franchise fee can be as little as $5,000 or as much as $100,000 or more. You'll also pay a percentage of gross revenues to the franchisor, usually from 5 to 8 percent. Sell a million dollars in a year and you send the franchisor $50,000 to $80,000 of your gross profits. Some franchises have lower fees in smaller markets or when they act as the sole wholesale supplier, with some fees buried in the costs.

⊛ Essential

Whether you opt to buy a franchise or decide to remain independent, knowing what a franchisee must pay in your industry will help you know how best to compete. Do your homework as if you were going to purchase a franchise. Then ask yourself whether your business profit from the franchisor will be more than enough to pay the required fees.

Make sure that you know in advance exactly what the franchise fees cover and what they don't. Big business operates on profits of just a few pennies of profit for every dollar of sales. Don't give away those pennies unless you get sufficient value for them. Pennies add up.

Advertising

One of the forgotten fees of franchising is advertising. No matter what your retail business is, you will need to spend money on advertising and promoting it. Most operating retail stores spend 1 to 3 percent of sales on advertising; that's $5,000 to $15,000 annually for a store grossing $500,000. If you sign a franchise agreement, most of that advertising budget will be controlled by the franchisor. Remember: A franchise is a brand, and brands must be advertised. The franchisor controls the brand, so it typically controls the advertising—or at least controls how you get to spend the ad dollars.

Location

Major franchisors don't want you to put their name on a building in a run-down neighborhood. And they don't want you to go out of business anytime soon. That means they will require control over where you site your store and how it looks. That's okay, because a successful franchisor knows more about locating and marketing its brand than you do.

Training

Another advantage of franchises is that many offer a training program for owners, managers, and employees. Of course, the training isn't free. There will be costs, possibly including travel.

What is included in the franchisors' training? Operating systems, methods, procedures, advertising strategies, employee recruitment and hiring, employee training, financial and inventory control, and other tasks of starting and running a retail store.

Buying an Existing Store

Starting a retail store from scratch can be daunting work, taking time and money to ensure success. Fortunately, you may not have to do all the work. There may be a retail store available nearby that fits your requirements. It may be ready to go and, depending on its profitability and the owner's situation, priced fairly.

Finding such a store is still hard work. You must know what you are getting into, and that takes some research. The advantage is that, if you choose properly, you can be operating a successful retail store much sooner than if you start from scratch.

Choosing the Store

How can you find out whether a retail store is available for sale? Most entrepreneurs start by checking local and regional newspapers under "business for sale." The ads frequently don't name the store, but they do identify the industry, the general location, and sometimes include an asking price. Sunday metropolitan newspapers and regional business publications are the best source for business opportunity ads.

❓ Question

Can I just go into a store and ask if it is for sale?
Yes, you can. Just make sure you are talking with the owner rather than a manager or clerk. Dave, who was thinking about opening a bookstore, asked the owner of a successful store if it was for sale. Yes, it was. Within a few months Dave owned it, saving himself the time, grief, and risks of building a store from scratch.

Business brokers and real estate agents represent businesses for sale. However, brokers often represent only businesses worth $100,000 or more, and real estate agents typically are selling the property itself, with a business secondary to the transaction.

Numerous websites advertise businesses for sale throughout the United States and Canada. You can check their current ads or sign up to be notified when the type or location of business you are interested in is offered. Some of the more popular sites are *www .bizbuysell.com*, *www.businessbroker.net*, *www.acquireo.com*, and *www.businessmart.com*. Regional sites include *www.bizben.com* (California) and *www.sunbeltnetwork.com* (southwest).

Analyzing the Store

Small businesses are presented for sale in a document called an Offering Memorandum (OM). Once you've signed a confidentiality agreement, you should be able to view the OM and discuss its details with the store owner or business broker. The typical Offering Memorandum will include:

- Executive Overview: Concise description of the opportunity
- Business Description and History
- Description of Product Lines and Customer Base
- Sales and Marketing Methods
- Competitive Analysis
- Retail Process Description
- Facilities and Fixtures
- Personnel
- Goodwill (name value)
- Industry Overview and Store Potential
- Financial Information
- Reason for Sale
- Price and Terms
- Contact Information (owner or broker)

The Offering Memorandum can help you determine whether the store is profitable, whether it fulfills the needs of the defined marketplace, and whether it is an opportunity you should consider.

Buying the Store

If the retail store is owned by a corporation, you will be purchasing stock in the corporation. You'll need an attorney and an accountant to make sure the deal is structured to your benefit.

If the store is owned by a sole proprietor, a husband and wife (often considered a sole proprietor), or a partnership, you will be buying the store's assets in an *asset sale*. Besides inventory, fixtures, and other assets, you may have to buy "goodwill" or the name value for the business. If it is operated profitably and the marketplace is stable or growing, the goodwill can be 5 to 20 percent of the price of the store.

Retail store purchases can be paid in cash, financed through a small business loan or home equity loan, or possibly purchased on a contract from the current owner(s). A seller contract will require at least 25 percent down and use the store inventory as security. It is more common for sellers of successful stores to require 50 percent or more down and a short-term (one- to three-year) contract. Your accountant and attorney can draw up the papers.

If you are able to purchase a running store that needs lots of work, make sure you budget to get that done. Taking over a struggling store can be more costly than opening a new one.

Operating the Store

Buying someone else's store isn't the same as starting one yourself. On the plus side you will be able to open your door faster and be profitable more quickly because the hard work of a start-up has been done (the exception being a store that is failing that you must rebuild). The minus side is that, because it already is successful, you probably shouldn't make significant changes to the operation until you have at least a few months of sales. It will take you that long to meet and analyze your primary customer groups and determine what *they* want. Remember: owning a retail store isn't about pleasing yourself; it's about pleasing your *customers*!

CHAPTER 5

Planning for Success

Y ou've made good progress. Through the first four chapters of this book you've learned how the retail business works, made a tentative decision on what store fits you, analyzed your financial and personal assets, and considered two viable options to establishing a new independent store: buying a franchise and buying an existing retail store. But there's still more to go. This chapter will help you look at "the numbers" of retailing more closely to determine whether your retail concept is profitable.

Pulling Out the Sharp Pencil

Retailing is about numbers. It's about buying at one price and selling at another. It's about making sure that the difference between buy and sell is sufficient to pay expenses, employees, taxes, and still have something for yourself. It's about knowing what you're getting into.

Profit isn't a bad word. In fact, it's a very *good* word. *Greed* is a bad word. Folks who start independent lifestyle businesses typically aren't greedy. They want to serve their customers with something that profits the customers' lives. And they expect to earn a financial profit for their efforts.

To ensure that your retail store is profitable, you must first understand what profit is and how it is earned in transactions. You need to identify and customize your store's profit model.

Profit Model Overview

Profit is excess revenue after expenses are paid. Buy 100 widgets for $50, sell them for $1 each, pay expenses (shipping, labor, rent, advertising) of $25 and you have $25 left—your profit. If costs or expenses go up, profit goes down. If you only sell 70 widgets, profits go down. If you sell them all for $1.50 each, profit goes up.

This basic profit model is simple. The key to any retail business, including yours, is determining what sales will be and what percentages of sales must be spent on expenses to keep sales and profits as high as possible.

The example ratios in the profit model discussed here are relatively accurate. Take a look at a product on a store shelf. You can approximate that half of the price is the cost of goods sold, a quarter is for retail expenses, and the final quarter is profit (including your salary) before taxes. The MBAs will disagree with this simplification, but it is a starting point for determining your store's profit model.

Profit Model Variations

If you are starting a new independent bookstore, for example, the cost of goods typically is about 60 percent of retail, rather than 50 percent. However, unsold books can be returned to the distributor for credit, so losses are reduced.

Some merchandise is purchased at wholesale prices that are 25 to 45 percent of retail. However, the higher profit often is offset by high shipping costs or other expenses that keep the actual costs of goods sold at around 50 percent.

Some products require more floor space, more expensive displays, more advertising, or other expenses that add to sales costs and potentially reduce profits. However, because the retail price of these products is higher, a fair profit is retained.

Customize Your Profit Model

Your research thus far may have helped you discover the profit model that works best in your type of retail store. If not, continue your research. All retail stores use a variation of the basic profit model outlined at the beginning of this section. The cost of goods sold may be slightly higher or lower (depending on whether shipping or returns are included), and expenses of operating your store will vary by location, employee costs, store overhead, and so on. Following segments of this chapter will help in your research for your store's profit model.

Another word about profit: It really isn't a quarter of every dollar that comes to your store. For small, independent retail stores owned by one or two people, the profit includes payback for what the owners invest as well as what the owners get to take home for their labor. And it includes income taxes that must be paid on store profits. Your goal, as a small retailer, is to get a fair salary and a fair return on your financial investment into the store.

Analyzing Retail Costs

Again, profit is excess revenue after all expenses are paid. This means that one of the best ways of increasing your retail store's profits is to control expenses: inventory, fixtures, equipment, overhead, taxes, and licenses. As your retail store matures, you will spend more time identifying excessive expenses and trimming them down. You may realize that you are spending 4 percent too much for your inventory, or you may find legitimate ways of reducing taxes. That will be your job. For now, during the start-up and initial operation, your responsibility is to identify and track your retail costs.

Inventory

The biggest expense in your retail store will be inventory. As merchandise sells, you will need to replace it—or determine that it wasn't sufficiently profitable and then find products that are more profitable and better fit your customers' needs. Starting with your customized profit model, you may determine that inventory costs you 55 percent of sales. The reason, you discover, is not what sells but what doesn't sell; there is too much waste. Too many products get damaged on the shelves and must be clearanced, or too many items just don't sell and you cannot return them.

Planning your store's success will require that you stay on top of inventory, knowing what is selling, what is not, and why. If you can reduce costs without increasing expenses, you profit.

Fixtures and Equipment

Fixtures and equipment for a small retail store typically are a one-time buy. They probably are your second-largest initial expense. You purchase them before you open, and you hope to keep them for many years. Some retailers opt to build at least some of their own store fixtures. Others buy used fixtures or equipment or lease them to reduce initial and ongoing costs.

How much should fixtures and equipment cost? Much depends on what type of retail store you decide to open. A bargain store will use basic or used fixtures. A jewelry store will have expensive display cases, a sturdy safe, and quality lighting. In some cases, the store lease will include built-in fixtures.

Overhead and Employees

Overhead is the day-to-day expense of keeping the store open. It includes the rent or lease payment, of course. But some overhead expenses change depending on how many hours your store is open. Also, depending on utility costs and climate in your area, the costs of lighting, heating, and air conditioning can fluctuate significantly through the year. These expenses and their variations must be calculated in your overhead budget. Many utility companies will put customers on a budget plan to reduce the fluctuation of costs with an average bill.

Employees are a significant expense to some retail stores, especially larger ones. For many small retailers, employees aren't an issue; the owner(s) run the store whenever it is open, taking infrequent vacations, and those only when the owner can close the store with the least income loss.

Taxes and Licenses

Taxes are unavoidable. If you make a profit you will pay taxes on it. In addition, taxes on inventory and equipment must be paid whether you make a profit or not. Therefore, taxes can be a significant management challenge to a small retail store.

Even if you plan to do your own recordkeeping (see Chapter 15), consider hiring an accountant or tax adviser before you set up your store so you can manage and budget taxes. Too many small business close because they don't pay attention to their taxes and licenses.

Calculating Target Profits

The lifeblood of your retail store is profits. If it doesn't pay expenses and give you a profit for your time, you soon will be looking for another job. How can you determine in advance what your store's profits need to be? Remember that profit is the excess revenue after expenses are paid. Calculate the store's revenue and deduct the expenses to determine target profits.

Target Income

Here are some initial calculations of profitability for your retail store. You will refine these numbers as you develop your specific business plan (see Chapter 6), but for now they will help you calculate potential profits.

If your profits (including your salary) are about 25 percent of sales and you need $50,000 a year to live on, your target revenues for the store need to be about $200,000 (50,000 ÷ 0.25) in annual sales. This may or may not be realistic for the first year of operation (unless you buy a franchise or an existing business), but it will give you a revenue target.

So the big question becomes this: Can your local marketplace support $200,000 in annual sales—nearly $17,000 a month, or more than $640 a day, six days a week? If so, you may have a viable business concept. If not, you may need to reduce your needs and your profit target. Or maybe you should develop a business concept that *will* support your profit target.

Target Expenses

Profits are reduced by expenses. If you estimate annual sales to be about $200,000, is your expense model of 25 percent realistic? Can you cover overhead and expenses for $50,000 a year? In addition, can you restock inventory for 50 percent, or $100,000 a year? If yes, you may succeed. If not, you may not. If you decided to reduce your inventory costs to 45 percent of sales your profitability would increase, but maybe you would lose customers to poorer quality stock. It's a tradeoff.

Figuring Rate of Return

To start and run a small retail business will take a large investment of capital. You could instead invest that capital in stocks, bonds, or other, lower-risk investments. It wouldn't be as much fun, but at least you would get a reasonable return on your investment.

⊕ Essential

Because inventory is the greatest expense you will have, you will reduce the risk of loss if you buy inventory that easily can be resold, even if it is at a minimal profit. In addition, purchasing fixtures and equipment that are already depreciated and are sold well below original cost will allow you to sell it, if necessary, with little loss.

How much return? That depends on the risk involved. If there is virtually no chance that you will lose any of your investment, the risk is low and the return on investment (ROI) will be low. If, however, there is a risk of at least partial loss, such as in the stock market, the ROI should be higher. The same goes for your retail store. If it is a risky venture you should get a higher rate of return than if there is little risk of loss.

The ROI for your retail store should be important to you. If you are borrowing any of the capital you need for this venture you can be sure that the lender will want to know that the ROI will be at least as much as the interest charged.

Typical ROI

What level of return should you expect on your investment in a store? Remember, this doesn't include the salary you will be taking from profits. To answer the question, you need to determine the approximate risk of failure in your business. If there's a 25 percent chance that your business won't be operating in one year, the risk is high. If your business has an excellent chance of succeeding a decade from now, the risk is relatively low.

As already mentioned, low-risk investments earn low returns. Bank savings accounts, one of the most secure investments available, notoriously pay low interest rates of just a couple of percent. Mutual funds can pay better, at least over longer periods, with common ROIs of 4 to 12 percent. Common stocks, too, pay higher ROIs in the long haul, with expected returns ranging from minus numbers to 20 percent or more.

Your ROI

Your investment in a retail store typically should return 8 to 12 percent, again depending on relative risk. That means if you invest $100,000 of your own capital in this business, you should expect the business to pay you $8,000 to $12,000 in interest, or ROI, in addition to a fair salary. Where does it come from? It comes from your target profit. If your target profit is estimated at 25 percent of sales, 8 to 12 percent of it will pay back the financial investment, and the balance will pay you a wage for your time and expertise running the business. (There will be taxes to pay out of that 25 percent, too, so don't spend it all just yet.)

That also means that any investor who puts money into your idea, such as a lender or limited partner, will be paid from the total ROI. For example, if the bank lends you $50,000 at 8 percent interest and your business earns an ROI of 10 percent, you as the owner, get to keep the 2 percent difference. Of course, if the business closes, you get to repay the loan personally at 8 percent!

Estimating Inventory Requirements

As you can see, inventory is the big expense for most retail stores. Therefore, accurately determining your store's inventory requirements is important. Following are some guidelines to help you estimate initial and replacement inventory requirements. As your business plan is developed and your store is operating, these numbers will need to be more specific. For now, they will help you set inventory targets.

Turnover

First, consider the store's inventory turnover rate. *Turnover* is the number of times that you will sell your inventory in one year. Of course, some departments will have a high turnover rate and others a lower turnover. For now, calculate a typical turnover rate.

The type of inventory you carry will suggest what turnover rate to expect. Many small retail stores with more common inventory expect a turnover rate of 2X, or twice a year. If the retail value of all inventory is $100,000, the owners expect to sell it twice, on average, for sales of about $200,000 a year. Some departments may turn over once a month, while others only once every three years.

You can discover the typical turnover rate for your type of store with a little research. Trade associations, major wholesalers, and distributor salespeople may be able to help you determine an expected turnover rate for your store. Wholesalers are familiar with establishing initial inventories and can help you pinpoint an expected turnover rate for your store by size and location.

 **Essential**

One of the most profitable ways of making your retail store grow is to increase your profitable inventory and reduce unprofitable inventory. Such fine-tuning depends on knowing the price, cost, and turnover rate for all departments within your store. Keeping good records (Chapter 15) will help you increase profitable inventory levels.

Even better, your accountant should have resources to accurately determine your store's target turnover rate. The actual rate may be different once you get the store up and running, but it should be close to the target.

Initial Inventory

Once you establish a target turnover rate, you need to determine how much inventory should be on the shelves on opening day. If, for example, the target sales for the store is $200,000 a year and the inventory is expected to turn over twice during that year, inventory at any given time should be $100,000 in retail value. Following the profit model defined at the beginning of this chapter, the wholesale value of the start-up inventory will be about $50,000. These are ballpark numbers, but they give you an idea of what you'll need to invest in inventory to get your store open. Remember that the calculation depends greatly on the turnover rate for your store. The more accurate that rate is, the better your inventory estimate will be.

Replacement Inventory

As inventory flies off the shelves, you'll need to replace it. The simplest method is to replace sold inventory with like kind. Sold fifty blue vases? Buy fifty more. However, smart managers carefully watch how inventory sells and replace it with products that offer, if possible, higher profits. If the profit on the blue vases is $1.00 each and the green ones is $1.50 each, the manager will consider reducing the number of blues and increasing the order for greens. It's this type of fine-tuning that makes a store grow.

In marketing, this technique is called *beating the control*. If a profitable product (the control) is selling well, a similar and more profitable product is added. If the new product beats it for profitability, more of the control product inventory is replaced with the new product. In fact, the new product becomes the control—the product to beat. You'll learn other techniques like this in Chapter 14.

Adjusting Your Business Concept

Few business concepts go from their initial idea to a business plan without changes and adjustments. In fact, some are thrown out based on limited market, limited profitability, excessive costs, low rate of return, and other valid reasons. Your business concept may morph from a high-end gift store to a specialty craft store. Certainly you must follow your dream, but unless customers decide to follow you, it will be an expensive dream. Don't believe simply that if you build it, they will come. Instead, think, "Build what customers want and they will come."

Toward that end, following are three questions that you need to accurately answer before you proceed to your business plan.

Will It Work?

The profit model and other guides in this chapter are offered to help you answer a single question: Will it work? You'll need market research as well, but by now you should have a good idea whether the local marketplace can support a store that wants to sell X amount of what you are offering. You will invest a large amount of money and significant time into this project, so asking if it will be profitable for you is an important question.

If you're still not sure whether it will work, you have more research to do. Who are your customers? Do they need or want your products? Will they find your store? Can you offer them something they can't easily find elsewhere? If you do sell lots of stuff, will you make a profit? Do you have the capital and personal assets to make it work? Lots of questions spring from this single, vital question: Will it work?

What Will Make It Better?

Maybe you *think* your business concept will work as designed, but you're not certain. Ask yourself what changes you can make to it that will improve it. What will your customers prefer? What will give you better profitability and allow you to serve more customers?

Retailing is about fulfilling the needs of a group of buyers known as "your customers." If you know your target customer group well, you know what they need and want. How can you modify your business concept to serve them better and more profitably? Here are some idea starters:

- Offer fresh-cut flowers in a prominent section of your gift store.
- Set up a bargain table near the back of your store to serve budget-minded customers.
- Add complementary products to your inventory to bring in a related group of customers.
- Make shopping at your store a more enjoyable experience than at any other store in your market.
- Revise store hours to meet the needs of customers who leave nearby offices after 6 P.M.
- Add a line of high-end products near the register area that enhance the customer's perception of your store.

You get the picture. If your retail concept is good but you think you may have trouble meeting your target goals, add lines, add services, and enhance the shopping experience so that sales will improve and you can succeed.

What Makes It Unique?

Even a dollar store requires some uniqueness to survive in retail. It may be the only dollar store in a specific neighborhood, or the only one in the area that doesn't look like a bargain store. Your store must be unique. In addition to the preceding suggestions on making your retail concept better, here are some toward making it unique:

- Offer the friendliest, most helpful service of all retail stores in your marketplace.
- Let customers know that yours is the only store within a hundred miles that offers specific products or lines (see the information about product franchises in Chapter 4).
- Paint the inside or outside of your store an eye-catching color to draw attention to it.
- Use exceptional signage to direct people to your store and within it.
- Focus your promotion on how knowledgeable, helpful, and friendly your staff is.
- If parking near your store is challenging, validate parking for customers.
- Promote your store's philanthropic efforts: donating unsold stock to local charities; offering a percentage of sales to a local aid organization during a special drive.
- Offer comfortable seating in front of or in your store for tired shoppers.

Give your customers and prospects a valuable reason to shop with you rather than your competitors. Make your retail concept unique.

CHAPTER 6

Writing Your Business Plan

Imagine starting a trip to a distant city without a map. You may eventually get to your destination, but you'll waste a lot of time and fuel on the way. Planning is even more important when you are considering a retail business. You need a business concept, some numbers, and some goals. They all come together as a document in your retail business plan. This chapter guides you through the intricacies of developing your business plan, marketing plan, and specific financial plan.

Business Plan Basics

A business plan is a document that will guide you through starting and running your retail store. To be worthwhile, the plan must be specific as well as accurate. If the plan simply says, "I'm going to open some kind of retail store in my city and make a million dollars," it's not really a plan—it's a dream. However, a plan that documents the type of store, how it will be different from other area stores, where it is located, how it will find merchandise and develop profit, including specific costs and goals—that's a plan.

Plan Audience

To be an effective plan it must meet the needs of the reader. So the first question in developing a business plan is, Who cares? You do, of course. You want to document your goals and path so you can stay focused. You want to plan out what you will do and how you will do it to reach your retail goal.

Who else cares? If you have a direct lender, such as a bank, the people who make financial decisions there will want to see a comprehensive business plan. If you are seeking other investors, they, too, will want to know how you will spend their money and, most important to them, how you plan to pay it back. Major suppliers may also need to see your business plan—or at least a summary of it—before they will offer you credit on initial inventory.

The definition of your audience also dictates what is included in your business plan. For example, a self-financed retail store may only require a two- or three-page business plan to help keep the owner on track. A lender or major investor will need more facts and figures. Especially important to them will be whether you really know your marketplace and have a profitable plan for reaching it. As you design your retail business plan, keep your reading audience clearly in your mind.

Plan Outline

A business plan can be as short or as long as is necessary, from one page to a hundred. The following are the most common components of a successful retail business plan:

- **Cover page** identifies the business by name, location, and its participants.
- **Table of contents** helps readers find primary sections of the plan.
- **Executive summary** is a concise overview of the business plan for readers who don't need the details.
- **Business concept** describes your store in detail including location, operating hours, staffing, and primary inventory. This portion of the plan will be its largest component.

- **Market analysis** defines your customers, who they are, where they live, and why they will buy from your store.
- **Management team** identifies the owner, manager, and primary employees of the retail store and includes their credentials and experience.
- **Financial projections** estimate the start-up and operating costs, sources of funding, sales estimates, cash flow, and other financial facts.
- **Call to action** is a concise statement of what you want the reader to do: invest X dollars, lend a specific amount, join the staff as manager, or offer extended credit on initial inventory.

Writing the Plan

By now, your retail notebook is bulging with notes on all aspects of your business concept. However, it's not complete, nor is it organized. The preceding plan outline will help you organize your thoughts into a document that you can share. Doing so will help you determine what facts and figures you'll need to make it complete. A sample business plan is offered at the end of this chapter.

Question

Are there any software programs that can help me write my business plan?
Dozens. Some of the more popular ones are Business Plan Pro (*www.businessplanpro.com*, *www.bplans.com*, and *www.paloalto.com*) and Plan Write (*www.brs-inc.com*). There are others, ranging in price from free (beware) to hundreds of dollars. Some include templates designed for specific types of businesses, such as retail and specialty stores.

To produce a quality business plan you may need outside help, primarily with local market research and analysis. Some chambers of commerce can provide the numbers you need and even suggest a local market research firm. Alternately, a local Small Business Administration office (*www.sba.gov*) may offer classes or services to help you with localized market analysis. If you are near a university or major college, contact the business department to ask whether they can provide low- or no-cost market analysis for you. There may be students who would love the experience.

Revising the Plan

Once your business plan is drafted, set it aside for at least a day or two before finalizing it. If possible, show a draft of it to friendly experts or principal funders and ask for feedback. What else do they need to know? They may point out holes that you missed or ask questions that you hadn't considered.

 Fact

The Small Business Administration (*www.sba.gov*) offers classes and documents on writing a business plan. Contact your local SBA office for additional information. In addition, the SBA and other entrepreneur services offer assistance at little or no cost to develop the concept, marketing, and financial data needed to write a successful business plan.

Writing a business plan is instructive. You may discover that your business concept needs adjusting to be profitable. Or you may find a supplier who can give you an even better wholesale package and start-up assistance. Also, you must remain flexible in your plan if you hope to succeed in business. You cannot ignore facts that indicate your business plan won't work. Spend as much time as you can developing and revising your business plan—it is your map to the future.

Planning Your Marketing

Marketing—how you will reach and entice potential customers—is a vital component of your business plan. In fact, many businesses make it a separate plan: their marketing plan. It can be a page or two within the business plan or an extensive document with branding information. It will focus on the two primary components of marketing: advertising and promotion.

Retail Advertising

Retail stores depend upon advertising to bring in new customers and help retain existing customers. Too many small businesses ignore advertising.

How much should your store spend on advertising? A common guideline for small retail stores is 2 to 3 percent of target sales. If you expect your retail store to sell $200,000 a year, your ad budget should be about $4,000 to $6,000 annually. Remember, your market may require more advertising, especially during start-up. Many new retailers allocate 5 percent or more of their initial budget for advertising. A $200,000-a-year store might spend up to $10,000 for the first year of operation to get its name out and draw customers.

Be aware, though, that not all local advertising media are profitable for you. In fact, smaller retail stores typically don't benefit from expensive television advertising. Radio advertising makes more sense for many, especially stores that sell impulse-buy products such as flowers and gifts. Price-conscious retail stores may focus their advertising budget on the local shopper publication.

You don't need to spend money on advertising just yet, but your marketing plan should outline how you will spend it, and where. As you open your store, advertise where your competitors are, and stay away from unproven ad media.

Retail Promotion

Promoting your store can be more cost-effective than advertising. It also can give you better results. The problem is finding something about your store that is newsworthy and entices a local media outlet (newspaper, radio, television, and so on) to promote it. It helps if you understand the structure and goals of your local media outlets.

For example, community newspapers frequently have a business column that tells readers about new businesses, local events and promotions, and other news. Make sure you read it, meet the writer or editor, and use the medium frequently. In fact, the columnist may give you guidelines for what is considered newsworthy promotion. Get the fax numbers or e-mail addresses of media editors and news directors so you can submit promotional material as needed.

Don't forget that signage is a cost-effective way to promote your retail store. Check with the local building department to learn what signs you can and cannot have on your store and where you can locate them. Most communities have limits even on how much lettering you can have in your front window or whether you can install neon and other lighted signs outside your store.

Alternately, include a budget in your business plan for hiring a promotional service to help you get the word out about your business.

Gathering Financials

Chapter 5 offered financial guidelines to help you estimate profitability of a business concept. Your business plan goes much further, with specific data that will guide you and inform other readers about the income, expenses, and profits of your retail store.

❓ Question

Are there any software programs that can help me build my store's financial plan?
Yes, there are. The most popular are Microsoft Small Business Financials (*www.microsoft.com/smallbusiness*) and MYOB (*www.myob.com*). Some accounting software packages offer templates for specific retail store operations. These programs can handle the day-to-day income and expense entries as well as common financial statements.

What do you need in the financial component of your business plan? Again, the answer depends on your audience. For yourself, a simple document of basic financial numbers will be sufficient. Lenders may require more. Following are the most common financial documents.

Projected Profit and Loss (Income) Statement

A profit and loss statement includes data on your business's projected income, expenses, and subsequent profit. Because you're not in business yet, the statement is "projected." It's what you're planning on. Commonly known as the P & L (profit and loss) or the income statement, this document summarizes the financial actions of your retail store. Once operating, you will use this document regularly to decide how to best increase profits.

A simplified income statement looks like this:

BOB'S WIDGETS INCOME STATEMENT

Income

Sales	$200,000	100%
Expenses		
Inventory	$100,000	50%
Overhead	$50,000	25%
Total Expenses	$150,000	75%
Net Profit*	$50,000	25%

*Before taxes

An actual income statement for a retail business will be longer and more complete, documenting the income by major departments as well as spelling out each component of overhead. It also will include specifics on the owner's salary or "draw" from the business, which is a component of the net profit figure.

Projected Balance Sheet

Another document vital to your financial plan is the balance sheet. The primary accounting equation that all businesses use is this:

Assets = Liabilities + Capital

Put a more common way:

Assets – Liabilities = Capital

That's the structure of your balance sheet. It makes sense: what you own minus what you owe is what you are worth, financially speaking. Business balance sheets are detailed. Here's a simplified example:

BOB'S WIDGETS BALANCE SHEET

Assets

Cash	$32,000
Accounts Receivable	$5,000
Inventory	$72,000
Total Assets	$109,000

Liabilities

Accounts Payable	$6,400
Notes Payable	$60,700
Total Liabilities	$ 67,100
Capital	**$41,900**

Chapter 15 offers more specific information about developing and tracking financial records. For now, your business plan should have a projected profit and loss statement and a projected balance sheet for your retail store. The detail required depends on who will use the document to make decisions. However, it's good advice to make it as detailed as possible even if you don't have to approach a lender. If needed, hire an accountant or other financial adviser to help you draft accurate financial statements for your business plan.

Sample Business Plan

Following is an example of a business plan for the fictitious business Bob's Widgets.

Bob's Widgets Business Plan

Table of Contents

Executive Summary

Bob's Widgets will be a profitable retail store offering better-quality widgets and related merchandise to customers in Thankful County, Arizona, and worldwide. The retail store offers a balanced inventory of common widgets matched to the local market. The online retail store will distribute uncommon and higher-priced widgets on the Internet via eBay and other outlets.

Business Concept

Bob's Widgets will be fully owned and operated by Bob and Donna Mulligan as a sole proprietorship (husband and wife) with DBA (doing business as) registration, Arizona seller's permit, and city business license.

Bob's Widgets will sell quality widgets in a wide variety of categories, selected to match the local market by tracking customer sales. There will be 20 primary departments, and sales records will be measured monthly to determine future buys. In addition, Bob's Widgets will sell widget repair kits and related ephemera. Bob's Widgets also will sell uncommon widgets online through eBay. Online widgets are selected from store inventory and special purchases, and priced between $20 and $100 each. Retail value of initial store inventory is estimated at $200,000 including the online inventory.

Operations

Bob's Widgets will price new widgets at twice the wholesale price (excluding shipping costs).

Bob's Widgets expects to sell about 1,500 widgets a month, tracked by department sales.

Bob's Widgets will accept Visa and MasterCard charge and debit cards as well as checks. It will allow open accounts with primary customers and limit credit to $500 per account.

Ongoing business consulting will be provided by the Smallville SBA and by Lewis Carroll, professional business consultant.

Facilities

Bob's Widgets will lease a 1,450 sq. ft. (apx. 20' × 73') retail store on the west side of South Jones St., just north of the famous Smallville clock. Lease payments will be $1,000 per month for three years. Utilities will be paid by the tenants. Bob's Widgets will be located in the middle of the block on the west side of the street. The store front has a full awning. Parking is available at the door, and a loading zone for larger deliveries is nearby.

The store will be laid out for optimum traffic including a transition area, self-directing signage, extensive categorization, numerous shelf labels, and clean facilities. The store will have a small back room with shelves, table, refrigerator, microwave, store music system, and supplies. An adjacent bathroom (toilet, hot and cold water sink) will include a storage area.

The store will include two comfortable chairs near the front of the store for shoppers to relax. Store lighting will be adequate for easy shopping. A skylight provides natural lighting. Exterior and window lights will be on a timer to present the window display at night. Fifty-three (53) primary shelving units will be purchased used from a closing widget store in Whatever, Arizona. Thirty-three (33) additional new shelving units will be added at the rear of the store within the first 30 days of operation. All aisles will be approximately 48 in. wide and wheelchair accessible.

The cash wrap area will be at the front and left side of the store with sufficient counter space for product sorting, for transaction equipment, and for storage. An extensive library of widget reference books and business books will be located below the counter. There will be two incoming telephone lines including one high-speed DSL. A computer with printer/copier/fax machine will be located at the counter with a second computer in the rear of the store.

Market Analysis

Smallville is the Thankful County seat, 108 miles (2 hours) north of downtown Phoenix. The only other retail widget store in Smallville is Village Widgets and Gifts, four blocks north of Bob's Widgets. It is owner-operated and open weekdays only. The only new general retail store in Smallville is Thankful Widget Company, 2 blocks northwest of Bob's Widgets, open six days a week. Tinyville, 23 miles north of Smallville, has one established widget retail store.

Numerous special events are held throughout the year in downtown Smallville, drawing visitors from around northern Arizona. Bob's Widgets' large and unique window display (designed to look like a giant widget) and neon WIDGETS and OPEN signs will draw passersby. A large WIDGETS sign will decorate the front of the building above the awning and will be seen for approximately two blocks. A reversible sandwich-board sign will be placed at the curb when the store is open; one side saying BOB'S WIDGETS OPEN and the other reading WIDGET SALE TODAY!

Bob's Widgets initially will be open 47 hours per week: Monday through Saturday 10–5 and Sunday 12–5. Bob's Widgets will be the only widget store in Smallville open on Sundays.

Bob's Widgets will use local advertising and publicity, window and neon signs, sidewalk signs, and window displays to promote itself. Bob's Widgets will advertise on the area PBS station, in the local shopper newspaper, and the weekly newspaper. Bob's Widgets will host the Second Sunday Widget Group monthly meeting with 20–35 attendees, promoted by press releases in local print and broadcast media. In addition, Bob's Widgets will participate in various downtown Smallville events.

Management Team

Donna Mulligan will be the store manager, working in the store four days per week. Bob Mulligan will work in the store three days per week and off-site the equivalent of one day per week managing business records. Both have extensive retail experience, and Bob is a certified widget repairperson.

Financials

Financial and initial inventory records, including projected income statement and projected balance sheet, are available to investors who sign a confidentiality agreement. Credit reports for the principals also are available.

Call to Action

Bob's Widgets seeks an investor who will provide $50,000 of initial capital in the business in return for a 25 percent equity in profits.

CHAPTER 7

Selecting a Profitable Location

The mantra of retailing is location, location, location. That's because location is a vital component of retail success. If customers can't find your store or it isn't convenient to their needs, it will have less traffic—and you will have fewer profits. On the other side, you can lease the best location in town and pay too much, dramatically increasing your expenses and reducing profits. There is no one single reason why retailers don't succeed, but a poor location is often a major cause. This chapter helps you select the appropriate location for your retail store, so it will have the greatest chance of success.

Location, Location, Location

How well would a major grocery store do if it were located in a rural area with no other businesses around it? Product sell-by dates would expire before they were sold. Shopping carts would sit empty. Layoffs would abound. The store would soon be empty.

That scenario can happen to your independent retail business if it isn't located where its target customers can easily find it, or if it is more difficult to find than your competitor's store. Yet owners of new retail stores think that they can disobey this law of retailing and locate their business wherever it is convenient to them. Retailing is about convenience. If your store isn't convenient, it won't be as frequently visited.

Importance of Location

One of the biggest decisions you will make as you start your retail store is where and how to locate it. Once in operation, you can change your store hours, increase or decrease expenses, even change your entire inventory and image. But once you've selected a location, it is very difficult to relocate your business without loss of time and profits. That's why it is so important to make the best location decision right now, as you are starting up.

Depending on your local retail market, the appropriate location for your store may not be available. What should you do? In most cases, wait. Many retailers fail because they try to overcome significant location problems, or an inadequate location, rather than wait. They rent a store that is just too small, or inconvenient to their primary customers, or in a declining commercial district. They hope their gamble will succeed. It rarely does. They learn a valuable and expensive lesson about location.

How can you determine the best location for your retail store? The planning you've been doing thus far through this book will help. To locate successfully you must know your customers, how and when they make buying decisions, and how to make your merchandise convenient to that decision.

Your Customers

The big stores know all about location. They have it down to the person and the penny. They can tell you exactly who their customers are, how they buy, when they buy, why they buy, what else they may be receptive to buy at the same time (impulse purchases), and more. They probably know how much money their typical customers (or customer groups) make, where they work, when they work, how frequently they make related purchases, and more. The success of their very expensive store is based on knowing all about their customers' buying needs.

Your retail store should, too. If you are your own store's best customer—you have experience buying and using the products you will be selling—you know a lot about your customers. But you need to know much more. As suggested in earlier chapters, contact your local chamber of commerce, merchant association, and city government, which can provide you with demographics of local shoppers. *Demographics* are the characteristics of a specific group of people, such as your potential customers. It typically includes their age, income, education, marital status, and where they live. Demographics can easily be quantified and are available through basic market research.

Also do your own research, talking with friends, spying on competitors, reading anything you can get your hands on about your retail specialty. In addition, consider hiring a marketing research firm to help you identify your customers, how much money they make, where they live, how much they spend on your type of merchandise annually, and related marketing facts.

📋 Fact

Psychographics is the study of the opinions, attitudes, and buying habits of people. Psychographics requires in-depth interviews and can be more costly than demographics, but may reveal information about your customers that can help you serve them better, or at least better than your competitors do. If you don't understand what makes your target customers buy, consider getting this additional market research, available through a local business consultant or SBA office.

Convenience to Customer Decisions

If you were setting up a small retail store with snack items, you would locate it along the path that customers follow in the morning, at noon, or after work, when they most want snack items. If you are selling gifts or impulse products, your store will be convenient to primary shops in hopes of drawing the shopper's attention to your wares. It may be in a mall or popular downtown area; it would not be located in an industrial complex.

As you research your customers, understand when they make the decision to buy the products you sell, and then be there. For example, a bookstore specializing in quality illustrated books would locate near art shops and craft stores. One that concentrated on children's books should locate near other shops that cater to adults with children. A store that sold whole bean coffee and specialty teas would locate near a large supermarket that draws food buyers but doesn't serve this customer.

Competitive Sites

Maybe in your search for the perfect site you discover that your competitor is already there. What choices do you have? First, you can go somewhere else, locating your store where it will successfully reach a similar market and customer base. Second, you can change your business concept to fill an unmet need and move in next door. Or, if the competitive store has a good location but isn't utilizing it, you can move in next door and draw its customers.

Don't let competitors easily run you off from a good site. By simply modifying your business concept you may be able to develop a cooperative competitor relationship that helps both of you build profitable stores.

Shopping Centers

For the first half of the twentieth century, individual stores and shops were the norm. The center of a community would be populated with retail stores, which centralized retailing. After World War II, shopping centers started popping up in suburban areas, near new subdivisions of homes. These shopping centers were convenient to where people lived, so they were often called convenience centers. As cities expanded outward and smaller communities were overrun and frequently became the sites of renewed communities with even larger regional shopping centers called malls. In four-season climates, these malls were indoors to protect customers from the weather—and to encourage them to shop in any weather. Big-box stores often were leased first at the edges of these malls; these stores were called anchor stores and were intended to draw large groups of buyers. Smaller stores filled in the spaces between the anchors and fed on the traffic drawn in.

Should you locate your independent retail store within a shopping center? Yes, if that is the best location for your success. Following is a summary of the primary types of shopping centers and their structures. Keep your own retail concept in mind as you review their functions.

Question

I *hate* shopping malls. Should I set up my store downtown?
Independent retailing is about what you want, but it also is about what your customers want. If you are adamantly opposed to shopping malls and there are opportunities for your store in nearby downtown areas, do your research and, if you will succeed there, go for it. Just be sure that your store or the downtown center has sufficient drawing power to meet your income requirements.

Convenience Centers

A convenience center may be as small as a few related stores located at a popular intersection. It typically includes a convenience market and a few other stores, most commonly service stores (such as a dry cleaner) or a small restaurant or fast-food outlet. They are designed to serve passing traffic, with a visible location and adequate parking. Every day, millions of people shop at convenience centers across North America.

Neighborhood Centers

A neighborhood center typically has one major store, such as a large grocery store, and twelve to fifteen smaller stores that depend on the larger store to draw customers. You'll also hear neighborhood centers called strip malls, plazas, or mini-malls. Like the convenience center, it is located at a busy intersection and requires off-street parking. A wide variety of stores can locate in neighborhood centers, including retail, service, and restaurants. A strong mix of small stores can draw customers from nearby neighborhoods.

Regional Centers

Often called malls, regional centers have at least two major tenants and as many as eighty smaller stores. Most regional centers are indoors or at least have covered walk areas. They frequently are located away from the downtown area and where land costs are lower—or were lower when the centers were built—because regional centers require extensive space for parking. Regional centers draw customers from other neighborhoods and even outlying towns. A strongly promoted mall will have seasonal events and entertainment to draw the widest number of potential customers for its tenants. The operating hours of stores within the mall are extended, and most are open for at least twelve hours every day.

Mega-Malls

The largest of the shopping centers are called super-regional centers or mega-malls. They range in total size from 750,000 to 1,000,000 square feet—that's seventeen to twenty-three acres in size! Each of the anchor stores in a mega-mall will occupy at least 100,000 square feet, usually on two or more levels. In between the anchors will be 100 or more smaller retail stores and restaurants. Mega-malls become destinations, drawing buyers from a wide region.

Downtown Stores

Not to be outdone, many communities have revitalized downtown areas into shopping centers. Most are built around anchor stores and even parks or other attractions. With urban renewal, dilapidated sections of downtown areas have been converted into business centers and parking garages. Where there are people, there are retailers. Many small retail stores have opted to set up shop in downtown stores. As stores began vacating downtowns, property values diminished until it was profitable for investors to buy up and remodel buildings into retail shopping centers. In some cases, the buildings were previously factories or warehouses.

In smaller communities, downtown areas still attract retail stores looking for lower rents and community traffic. They rely on courthouses, government offices, medical centers, office buildings, and other draws to attract customers.

You have one other option in locating your retail store. You can have it in your home. However, your customers may not like driving to your location to shop. For that reason, most small retailers instead locate their store where the customers frequently are. If you happen to own a home in a retailing area or are willing to live in the back room or upstairs above your retail store, it can be a good opportunity. Alternatively, you can set up a home-based retail store that exclusively sells online. In this case, you *can* locate your business at home—as long as local zoning laws allow it. If selling online interests you, contact your city or county building department about regulations for home-based businesses in residential zones.

Store Types

Where you set up your store is extremely important to your success. The type of store also is vital. You have choices. You can establish a small standalone store, have a store adjacent to other stores, have a store within a store, or a small standalone store within a mall, called a kiosk. Following are guidelines for selecting the type of store that you will set up.

Standalone stores are unique stores that don't require other retailers or businesses to draw customers. They are destinations. A jewelry retailer can have a standalone store. The advantage is that they don't have other stores nearby to detract from them. Nor, however, are they able to draw from other businesses. Given the advantages of cooperative retailing, few modern retailers opt for standalone stores.

Adjacent stores are the most popular. Whether in a neighborhood shopping center, a mega-mall, or in a downtown retail area, adjacent stores offer convenience to shoppers. However, poor neighbors can ruin the neighborhood and drive your business away. Be cautious as you select an adjacent store location, paying attention to who your neighbors are and how successful they are. If a weak neighbor store goes out of business it may mean a stronger store will move in—or it could mean that the store will sit vacant for months or years and hurt your business.

Store within a store is a unique opportunity for smaller retail concepts and specialty or niche retailers. For example, a jewelry retailer can set up within a big-box store or a mercantile, paying a rental fee and percentage of sales to the primary store. This structure works best with merchandise that is smaller and more unique. High-end brand names offer drawing power.

Kiosk stores are standalone stores within a mall. A kiosk is a booth. Similar retail opportunities include portable carts for selling merchandise from the sidewalk. At indoor malls, a kiosk or booth offers the advantage of being protected from the weather. Security can be an issue, because pilferage, especially when selling products that are small, can be high.

Landlords and Leases

With all this talk about location comes a frank discussion of how to rent or lease a site to your advantage. Some small retailers in downtown areas may be able to purchase their stores, but the majority of retailers—especially those in shopping centers—must sign a lease.

A *lease* is a property rental contract with a specific term or length. There are three common types of leases: fixed rent, straight percentage, and percentage with minimum. Following is a discussion of how they work.

Fixed-Rent Lease

Under a *fixed-rent lease*, the tenant pays the same amount every period (typically a month), regardless of the sales volume. The lease payment, sometimes referred to as rent, usually is based on the size of the store in square feet. In fact, most commercial properties are priced and compared using square footage.

Many tenants prefer fixed-rent leases because their rent costs do not go up if their sales increase. It is a fixed expense for their business. Tenants also prefer longer leases, such as three or five years, though the term can be an obligation if your store closes before expiration. Some fixed-rent leases are adjusted annually, based on indexes such as the Consumer Price Index or other economic indicators.

Downtown stores and smaller shopping centers, especially in outlying areas and small towns, tend to be offered on fixed-rent leases. Retailers who prefer fixed-rent leases may lease a downtown store rather than a mall location because the downtown location has fixed rent.

Before you select a retail site, do some research on the local rates so that you can accurately compare them. Talk with property managers, landlords, and other retailers to determine what fair market rates are in your area.

Straight-Percentage Lease

Under this less popular agreement, the retail tenant pays rent equal to a stated percentage of the periodic sales figure. Quarterly payments are common, though monthly and even annual payments are done.

For a tenant, a straight percentage can be great or a drain. If sales increase, you will be paying higher rent. If they fall off, you will pay less. Because a straight-percentage lease is riskier for landlord and tenant, it is not as popular as other lease forms.

Percentage-with-Minimum Lease

A percentage-with-minimum lease is a combination of the previous two lease forms. Rent is a percentage of sales, but there is a minimum that must be paid even if sales fall off. There is less risk for the landlord and more for the tenant, so the percentage is less than in a straight-percentage lease. If your store's sales dramatically exceed expectations you will pay a higher rent.

Percentage-with-minimum leases are the most popular type of shopping center leases. It protects the center owner from an unsuccessful tenant yet rewards the landlord for higher sales levels. The shopping center has an incentive to increase sales for tenants through advertising and promotions.

How Shopping Center Leases Differ

Larger shopping centers and malls use a modified version of the percentage-with-minimum lease structure. The primary reason is that they provide not only the retail space, but also common space and services shared by all tenants within the mall.

Shopping center leases get more complex as the landlords and tenants divvy up the risks and rewards of real estate and retailing. The lease for your retail space will be dictated more by the landlord than by you, the tenant. However, you must know what common leasing terms mean:

Net or single net lease: the tenant pays the base rent plus property taxes. The leasor pays the building insurance and building maintenance costs.

Net-net or double-net lease: the tenant pays the base rent plus property taxes and building insurance. The leasor pays the building maintenance costs.

Net-net-net or triple-net lease: the tenant pays the base rent plus property taxes, building insurance, and maintenance.

Under a triple-net lease, the risks are reduced for the landlord and shifted to the tenant. That means the total rent paid to the landlord is lower. It also means that the tenant can shop around and reduce secondary (net) costs rather than rely on the landlord to do so, thus saving money that adds to the profit.

In addition to rent, shopping center tenants typically must pay into a tenant association that coordinates cooperative advertising and funds other common promotions. Make sure that you are aware of these costs as you sign a lease. They must be in your budget, as they are expenses that will reduce your profits. Also, if you are comparing two locations, make sure that you compare the occupancy costs (fixed rent, overhead, common area costs) and the promotion costs (advertising, signage, and so on) as well as estimated traffic to determine a cost per customer.

Negotiating the Lease

Though you are a first-time retailer with a small business, you still have power as you negotiate an optimum store lease. Your greatest power is knowledge. You're learning about the retail process as well as how to select and lease a profitable retail location. There's one more component you need. You must understand basic negotiating techniques as you agree to the terms of your store lease. You are negotiating against professionals, so you probably won't get the very best lease terms, but you also don't want to get the worst. Following are some guidelines and tips for negotiating your store's lease:

- Good negotiators are good planners. Know what you want to achieve in the negotiation before you begin.
- Know your bottom line. Based on estimated retail sales and typical expenses, how much should you expect to pay for rent, and what will it include?

- Learn as much as you can about the landlord and property manager. Who are they? What problems have they had in leasing this property?
- Learn what you can about the property. How old is it? How long has it been available?
- Find out about your neighbors. Who are they? What is the size of their stores? What do they pay for rent? What are the lengths and terms of their leases?
- Contact local government offices to verify that the property is properly zoned for your commercial venture before you sign a lease.
- Get a renewal option that allows you to renew the lease at the end of the term for a specified amount rather than having to renegotiate the lease.
- If you are joining an existing shopping mall, how stable are the primary tenants? Will they be leaving soon?
- If your business doesn't work out and you must close, can you sublet your store to another tenant? If so, under what conditions?
- Determine what terms you need to make your venture profitable. Do you need free or lower-cost rent during the two months it will take you to set up your store? Many landlords provide this concession—if asked.
- Make sure you are clear on all terms of the lease and that they all are in writing. There are no verbal agreements in real estate.

Remember: Information is power. The more you know about your target property and landlord, the better position you will be in to negotiate a fair and profitable lease.

CHAPTER 8

Setting Up Your Business

You're getting closer to opening day for your retail store. The next step in this process is to set up your business as a unique entity. That means handling the legal and financial requirements, getting needed licenses and permits, determining what you legally need to do about employees, setting up your financial accounts, and related matters. This chapter covers these topics and more.

Logistics of Retail Start-Up

There's much to do in starting up a retail store. You must make sure it follows the laws and regulations that govern businesses in your area. You must plan for the inevitability of employees. You need to get your bank accounts set up. And you must make sure you have adequate insurance to cover possible major losses due to damage, theft, or lawsuits.

Fortunately, the road to retail start-up is well paved. You're not the first. And you're not alone. The following information will help you feel more comfortable and productive as you set up the legal and regulatory sides of your retail business.

Legal

A *law* is a rule of conduct. Laws govern nearly all aspects of our lives. Business is no exception. The laws that rule business include protections for consumers, transactions, and safety. Without a codified set of proven laws, business would not be conducted as it is. However, that doesn't mean laws are easy to implement or follow.

The legal system considers a business an entity. If you are the owner, it is a part of your assets. If it is owned by a corporation, it is a separate entity, almost as if it were a separate person. Business entities will be covered later in this chapter.

Licensing

The law requires that all business enterprises be licensed in some way. A *license* is a legal permission to do a specified thing. A business license, for example, allows you to conduct business within the jurisdiction. Most business licenses are issued by a county or city, while others may be issued by a state or province.

 Fact

In addition to a business license, some businesses require specialized licenses. If your business sells liquor, for example, a liquor license must be obtained. If you sell products that may have safety issues, another license may be required. The license is designed to help control the appropriate sale of products for the safety and well-being of the buyers and the general public.

The first place to check about licensing is your city or county offices. Given a brief description of your business, they can tell you what licenses will be required. In addition, they can refer you to other sources of licenses and regulations that govern your type of business.

Employment

Even if you plan to run the store yourself or with a spouse or family members, you need to know the employment laws that impact your business. Are business partners or family members exempt from employment laws? What are the laws? What employment information must you post in your store? What is the minimum wage, and does it apply to your business? These and other questions can be answered by your state employment department, which you can contact by telephone, online, or at offices located in larger cities. Identify yourself as a retailer and ask for an appointment to discuss employment law and requirements.

Financial and Banking

An important step in setting up a business is establishing a banking account and getting financial records in place. Later in this chapter there will be more specifics on selecting a bank, establishing a merchant (credit card) account, and identifying other banking services you'll need. For now, be aware that there are laws and regulations regarding financial records that you must follow.

The most critical legal aspect of business finance and banking is taxation. You will be required to pay income tax on your profits (in most states) and pass on the sales tax (in most states) that your customers pay. To stay within the law you must maintain accurate records and share them with the powers that govern these taxes. There will be more on this topic later in this chapter and in coming chapters.

Insurance and Security

Business is risky. Your business may not succeed. A natural catastrophe may wipe out your store. A customer may slip and fall while shopping. A major supplier may sue you. All sorts of things can happen that jeopardize your business. That's why you will need insurance coverage for your business. Basic business insurance is covered later in this chapter.

Security is also a business issue. A shopper—or an employee—may steal from you. Insurance is available to help reduce the costs, but the most important thing you can do is minimize potential security losses. Ask your local police department if it offers training for retailers on how to minimize shoplifting and employee theft.

Business Structures

A business can be a legal entity. It may be totally your entity and responsibility, it may be shared with partners, or it could be a separate entity in which you and others own a share. When you wrote your business plan (Chapter 6) you may have decided which business structure you will take (sole proprietorship, partnership, and corporation). Following is a discussion of these forms to help you make the right decision for your business.

Sole Proprietorship

A *proprietor* is an owner. A sole proprietorship is a single owner. If you start a business by yourself you automatically are the sole proprietor; the majority of small businesses are sole proprietorships. It means that you are personally liable for all debts and commitments made by the business. It also means that your financial and credit resources are the only resources the business has available. It doesn't mean, however, that you must be the only employee. A large sole proprietorship can have hundreds of employees and numerous locations.

A sole proprietor has the greatest freedom of action, not requiring the permission of other owners or stockholders to make decisions. In addition, a sole proprietorship is the least expensive business entity to establish.

A major reason why businesspeople select one form of business over another is taxation. Sole proprietors pay income taxes on the profits, if any, of the business. If the store has $200,000 in annual sales and the store expenses (including inventory) are $150,000, the sole proprietor will be taxed for an income of $50,000.

Another reason to select a specific form of business is liability. Sole proprietors are liable for anything that their business does. That's why they buy insurance. However, if insurance doesn't cover major damage or a lawsuit, the proprietor must. Riskier enterprises can get more legal protection by establishing partnerships or corporations—at a cost.

 Fact

A sole proprietor is not always limited to one person. In some states, a husband and wife who equally own a business can be sole proprietors. In other states, a spouse is considered a partner in the business whether he participates or not. Check with a business attorney to determine the best business form to take for your retail store.

Partnership

Need additional capital to start and run your retail store? Need some expertise and management help? Maybe a partnership is the best business form for you. A *partnership* is an entity wherein two or more people own a business. How they participate in the partnership depends on what type it is: general or limited.

A *general partnership* consists of two or more partners, each of whom has equal legal responsibility for the company's actions and debts. The partners don't have to contribute the same amount of capital or skill, and they aren't required to split profits evenly. General partners, typically, have unlimited liability, just as sole proprietors do. The details of capital and profits are included in the partnership agreement.

A *limited partnership* has at least one general (active) partner and one or more investors whose liability is limited to the amount of their financial contributions. If they invest $50,000 and the business somehow loses $200,000, the limited partner only loses the $50,000 while the general partner loses the rest. However, in most partnership agreements, the limited partner has no power in the day-to-day operations of the business.

The way in which partnerships are taxed is based on the partnership agreement. If it is an equal general partnership, the year's profits are split evenly and each partner must pay taxes on the amount received. In a limited partnership, the partners are taxed based on their share. If a limited partner receives 25 percent of profits, that is the amount the partner must pay taxes on, not on the entire profit of the business.

An Agreement of General Partnership includes the name and place of business, purpose of the business, and term (length of the partnership agreement). It also identifies the general partners, states how profits and losses will be distributed, notes how partnership interests can be assigned to others (if at all), and lists the rights and responsibilities of the general partners. In addition, there are terms that specify what will happen at the death or retirement of a general partner, as well as how the partnership can be terminated. Drawn up by a business attorney, a partnership agreement is a binding contract that will guide your business decisions.

Corporation

One of the disadvantages of both sole proprietorships and general partnerships is the owner's liability for business debts. If the business loses a $1,000,000 suit, the owners must pay it out of their own pocket (or insurance coverage). A corporation is different. A *corporation* is a legal entity that can buy, sell, and enter into contracts as if it were a person. It is responsible for its own debts, theoretically freeing the owners from this obligation. Practically, many smaller corporations are required to have primary stockholders cosign for major debts, minimizing the risk to lenders if the corporation fails. Legal advice is necessary in setting up a business corporation.

There are many types of corporations, including public (stock is sold to the public), nonprofit (actually, not-for-profit), and S corporation. Most large corporations pay income tax on profits; stockholders then must pay taxes on their share of profits—double taxation. An S corporation is a smaller corporation structure with a limited number of stock owners. It *does not* pay income tax on profits. Instead, it passes all profits on to owners, who must pay taxes as individuals. Which form is right for you in your unique situation? Ask a business attorney.

Corporations, even S corporations, can be expensive to launch because of all the legal advice and paperwork required. Make sure that your retail store requires the advantages and can accept the disadvantages of corporate structure before filing.

LLP

A newer option when setting up a business entity is the limited-liability partnership (LLP). It combines some advantages of partnerships and of corporations into a single entity. An LLP limits the *liability* of partners to the amount of their investment. Partners are *not* limited in their participation in business decisions. This structure is set up primarily for professional groups such as doctors, attorneys, and so on. Your state may or may not allow LLP ownership of retail stores. Some states allow limited-liability companies (LLCs). Check with your state's department of corporations for specific information.

Sales Taxes

"In this world nothing can be said to be certain, except death and taxes." Benjamin Franklin knew it in 1789, and it is more obvious today. The national tax bill is staggering and touches everything you own, purchase, or use. One of the most common taxes is the consumption tax—also known as the sales tax—which is collected on the purchase of goods and services.

Most sales taxes are collected by state governments, though municipalities and counties often get a share of the tax based on where the sale was made. As of 2007, only Alaska, Delaware, Montana, New Hampshire, and Oregon do not have state sales taxes. The other forty-five states and District of Columbia have sales taxes that range from 2.9 to 7.25 percent of the sale. Many states exempt or reduce sales tax on food or drugs.

As a retail store owner you will likely be faced with collecting sales tax from your customers. How much and on what depends on your state's regulations. Your business will be issued a sales tax permit with a unique account number. You will be *required* to collect sales tax, and your customers will expect you to add it on the sale and collect it. Then what? Periodically, you will send the collected sales tax to a governing body, typically a board of equalization or similar department within your state government. Reporting and payment requirements differ from state to state. Check with your state sales tax agency for specific information. In general, the money you collect from customers in *their* payment of sales tax must be set aside and paid to the state monthly, quarterly, or annually, depending on state regulations. In most states, the lower your store sales level (and sales tax), the less frequently you will need to pass it along. You will complete a sales tax reporting form and send a check or make an electronic transfer of funds as dictated.

 Fact

As a retailer, you aren't required to pay sales tax on anything you purchase for resale to a customer. The end-user (customer) is required to pay the sales tax in states with sales tax. For example, there is no sales tax on your wholesale inventory. Nor is there tax required on merchandise you buy from another retailer that you intend to resell at your store. The retailer you buy from must record your sales tax permit number with the sale in order for you to qualify for the exemption on the sale.

Sales tax collected on Internet and out-of-state sales are handled differently. Contact your state's sales tax agency or board of equalization to determine when and how you must collect sales tax from customers.

Employees

Your retail store probably will have employees at some point in its operation. When it does, you will be subject to employment laws for your state. An employee is someone who works for you for hourly wages or salary. You are responsible to pay the employee for work, to provide a safe working environment, and provide required benefits. The benefits required may be as basic as worker's compensation insurance (to cover injuries) and employment insurance, or can include mandated health benefits. Of course, you can offer additional benefits to attract and retain employees, but you cannot offer less than the state requires.

Employment requires a contract, a definition of duties, and a wage or salary. The agreement is binding on all parties.

Employment Contract

Employment is a contract between two parties, the employer and the employee. They agree verbally or in writing to the terms of employment. Most employment contracts or agreements are *at will*, meaning that either can cancel the contract with a specified notice. If the termination is considered unjust, the employee may take legal action against the employer. If the termination is for theft of property, the employer may file criminal charges against the employee.

Employment law can be complex, and you will need assistance from your state employment office and possibly an attorney who specializes in employment to define your rights and responsibilities. Every state has its own employment rules and regulations, which you must follow if you hire within the state.

Setting Wages and Salaries

Establishing a wage for employees depends on varying factors, including the profitability of the business. However, too many stores pay "the going rate" or lowest amount that will draw employees without considering costs of living. As an independent businessperson, you have the privilege of hiring higher-quality workers, training them well, and paying them a living wage. Managers of big-box stores don't have this opportunity. They must pay whatever the corporate office says they can pay and no more. In that situation, employees are commodities. Your retail store can reward employees for valuable service, ingenuity, and caring for your customers. In fact, one of the benefits of shopping at your store over big-box stores is the higher level of knowledge and service that customers will receive. Expect to pay for it. Minimum wage will earn, at the most, minimum effort.

Because small businesses view their employees as retail associates, they expect more of them and they pay accordingly. How much? The answer depends on the value that the employee can bring to your business. If the employee is a manager, the value will be greater than for a clerk. Local business associations can tell you what the typical wages and salaries are in your marketplace. Remember: to get better employees, offer better wages.

Hiring and Firing Employees

Much of employment law covers the hiring and firing of employees. Its primary intent is to protect employees from discrimination and harassment, though the law also covers employer rights. Before you hire your first employee, find an employment adviser who can help you understand what you can and cannot do. A discrimination suit, for example, can damage your business before it even gets started.

Firing an employee also can be a legal problem depending on state employment laws and enforcement. Know what you can and cannot do in releasing an employee. Numerous books about employment law are available. Make sure that the books you choose cover your state's employment laws.

Hiring Family

Can you legally hire family members to work in your business? Of course you can; it's *your* business! Whether they are considered employees and subject to state employment laws depends upon the state. Even the matters of wages and minimum age are impacted by state laws. You may be able to hire a younger family member in exchange for room and board—if your state law allows it.

In states where a husband and wife work together in a sole proprietorship, neither are employees. Check with your state employment office to determine how the law governs the work of spouses, partners, and other family or living-group members.

Business Banking

Even if your retail store sells only to cash customers, you'll need somewhere other than a sock to store your cash. Add to this the complexities of personal checks, traveler's checks, credit cards, and debit cards, and you have even more need for a bank.

A *bank* is a commercial or state institution that provides various financial services. Most banks take deposits, make loans, and offer related financial products. Business banks specialize in the needs of businesses rather than consumers. A small retail store doesn't require a business bank to handle its financial account unless large amounts of cash and credit are involved. If possible, set up a small business account at your current bank or credit union. Most financial institutions usually will be more responsive to existing customers. If you plan to do much of your banking online, make sure the bank you select has capability for it.

When setting up a business account, you will need documents that show you have filed for a fictitious business name (DBA) and that you are its owner. In addition, you will need an address, preferably of your store, but it could be a post office box or temporary address. You also will need personal identification, which is an easier task if you already have an account at the bank.

At the time you open your account, ask about other financial services the bank offers to small businesses. You may want to use them someday. In addition, find out how to prepare deposits and deliver them to the bank. Most banks have a night deposit box where you can leave one of their deposit bags anytime, day or night. If you've not done a business deposit before, ask your banker or a teller for assistance.

Merchant Account

A merchant account is a financial service that accepts credit and debit card transactions from customers and deposits them in your business bank account. Nearly all retailers accept card transactions, and most customers expect them to be accepted everywhere. You will work with your bank to set up and manage the account. The fees you will pay depend on the agreement you sign. Following is an overview on merchant accounts for small business.

Setting Up an Account

Setting up a merchant account is relatively simple, though it may take a few weeks to get it activated as the service checks out your credit rating, coordinates with your bank for electronic deposits, and sets up your card machine.

A card machine can be a standalone machine that ranges in cost from $200 to $500 or it can be built into your POS software with a basic reader nearby. Alternately, some card machines can be leased through the merchant service. Make sure you get full instructions on how to set up and test the machine prior to your opening day.

Fees and Reports

The fees for processing credit and debit cards typically include a monthly charge and a percentage fee. The actual percentage depends on the transaction size, the card (Visa, MasterCard, Discover, and a few others), and the type of card.

Example, one major merchant account service sets a flat charge of $12 per month to cover reports. Larger businesses with more requirements may pay higher charges. Some services will waive the monthly charge under certain circumstances. The fee is based on a variety of factors, including whether the card is passed through the card reader (swiped) or keyed in and whether the card is a "rewards" card. The transactions frequently are classified as qualified (best rate), mid-qualified (medium rate), and non-qualified (highest rate). With so many variables, how can you budget for merchant card fees? The best answer will come from your merchant account representative or your banker. Otherwise, if you budget about 3.5 to 4 percent of the sales total for merchant account fees you will be close. Your goal will be to manage the account for lower costs—every dollar you save will go toward profits.

Business Insurance

Business insurance is big business! There are many types of risks in business, and for every one there is at least one type of policy. There are policies that protect business owners against loss from fire, theft, natural disasters, customer injury, employee theft, errors and omissions, and many other acts that can injure or destroy a small business.

Following is a short list of the primary types of business insurance policies available to small businesses:

- **Property insurance** pays if specified business property (building, fixtures, inventory) is damaged.
- **Personal injury insurance** covers costs of an injury to people or damage to personal property while on your business premises.
- **Business income insurance** pays if the business loses income due to an uncontrollable event.
- **Physical damage insurance** made to the landlord's property by a customer, employee, or other person.

- **Employment practices insurance** covers damages or settlements based on employment law.
- **Key insurance** protects against the loss (death or disability) of a key employee.
- **Succession insurance** pays the lost share of a partnership on the death of a partner.
- **Errors and omissions insurance** pays if a business principal makes a costly error.
- **Cyber liability insurance** pays on the loss of valuable data due to a computer security breach or catastrophic damage.

These are just a few of the more common insurance products available to small businesses. The most economical choice is to purchase a bundle of common business insurances in a package, sometimes called an *umbrella policy*. Rates are lower than for individual policies and can give you more protection than à la carte insurance.

How can you find adequate and cost-effective business insurance? Start with whatever company you use for your household and automotive insurance. It may or may not carry a business insurance line. If not, your agent probably can recommend a business insurance agent or company that can advise you. Your business success requires having an insurance adviser you can trust.

How much should you budget for business insurance? The answer depends on many factors— including where your business is located, the value of your business, the risks involved, and what inventory you carry. As a starting point, set aside about 1 to 2 percent of your estimated gross sales for annual insurance premiums on an umbrella policy for a typical small retail store. That's $1,000 to $2,000 annually for gross sales of $200,000.

CHAPTER 9

Planning Your Retail Store Layout

Your retail store should be as comfortable to your customers as their own living rooms. That doesn't mean you need a dog relaxing on the sofa or kids sprawled across the floor playing video games. It means that they should feel welcome, relaxed, and intuitively know where to find things. Even if it's their first visit, customers should be able to find what they came in for—and a few things more. Your store layout will offer them logical and emotional choices. This chapter offers you choices to help you design your store for success, as well as tips that can increase your profits.

The Process of Selling

The reason you've worked so hard establishing your retail store is to sell something to people who need or want it. You may be selling candles, jewelry, books, telephones, computers, office supplies, picture frames, sunglasses, car parts, or whatever you choose. The sales process is the same. If you are good at it—and your store layout facilitates it—you have a greater chance of retail success than if you just open the front doors every morning and hope that someone comes in to buy your stuff.

The process of selling at the retail level is really about helping customers buy. In fact, few independent retail stores use hard-core selling techniques to move products. Many instead use consultative selling methods. They help customers identify their needs so they can then make the best purchase decision. No pressure.

 **Essential**

> One of the best ways that an independent retail store can beat the big-box stores nearby is to help customers by using consultative selling. Consult with them to help satisfy their needs and make good buying decisions. This technique is rarely used by clerks in large stores and will be welcomed by many customers. Know your products thoroughly and help your customers choose the most appropriate ones.

Customer Needs

What does your customer need? Because you will have many types of customers, each with a variety of needs, this question may seem difficult to answer. It is. In fact, it's not within your power to know what your customer needs until the customer expresses it by a purchase or a question. With experience you will be able to make a good guess at your customers' current needs, but not until they act or ask will you know.

Of course, when a customer comes into your widget store, you know that he probably wants a widget. That's obvious. But which widget? For whom? What is his budget? Would he like suggestions? The overall question is: Why did he come into your store today?

The Decision Process

For some retail products, the decision process is simple: a red widget or a blue one. For others, making a purchasing decision can get more complicated: red, blue, yellow with orange stripes, large, small, portable, under $10, less than $50, and so on. Within your retail store, you probably will have merchandise that requires simple and complex decisions. In addition, you will have customers who are more comfortable with making these decisions on their own, while others prefer some help. So let's break down the decision process into three easy steps: need, choice, and commitment.

As an example, a new customer comes into your store and walks to your widget section indicating a perceived need for a widget. There are four types on the shelf, and the customer picks each up to examine it and the price tag. Based on the need for a medium-size widget costing about $5, the customer picks one up, walks over to the cashier, and makes a commitment by purchasing it. Simple enough.

Another customer soon walks in and looks around the store for ten minutes, then stops in front of the widget section and stares at them for a couple of minutes, obviously thinking. Surreptitiously, you walk by to make yourself available for questions. The customer asks you which widget would be best for a specific task and you offer your knowledge (without explaining the history and various uses of widgets). The customer then makes a decision and hands you the product to ring up the sale.

These are different customers with different needs and methods of making a decision, but the process they followed is the same: need, choice, and commitment.

Guiding the Decision Process

As you answer questions for a customer, you are assisting him in making a buying decision. However, it is not the only way you guide the decision process. In fact, as you laid out your retail store for customers, you were thinking about their needs, their choices, and their commitments. You placed the popular widget department in an easy-to-find location with lots of signage to help customers quickly fulfill their need. (Or you placed popular widgets in the rear of the store so that customers must walk past other merchandise to get to them.)

The bottom line is that you will design your retail store layout to meet customers' needs and help them make and commit to buying choices. You *won't* design the store for yourself. You will design it for your *customers*. To do so, you must understand and guide their buying decisions.

Designing for Your Customers

Your customers are the resources that keep your retail store open—and profitable. Without them you will be surrounded by more widgets than you can ever use. By helping customers fulfill their needs you will be fulfilling yours.

Think of it this way: It's your *customers'* store and you get to run it! Keep your customers—your "employer"—happy, and you will be gainfully employed for a long time.

Your Store

Before getting into the details of store layout, take a look at your store's shell—the walls, floors, and other components that will hold your store. How large is it? What is its shape? What is its condition? Are there barriers or limitations that will restrict store layout? What do you have to work with?

There are no specific requirements for how much floor space you will need in your store. For practical purposes, most small retail stores range in size from 800 to 2,000 square feet. Medium-size retailers need 2,000 to 10,000 square feet total, including sales floor and back room. The ideal size is one that fits your income goals for annual sales per square foot. An analytical look at your competitors will help you in sizing your store. If you estimate that a competitor has $300,000 in annual sales in a 1,500-square-foot store, the annual income is $200 per square foot (300,000 ÷ 1,500). If your sales goal is $200,000 a year and you want to meet the goal of $200 per square foot, you'll need a store of at least 1,000 square feet (200,000 ÷ 200). There are many variables, of course, but this comparison is a guideline.

Your Customers' Store

How would your customers lay out your new store? If you know lots of people who are your target customers, you can ask them. If you are your best customer, you can ask yourself. Visit competitors' and non-competitors' stores and take notes that answer these questions:

- What do you like or not like about shopping there?
- Are products convenient?
- Are they easy to find?
- Is the store comfortable and well lit?
- Are the display fixtures too tall or too short for typical customers?
- What would you change about the store to make it more customer-friendly?

Make more notes in your retail notebook and review the notes you made as you began research on starting a store. Then use your notebook to begin making sketches of how you can lay out your store for optimum sales. Unless you are starting a bargain or warehouse-type store, include some features that make your store comfortable, such as chairs or small tables where the customer can place products they wish to buy rather than carry them around.

Directing Traffic

Retail stores should be designed to make navigation easy for customers. Not only should merchandise be placed logically; it should be easy to get to the merchandise. The simplest flow is rows of shelving along the walls and evenly spaced on the floor. However, a store of straight rows can be boring for customers. Instead, design the store layout to encourage traffic, yet offer a variety of paths. For example, if an aisle is blocked by numerous customers there should be alternate paths that other customers can take to reach the back of the store. Aisles must have adequate width for customers to freely move, but not take up too much floor space. Common widths for retail aisles range from 36 to 48 inches.

The three primary areas within a retail store are the entry and cash wrap, the sales floor, and the back room. Following are some guidelines for designing each.

 **Question**

What should I do in my store to accommodate disabled customers?
Aisles must be of adequate width to allow passage of a wheelchair.
Steps to and within a store may be required to have a ramp, or an
alternate entry with a ramp may be needed.

Your local building department can answer questions about
conforming to Americans with Disabilities Act (ADA) equal access
requirements.

Entry and Cash Wrap

Your store's entry is analogous to your home's entry. You want
it neat, attractive, and inviting to visitors. The entry area of your
store includes the front display window, the transition area, and
the cash wrap or cashier area.

The front window must be inviting, just as your home's front
porch or doorway is. It should say, "Welcome! Please come in." The
window should display merchandise that indicates the width *and*
depth of your inventory. That is, one section can display representatives from all departments while another section can feature a variety of merchandise from a single department, frequently changed.

The transition area is an open and attractive space near the
door where new customers can stop and quickly look around.
Signage and merchandise within the store will draw them further.
Use the transition area to impress customers with your store's attitude: neat, clean, and helpful, with lots of treasures inside. Some
customers will ask for assistance, but others will simply locate a
department that may meet their need and head for it.

The cash wrap or cashier area should be near the front door
and next to the transition area. It offers the owner or clerk an
opportunity to smile at the customer. Some customers will then ask
questions and others will not, but the nearby clerk is an implied
offer to assist.

Sales Floor

The purpose of a retail store is to sell merchandise to customers. More accurately, the purpose is to help them buy. The sales floor is the presentation of your merchandise in a logical and accessible form. Aisles should be clear of clutter and trash.

Besides making the buying decision easier for a customer, the sales floor also should suggest related products that fulfill similar needs. For example, near the widget department should be a rack of widget repair tools or widget cleaners. The customer may be reminded of a related need and buy additional products.

The sales floor actually extends to the cash wrap, where customers pay for their merchandise. This area can have related merchandise (widget tools) or unrelated products (snacks). In most cases, these impulse-buy products are attractive and offer a high profit for the store. For security, the cash wrap typically has sales display space behind it where the customer can see higher-priced or breakable merchandise.

Back Room

Your store's back room is important to your success. It must be designed logically to fit the needs of your retail operation. If you must have extensive inventory that cannot all be on the sales floor, it will be stored in the back room. If your business requires shipping merchandise to customers or returns to distributors, it will need a shipping table and supplies. In addition, you can store out-of-season merchandise and displays in the back room.

The back room also is where employees can take a break and relax. At the minimum it should include a small table and chairs. Depending on how many employees you have (if any) and the store's hours, you may want a small refrigerator in the back room. Cooking facilities are not advised, as cooking food can distract customers.

The back room also should have personal storage for employees where they can safely place uniforms, street clothes, purses, and other personal items. Finally, most stores should have a bathroom unless they have made arrangements to share one with an adjacent store.

 **Question**

What facilities am I required to provide for employees?
Check with your local state employment office or your business attorney for advice on requirements that employers must meet for employees. Remember that these regulations are minimums. You can improve employee relations by doing more for their comfort, which may be reflected in the quality of service they give to your customers.

Signage

Good signage can make a significant difference in traffic, sale, and profits. Signs don't have to be expensive, but they do have to reflect your store's image accurately. Cheap signs suggest a cheap store. Quality signs suggest quality merchandise.

There are two types of signs used in retail stores: informational and directional. Informational signs tell you *what*; directional signs indicate *where*. The signs out in front of your store are informational; they tell customers what the store is: Bob's Widgets. Inside the store are directional signs: Bargain Widgets and Left-Handed Widgets, each above the appropriate merchandise. Informational signs on the shelf in front of the merchandise will name the product and indicate the price: 4-inch Left-Handed Widget, $9.95.

Use signs whenever you want to inform or direct customers. Having a sale on yellow widgets? Are your widgets guaranteed? Can customers special-order widgets? How can customers select the best widget for their needs? (Make the answer short.) Which credit cards do you accept? How about local checks? In each of these cases—and many more—a sign can inform or direct your customers without the need for questions.

The majority of shoppers prefer to shop without help but like to have help nearby if they have questions. You're probably that type of customer. Help your customers by providing adequate informational and directional signage in your store. It's another form of consultative selling, which is explained later in this chapter.

Working Around Limitations

The ideal retail store may not be available to you. Or it may be so expensive that you must settle for a store that has a few limitations or challenges.

Some of the most common challenges in store design involve pillars and posts. Older buildings and multistory buildings often have supporting columns within the store, especially if the store has been remodeled from a larger store. Fortunately, many of these intrusions can be incorporated into the sales floor without significant problems. An obstacle may require that a row of shelves or fixtures be installed around it so it doesn't obstruct foot traffic. Having a pillar in an aisle is just poor planning. Instead, redesign the area to take advantage of the obstruction—or to at least reduce its impact on the sales floor.

🅴✴ Essential

One retail store had a liability: the electrical panels for three stores were mounted in the front corner next to the display window. Creative store owners built a shallow closet around the panels, then hired an artist to paint the door to look like a fireplace. The display window was remodeled to look like a cozy den with the store's merchandise displayed on tables and chairs. A liability became an asset.

Not all retail store sites are square or rectangular. Older commercial buildings that have been frequently remodeled may have pockets of wasted space that are difficult to use or even to access.

If the store location you select has these wasted areas, think creatively to find ways of productively using them. A small space that is not easy to access can be used for seasonal display storage. An attic can store old business records. High perimeter walls may be too high for shelves, but they can be used to display sample merchandise or to attach informational or directional signage.

Some small retail stores are challenged by not having a back door to accept deliveries. All freight and packages must come in the front door. This can be a significant problem if your store will receive numerous shipments. One solution is to have delivery people immediately take shipments to the back room, where storage space is available. Another solution is for the store to have all merchandise delivered to another site, such as a home address, where you can pick it up when the store closes.

Planning for Utilities

Your store will require a variety of services: water, sewer, electricity, gas or fuel oil, telephone, and related utilities. Planning your store means planning for these services as well. Before you select your store, you must identify what utilities you need and determine which are available at your prospective location. Limitations such as insufficient electrical outlets or not enough telephone lines can be resolved, but this should be done before fixtures and merchandise are placed. Also make sure that your computer system is adequate for current and future needs.

Electrical Services

Most retail stores only require 120-volt electrical service, just like that in your home. However, some equipment or machines may require 240-volt service, which is what electric stoves and clothes dryers use. Before finalizing your store plan, have an electrician review it to verify that you will have adequate power. List the store components that require electricity, and how much: lighting, computers, cash register, displays, and so on. In addition, you'll need wall outlets for plugging in a vacuum, fans, power tools, or other portable devices.

For the majority of retail stores, lighting is the primary user of electricity. Make sure your store has adequate lighting fixtures or electrical outlets that allow you to expand lighting as needed. Use energy-saving (and money-saving) lighting where possible. Your local electric utility may offer to audit your store's lighting needs and make recommendations at no cost.

Water and Sewer

Aren't you glad you're not opening a restaurant, which requires extensive water and sewer services? Even retail stores may need these services, especially if the store has a bathroom or two. Does your store need a water source for making coffee, or hot water for other purposes? Does your store have an evaporative (swamp) cooler that requires a water source? Make sure that the store you rent has adequate water and sewer services—in good repair. You don't want to set up your store, then have it all damaged by a broken pipe.

Heating and Cooling

There are few retail stores that don't require a heating or cooling system during the year. Make sure the system in your selected store is operating *before* you move in. It will be more difficult to repair once your store is in place—and it probably will be more difficult to get your landlord to do anything then. If you're not certain whether the system is adequate or in good repair, hire a heating, ventilation, and air-conditioning (HVAC) technician to check out the system. You may be able to get the landlord to pay for the inspection.

Telephone

Depending on your retail business, the telephone may be your most important utility. Customers will call to find out your store hours or to order merchandise. Employees will call in sick. You will use the Internet to check on wholesale orders and shipments.

Fortunately, telephone equipment is relatively inexpensive. You can purchase a two- or three-unit wireless phone with an answering system for under $200.

How many lines will you need? Plan for one or two voice lines, a fax line (if your business requires frequent faxing), and an Internet line. Alternately, you may be able to share a DSL (digital subscriber line) or T1 line among many phones and devices. Ask your phone company.

Computer

Computers are necessary to business, especially for keeping track of sales, inventory, and financial records. This book isn't a primer on computers or software; there are numerous retail computer stores that can help you make your selection. Be aware that the technology changes quickly and that your system will be outmoded within a year or two. You can still use it, of course, but you won't be using all of its potential without periodic upgrades of hardware (the computer, printer, network) and software (programs run on the computer).

One of the most useful advances is wireless technology. You can have a primary computer (the server) anywhere in your store— even hidden in the back room—and it can share information with computers throughout your store, including laptops that are networked. Just make sure that you have adequate security software so you aren't sharing your valuable data with other nearby wireless networks. Again, your computer store can give you advice and get you set up.

CHAPTER 10

Furnishing Your Retail Store

In reality or on paper, your retail store has a concept and a location. Now what? Just as in your home, it's time to furnish your store with specific fixtures and supplies. These components will add function and personality that will make visitors feel comfortable. Chapter 9 helped you lay out the store efficiently. This chapter will guide you in selecting, installing, and using fixtures for your selected retail store. You should read it before you make any decisions about fixtures so you'll choose the best fixtures the first time.

Make Your Store Sell for Itself

In furnishing your home, the goal is to make it comfortable and convenient for those who live there and those who visit there. Furnishing your retail store has the goal of making it easy for customers to buy what you are selling.

How do you come up with a plan to furnish your retail store? You study similar stores, get ideas from various other retail stores, make up your best plan within the given space, and then take some time to make modifications until you're confident that the furnishings will help you sell more merchandise.

Study Similar Stores

Now that you've decided to open your own retail store, your viewpoint will change. As you walk into a store, you will locate the cash wrap, look at the transition area, identify the primary and secondary departments, critique the signage, and recognize the store's ambiance. You now are a perceptive shopper.

You probably have done market research to identify your competitors in the area. Some stores will directly compete with you in your marketplace, while others do not compete. Non-competitors can be a good source of specific information on furnishing your store. Some may even have extra fixtures that they will sell you. Approach non-competitors; study competitors; and learn from both.

Question

How many stores should I study?
As many as you can. One retail candidate used a map to identify a dozen similar stores within 150 miles, then took a two-day road trip to visit each one. Once a model store was identified, she used her notebook to sketch the layout, make notes about inventory, and to record the sizes of primary fixtures.

Study Other Stores

Retailing is retailing. Though stores near you may not sell similar merchandise, their furnishings and fixtures have the same function as those in your store: to help in the buying process. Walk through stores, take notes, and learn how you can serve your customers as well or better.

How can you get assistance from the owner? First, make sure that you identify the owner or manager before you ask business questions. Offer an appropriate compliment on the store, tell them what you are doing, and assure the person that you are not a direct competitor by offering information on what kind of store yours will be. Then ask an open-ended question, such as "How do you like the layout and fixtures in your store?" If the retailer is receptive, you can then ask more specific questions. Just as you will do with customers, build a relationship of trust before you ask more revealing questions. In the process you may build some retail friendships that can help you build your own store.

Make Your Plan

From your work in Chapter 9 you have a sketch of your store. It will indicate the location of doors, windows, utilities, and limitations. Be sure that dimensions are on the sketch. Once you are sure it is accurate, make numerous copies of it so that you can test various ideas. Identify each copy, such as by a letter or number, and then draw in various retail functions and components: cash wrap, back room, primary sales floor, secondary sales floor, and so on. Next, populate the sketches with specific fixtures. (If you're not familiar with the types of retail fixtures, see the list of fixture types in the following section.)

Then, try variations. Move the cash wrap or transition area to the opposite side of the store. Move the main entryway. Angle the aisles. Relocate or reduce the back room. Imagine customers moving through the aisles. It helps if you can visualize your efforts.

Fine-Tune Your Plan

Your store plan isn't ready until you can visualize it from your customer's perspective. It may mean taking time shopping in a store or a department that is similar to yours. Or you can use empty boxes and home shelving units to place and test the layout. Will your customer benefit from the design? If not, make changes.

Of course, the most critical placement decisions involve fixtures that cannot easily be moved. They are placed first. Then movable fixtures are located. A few months after opening you may see where some of these movable fixtures can be relocated to make the shopping experience better for your customer and more profitable for you. Keep in mind, however, that shoppers quickly get used to finding things in a specific location.

Select Primary Fixtures

Just as in your home, there is a variety of furniture and fixtures available for retail stores. What fixtures does your store need? That depends on what you are selling.

Fixture Types

Following is a list of the primary types of store fixtures:

Bookcases are specialized fixtures for bookstores and similar merchandise. Wall bookcases are up to 7 feet tall and 36 to 48 inches wide. Island bookcases are 5 feet tall and 36 to 48 inches wide. The depth depends on the type of books displayed and whether shown cover-out, spine-out, or both.

End caps are installed at the ends of gondolas or other shelving units.

Garment or apparel racks hold clothing either on hangers or on shelves similar to a gondola. Most are circular for maximum merchandising. Some are smaller and flat to better display higher-priced clothing. Mannequins also are used to display garments.

Gondolas are open display units with shelves on two or four sides. They also are referred to as islands. The most common size is 54 inches high, 48 inches wide, and 36 inches deep. Shelving is adjustable.

Pegboards are boards mounted on walls and frames with rows of holes in them to accept display pegs. Packaged merchandise is then hung from these pegs.

Racks are wire or wood display units of various sizes. Some stand alone; others are tables with a bin on the top surface (also called merchandisers); and some hang from retail wall paneling, called slatwalls. Others hold magazines, videos, or other products that have decorative fronts.

Showcases are cases with glass or plastic tops or fronts to show merchandise. Typically 34 inches high, they range from 36 to 60 inches in length. They are used for showing smaller and more valuable merchandise, accessed with a key from the rear of the case by the clerk.

Tables are flat surfaces that easily can be set up to display products. Portable tables are also known as impulse tables.

Bins, barrels, and baskets are miscellaneous display fixtures that you can scatter around your store to show off some types of products.

There are many other types of specialized display units for various types of products. A video store, for example, will have wire racks sized for DVD and video boxes. Some merchandise will come with its own display unit. As you begin shopping for retail fixtures you also will see new and unique displays that can help your customers find what they are looking for.

Don't forget flooring. It's not a sales fixture, but it can impact how customers perceive your store and whether they enjoy their shopping experience with you. It may seem subtle, but it can have an impact on your success—and it can get expensive to change once you're moved in. A local flooring company can offer suggestions and pricing. As flooring is a long-term commitment to the building, your landlord may give you a flooring credit or even pay for the flooring, especially if you have a long lease.

Fixture Sources

Where can you buy retail store fixtures? You might be surprised. In most metropolitan areas there are numerous showrooms and warehouses full of new and used retail store fixtures. Often located in industrial complexes, these sources cater exclusively to retail start-ups. Some are custom cabinet shops or factories that produce various retail fixtures as a primary or secondary business. Others import and assemble fixtures from foreign manufacturing companies. In addition, fixture warehouses will buy fixtures from closing stores and sell them to new stores. This can save you 50 percent or more over the price of new fixtures.

Retail fixture stores can be found in the telephone book and through ads in business publications and classified ad sections. If you are careful, you can purchase fixtures from closing retail stores through eBay and other online sources. Make sure you can inspect the fixtures before purchasing, and plan to pick them up if you're the winning bidder.

Select Secondary Fixtures

In addition to the large fixtures that your store will require to display merchandise, there are many other fixtures and components that can make the job of selling easier. Following is a short list of some of them:

- Bags
- Bar-code labels
- Bar-code scanners
- Cash box
- Cash register(s)
- Cash register supplies
- Coin and bill counters (optional)
- Counter displays
- Dollies and hand trucks
- Gift certificates
- Open/closed/hours signs
- Portable sign frames
- Pricing guns and labels

- Safe
- Security devices
- Shopping baskets
- Shopping carts
- Sign holders
- Storage bins

Where can you find these supplies? There are many sources, including nearby office supply stores. Larger ones have a wide selection of behind-the-counter supplies. Many online store fixture suppliers also can provide secondary fixtures and supplies (bags, etc.).

Essential

Environmentally conscious retailers are finding creative ways to offer customers containers for their purchases that don't require new paper or plastic bags. For example, you could collect and reuse plastic bags that otherwise are thrown away after one use; purchase bags made from recycled plastic or paper; or sell canvas bags that can be used to package purchases.

In addition, look to office supply stores and even furniture stores for customer seating and tables, if needed. You can find functional chairs on sale at furniture stores for less than what they cost at many office or retail supply stores.

Support Equipment

In addition to primary and secondary store fixtures for the sales floor, your retail store also needs support equipment. What that is exactly depends on the type of store you're setting up and how many employees you expect to have within the first couple of years. The support equipment will be used in work areas, rest areas, and in keeping your store clean and sanitary.

Work Areas

Support equipment for work areas includes shipping and receiving equipment, product preparation tables and storage shelves in your back room, and any work equipment that sales clerks need at the front counter. Components you may need range from shipping and metering scales and shipping boxes and tape to inventory shelving, display storage, security tags and removal systems, supplies storage, and lighting. The products you sell may require some preparation before they can be displayed or sold. For example, some clothing may require steaming or pressing, or labels may need to be removed. Think through your retail process thoroughly to determine what support equipment you will need and where you will use it.

Rest Areas

Your enjoyment of retailing and the enjoyment of your employees will depend somewhat on the level of comfort while working. No one wants to be on her feet all day long. Rest breaks are necessary, and, depending on the length of the workday, taking time for lunch can be renewing.

Make sure that your store has adequate rest areas for its employees. If your employment policy allows smoking in designated areas, provide a comfortable and safe location for this activity. If your policy allows employees to eat food or drink beverages while on duty, provide a place to do so.

Sanitation

In addition to a well-stocked restroom (if available), your store should have equipment and supplies to keep it clean. An alternative is to hire a janitorial service to handle regular cleaning. However, you still will need supplies for emergencies, such as a person spilling a beverage in your store.

With hundreds of people visiting your store daily, the floors will get dirty—especially during inclement weather. Displays also may need periodic dusting. At the least, have a broom and dustpan handy for the most obvious dirt in the store's transition area; the janitorial service can get the rest. Better yet, have a vacuum cleaner and a regular schedule for an owner or employee to clean all floors. Vinyl composition tile (VCT) flooring will require periodic mopping, which means that you need a mop and other supplies. Your store also may need glass cleaner and other specialized cleaning products—and a storage place for all of them.

Music

A popular service of many independent retailers is music for customers. Appropriate music can enhance their shopping experience and even keep them in the store longer. What kind of music? How do you provide it at nondistracting levels? Here are some proven ideas:

* Don't broadcast your music from a commercial radio station. Not only is the announcer's talk distracting to shopping, the station may be running commercials for your competitors.
* Place speakers in multiple locations around your store so the sound isn't too loud in one area and too soft in another.
* For most stores, use instrumental music rather than vocals, which can distract a customer. Avoid broadcasting a news program or talk show.
* Make sure the music selected is appropriate for the age group of your primary customer base. You don't want customers leaving early because they don't like the music. Smooth or cool jazz instrumentals and moderate new age music are a good choice for most retail stores.
* Stay away from familiar songs that can distract the customer's thinking. Instead, use uplifting or neutral mood music.
* Satellite radio services have hundreds of commercial-free music channels from which to choose.

- Consider a multidisk CD player (at least ten CDs) that can play songs randomly.
- Have a remote controller at the front counter for any music systems so the clerk can control the music or the volume as needed.
- Ask target customers whether they like or dislike music being played. If they didn't consciously notice the music or say that it was enjoyable, you've met your goal.
- Remember: Don't play the music you like; play what helps your customer relax and make better buying decisions.

Making Your Own Fixtures

Depending on your do-it-yourself skills and your budget, you may find that building fixtures is the best option. Be aware that it is not always the least expensive. If you purchase quality materials and need additional power tools, the costs of building may be greater than having a cabinetmaker or other craftsperson build your fixtures for you.

In addition, you may elect to build only a few specialized fixtures. If you have experience building with wood, you can build a unique cash wrap. If not, you may decide to build storage shelving for the back room.

How can you make your own store fixtures? First, you need a plan. Using your store layout (see Chapter 9), your retail notebook, and notes from visiting other stores, you should have a good idea of what fixtures you can or want to build and their dimensions. Following are some guidelines.

Building the Cash Wrap

The cash wrap in a small retail store serves many purposes. It serves as a customer counter where buyers can place their purchases. It holds the cash register or POS computer, the merchant card equipment, and related equipment used during the transaction. It also will have signs, reminders, and even product displays, especially for impulse items.

Cash wraps are typically about 32 to 36 inches high depending on the size of the merchandise being sold. For example, if the customer buys products in large boxes or shops with a hand-held basket, the countertop should be shorter. Smaller items can be sold at taller cash wraps. If necessary, the cash wrap can be double-decked, with one height for customers to place purchases and another for the transaction equipment. Cash wrap depth can range from 18 to 24 inches for most units.

A secondary use for the cash wrap counter is storage. The area below and behind the counter can house shopping bags, waste bin, pricing equipment, cash register supplies, a computer, a printer or fax, and telephone equipment. You also can install a music system under the cash wrap for easier control.

Building Shelving

You can build sales shelving or storage shelves from wood or composite materials with basic power tools. Many small retailers place their best fixtures at the front of the store and use home-built fixtures in rear departments and the back room. In all cases, the shelving must fit the need. For example, uniform products that are 12-inches deep can be displayed in a simple shelving unit of that size. Products that vary in size will need shelving sized for the largest units.

Alert

Make sure that shelving you build is stable. Wall cases can be anchored to the wall. Island cases can be built back-to-back to widen their base and keep them from tipping over. You don't want customers or employees hurt by unstable fixtures.

The side-to-side width of shelving depends on several factors, including the combined weight of products. Books, for example, require narrower or reinforced shelves. Clothing shelves carry less weight and can be wider. Common widths are in one-foot multiples: 24, 36, and 48 inches. Shelves that hold heavier merchandise can have additional support in the middle or from behind.

Building Racks

There is a wide variety of racks for displaying retail merchandise. Many are made of metal and will require equipment that most people don't have in their home garage. However, the fixtures that hold the wire racks or pegs can be built by handy do-it-yourselfers.

For example, retailers that rely extensively on movable pegs to hang merchandise on walls can purchase pegboard at building supply stores, build a frame, and install it on the store walls themselves. In the same way, shorter, double-sided pegboard or shelving fixtures, called islands, can be built.

Building Tables

Display and impulse tables are handy sales aids that can be built by most do-it-yourselfers. Alternately, office tables or even antique tables can be purchased and rebuilt to serve a variety of purposes in your store. The most useful tables are those with folding legs that can be stored in a small space when not in use. Storage space is valuable in a retail store and shouldn't be wasted. If you are designing your own table, you can purchase folding legs at larger office supply stores or simply buy an inexpensive table and remove the legs for your own design. Make sure that tables are sturdy and will not injure customers or employees.

Computerizing Your Store

There are numerous applications for computers and software in even the smallest retail stores. That's good, especially because the cost of a basic computer is under $1,000. In fact, you may be able to use a second computer from home as your primary retail computer and save money.

The most important question to ask when setting up your retail computer is, What do I want to do with it? This in turn brings up other questions: Will it use specialized POS software? Will it print out receipts and invoices? Will it be used to scan credit cards and send the data by phone to your merchant account provider? Will you be tracking all store inventory on the computer? Will you use it for accounting software? Will you do all of your own accounting or send it electronically to an accountant?

The bottom line is to determine the computer requirements of the software you will be running, then buy or bring in a computer that at least fits the minimum. Many of these software programs are widely available, but the POS and inventory program you buy may be specialized to your type of store, so make sure that the computer meets its requirements.

Buying Retailing Software

Where can you find retailing software? Start with a search on the Internet, such as "retail POS," or "_____POS," filling in the blank with your retail specialty. There are numerous programs for most types of retail stores, and dozens more that are generic but can be modified for your use. Your choice may depend on your budget.

How much do specialized retail software programs cost? Retail specialty packages that handle transactions and basic inventory tasks can range in price from $300 for generic to $10,000 or more for specific applications. If your store has simple transactions and inventory needs, a budget of $5,000 for software should be adequate. If this is too much, look at the generic packages that are customizable and then plan to spend some time setting up the software and learning how it works.

Programs within Microsoft Office, such as Excel spreadsheet, can be sufficient for many financial tasks for your store. Microsoft Access is a database program that you can use to keep track of your store's inventory.

 Fact

If you're not a Microsoft fan or you just like saving money, consider OpenOffice (*www.openoffice.org*), a suite of practical software programs similar to Microsoft Office—and they are free. Included are word processor, spreadsheet, database, drawing, presentation, calculator, and other useful programs compatible with Windows. OpenOffice is an open-source suite of programs developed by Sun Microsystems.

Networking

Networking allows computers to share data with each other. In a small retail store, networked computers can share transaction information instantaneously. The manager can track sales in real time even if she is at a remote location (such as on a sunny beach!). In addition, wireless networking equipment is available so another computer within range that passes the security requirements can exchange vital data with others.

Computer networking advances so fast that your best choice is to decide what you want your system to do, then go to a trusted computer store and ask how to do it. The experts there can provide you with the equipment and know-how to network your store's computers.

CHAPTER 11

Selecting Initial Inventory

Your retail store is coming together. At least on paper, you've developed a business concept, selected a location, planned store layout, and chosen necessary fixtures. The next big step is selecting your initial inventory. The profitability and success of your retail store will depend on choosing products with adequate profit and turnover. Who will you buy from? What will you pay? How will you price your inventory? These and related questions will be answered in this chapter.

Define Your Primary Lines

Many new retail stores get lost at this point. They have been so focused on setting up their store that they are not ready to stock it. Others are chomping at the bit and already have purchased their wholesale stock, which is now sitting in storage. Some will find that the initial stock they purchased doesn't quite work in the store they designed.

Fortunately, you have developed a comprehensive business plan (Chapter 6) that answered the questions of what business you are in. Now you need to focus that plan toward buying the stock you need to open your store.

What Are You Selling?

It may seem to be an obvious question—What are you selling?—but it is more complex than that. Gift stores sell gifts, yes, but *which* gifts will your target customers buy? Before you invest thousands of dollars in buying the inventory, make sure you know exactly what your customers want.

For example, there are many wholesale sources that will attempt to sell you what *they* want to sell rather than what your customers will buy. You'll get a wholesale lot of 1,000 purple widgets that the wholesaler has been trying to unload since buying it from the manufacturer three years ago, when purple was the hot color for widgets. Therefore, it is critical that you know what your customers will ask for before they recognize their own needs.

Question

What if I'm not totally sure what my customers will buy?
Stock what you're sure of. One retailer put up a false wall at the back of her store and stocked the front with what she was sure would sell. Within two months, when she knew her customers' tastes, she moved the wall back farther and added more stock. Alternately, you can take merchandise on approval or consignment that you're not certain will sell. Make sure you understand the terms of the return agreement.

What Are the Wholesale Sources?

In some retail businesses, wholesale sources are a guarded secret. If that's the case for you, you're going to have to do some sleuthing to learn where your competitors buy at wholesale. For most, however, the sources are easy to identify. Here are some proven ways that you can find primary wholesalers for your merchandise lines:

- Attend trade shows for retailers as well as for consumers.
- Identify trade associations that cater to retailers in your field. Find out about membership requirements.

- Read the trade magazines for your type of retailing. Wholesalers advertise there.
- Check the ads in regional business magazines and newspapers.
- Look up your product line in your area phone book and check for "wholesale" sources: Widgets—Wholesale.
- Search the Internet for online wholesale sources.
- Snoop around your competitors' stores, looking for address labels on shipping boxes for received merchandise.
- Ask. Some retailers and clerks will tell you where they get their stock. This is easier to do if you identify yourself as a non-competing retailer from outside their market.
- Work for a competitor and learn about wholesalers, being sensitive to the legal and ethical issues.
- Ask a business counselor at your local SBA office to help you identify potential wholesalers.

How Is the Product Delivered?

The cost of shipping wholesale product to your store can be as much as 5 to 10 percent of the wholesale price. This expense cuts into your profits, so make sure you consider the cost of shipping (smaller lots) or freight (larger lots) for your initial inventory. The price can be significant when importing wholesale product in small lots.

A related issue is time. How quickly can you get the product once it is ordered? If the wholesale ordering process is slow and the shipping method also is slow, it can be weeks or even months between your order and delivery. If ordering for a specific customer, delays can end the sale and you're stuck with a special order.

Many wholesalers are sensitive to the delivery issue and have regional warehouses from which stock can be shipped within one business day of an order. Some even have their own delivery trucks and build the delivery expense into the wholesale price. Expect to pay a little more for the convenience. Of course, if you're not opening your store for two months, you can have stock shipped by a slower and less expensive method.

When choosing sources for your inventory, look for more than one source for each line and test them. One may be less expensive, while another may offer faster delivery. Or one may offer you a better price if you buy from that company exclusively.

Be aware that many wholesalers (and retailers) keep their pricing low by padding the shipping and "handling" costs. Make sure you are comparing prices delivered to the destination—your store.

Consider Line Profitability

At what retail price will you sell your products? It's a vital question. As introduced in Chapter 1, pricing used to be simple: double the wholesale price. Today's retail pricing is much more complex and competition has reduced the opportunities to price at "whatever the market will bear."

What are the options in setting a retail price? Following are some of the most common methods of computing a retail selling price:

- Break-even point
- Cost-plus pricing
- Rate-of-return pricing
- Demand pricing

Break-Even Point

Break-even point means that the income covers the expenses. If your store has to sell 120 widgets to cover the wholesale and overhead costs of a 400-widget order, that's the break-even point. Your profit will begin when you sell the 121st widget. Break-even calculations are more common to retail stores that buy large wholesale lots, such as dollar or bargain stores, though a break-even analysis can be calculated for any product.

Cost-Plus Pricing

Cost-plus pricing is more common among smaller retailers. Products are priced at a predetermined percentage above the direct costs to achieve an expected gross margin. To understand this method, some terms need to be defined.

The *gross margin* is the relationship of the profit to the <u>cost</u>. A widget with a wholesale cost of $6 is sold at a retail price of $10. Calculate: $(10 - 6) \div 10 = 40\%$, the gross margin.

The *markup* is the relationship of the profit to the <u>selling price</u>. It's the percentage added to the cost to get the retail price. Consider another widget with a retail price of $5 and a wholesale cost of $2. Calculate: $(5 - 2) \div 2 = 150\%$, the markup.

⊛ Essential

In the real world, most retail stores have a number of gross margins and markups. Primary merchandise may have one gross margin or markup while an impulse department or one that has less local competition may have a higher gross margin or markup.

Should your store use gross margin or markup? There are two ways of looking at cost-plus pricing. Many stores prefer using markup. It's easier to calculate. For example, if the wholesale cost is $4 and the markup is 100 percent, simply add 100 percent of the cost to get a retail price of $8.

Rate-of-Return Pricing

Your business plan helped you calculate a rate of return on your initial investment. Maybe you selected 12 percent. That means a $100,000 investment should pay back $12,000 a year or $1,000 a month in interest from the profit. The same method can be used to calculate a price as long as all other fixed and variable expenses, including payroll and your salary, are already factored in.

Retailers with large sales volumes, such as $1,000,000 a year or more, frequently use ROI (return on investment) pricing. It's also more common for stores that require an extensive initial investment in land, fixtures, and other costly components.

Demand Pricing

Airlines are notorious for demand (or yield) pricing. Buy the ticket well in advance and the price is lower than if you walk up to the counter on the day of the flight. Retailers can't use this method as easily unless they sell hot/cold merchandise. If your store gets the hottest new widgets in and everybody knows that supplies are initially limited, your price can be high—maybe even higher than the manufacturer's suggested retail price (SRP). When supply catches up and the market is saturated with these widgets, prices will slide until the merchandise hits the clearance table at prices below wholesale.

There are many other types of retail pricing methods. As you research and develop your own store you will find those that are most popular for your type of store. Remember that the key to pricing is profitability more than ease of use. That's why there are hand-held business calculators and software to do the figuring for you.

Contact Wholesalers

You probably have identified numerous wholesalers who can supply you with the merchandise you need to initially open your retail store. It's now time to contact them for further information and to establish wholesale accounts.

Be aware that wholesalers are inundated with requests from people who have a dream of opening up a store someday. Most have good intentions, but it can be burdensome for wholesalers to attempt to train people who probably won't start a store. They are understandably skeptical of anyone who approaches them. You are going to have to prove yourself to them before they share much information with you. Thousands of dollars are involved. You may become a competitor to a wholesaler's best customer. Most wholesalers are cooperative once you have established your intent and credentials, but don't expect the red-carpet treatment until you do.

⊕ Alert

Be cautious what you sign. Don't sign an exclusive contract with a specific wholesaler unless you clearly understand what you are getting into. What if the wholesaler drops some of the merchandise you sell best? What if the wholesaler dramatically raises prices? What if your supplier goes out of business or gets negative publicity?

If you are a member of one or more retail trade associations or have letters of recommendation from your new landlord or a local chamber of commerce, the task of impressing wholesalers will be much easier. Alternately, you may get a referral from a retailer you've met in your research. A business consultant can help prepare you for the tasks of finding and applying to reputable wholesalers who handle primary merchandise.

There are wholesalers who specialize in stages of retailing. For example, some will specialize in helping customers start and stock a specific type of retail store. They may even offer fixture packages and operating manuals comparable to the services of a franchisor. The only difference is that you don't have to use their name brand or follow their guidelines to the letter as you would with most licensed franchises. These are called packaging wholesalers or start-up wholesalers. They aren't available for all types of retail operations, but they can be found in the most popular. Keep in mind, however, that the easier it is to set up a store the more retail competitors you may have.

Other wholesalers will specialize in restocking your shelves (see Chapter 12). You will probably pay higher wholesale prices because you are buying in smaller quantities, but it will be more convenient for you.

Set Up Wholesale Accounts

Applying for an account with a primary wholesaler is like making a loan application with your resume attached. Because wholesalers are trusting you with thousands of dollars of their merchandise, they must know how you are going to pay for it. That's why they want financial information (to make sure you have adequate assets) and a resume of experience (to verify that you know what you are getting into).

Account Application

First, identify your primary wholesale candidates. You may not apply to all of them, but you want to know who the best wholesalers are, and what they require to give you an account. Most have a standard wholesale account form. You can attach additional information as needed to make the best impression. For example, you can attach the executive summary of your business plan or a summary of your retail or business training and experience.

 **Question**

Should I use a credit card to purchase my store's initial wholesale stock?
Probably not. First determine the interest rates for transactions funded by your card and by the wholesaler. Chances are that the wholesaler's interest rate (if any) will be lower. That's because the wholesaler may opt to be the owner of the merchandise until you pay for it. If something goes wrong, the wholesaler can pick up the unsold merchandise. The credit card company doesn't have that option, which means it carries more risk, and so higher interest.

Ordering

Once your account has been approved, you can begin placing orders. For some wholesalers, the application can be approved in as little as forty-eight hours, though others may take two weeks or more. Make sure you know how long the process will take and plan your inventory needs accordingly. Alternately, you can make your initial wholesale purchase with cash or certified check. Some wholesalers require this of all new accounts.

The ordering process varies among wholesalers. Here are a few of the primary ways that you can place your initial wholesale orders:

- Sales representatives will visit your store and help you plan your initial order based on their experience in helping a similar store setup.
- A wholesale representative takes your order by telephone, answering questions as needed.
- An order catalog will be mailed to you with an order form that you complete and mail or fax to the wholesaler.
- An online catalog (accessed by your username and password) describes products, pricing, and ordering information.
- A retail catalog is provided with printed pricing that you can show to your customers. A separate sheet tells you how to order and what wholesale discount you get.

Some stores, especially those that buy from a variety of wholesalers, may place orders using all of these methods. A sales rep may help with the initial inventory planning, then turn the account over to an inside sales representative or suggest that you place the order online. Specialty items may be ordered using a variety of retail catalogs with wholesale sheets.

Freight and Delivery

Depending on what you are selling, receiving initial inventory can be relatively easy or a nightmare. For example, some wholesalers who specialize in start-ups may have their own trucks with drivers who can help answer inventory questions and contact the warehouse with your problems. Other large deliveries will be made by freight truck drivers who don't know (and really don't care) what they are delivering. Pallets of boxes get set on the sidewalk out front and it's up to you to get them inside. Smaller orders will be walked up to your door and handed to you by a van driver or postal employee.

⊛ Essential

Some of your secondary inventory may come by means other than freight, such as United Parcel Service, FedEx, or the postal service. Be aware that each of these services have weight and size limits, so don't use them except for smaller and lighter inventory. Per pound they are much more expensive than freight services.

Cost is the primary reason why there is so much difference in the service level among delivery systems. The more service, the greater the price. Following are some proven tips on how to keep the delivery of your initial orders from becoming nightmares:

- Get an estimate of the space you'll need for initial inventory and decide where it will conveniently go while awaiting shelving.
- If your store doesn't have a rear loading dock and area, make sure the delivery truck has a power lift gate and a two-wheeled freight dolly or pallet jack, as needed.
- Delivery drivers are paid by the hour or mile, so don't expect them to wait around while you prepare an area to receive freight. Know when it will arrive, and be ready.
- Unless absolutely necessary, don't have the delivery made to your home garage. Residential deliveries are more expen-

sive than deliveries to commercial locations—and you'll still have to move it to the store eventually. Get the inventory delivered to the final location the first time, or rent storage space nearby.

* When you sign freight bills for delivery, add "Subject to inspection" so you will have some recourse if unpacking reveals freight damage.

* Make sure you know who is responsible for any damage to merchandise. Is it the manufacturer's responsibility until the freight company picks it up? Does the freight company assume liability for damage in transit? Does the freight company's liability end when you sign the shipping documents, or after inspection?

Computers and the Internet now allow you to track packages from their origin to destination. Each delivery system has a website for tracking. Simply enter the tracking number provided by the shipper and you can virtually watch the package as it moves toward your location. Some wholesalers have an automatic link on their site that will show you where an order is in the process at any time. This can be valuable if you're trying to coordinate incoming inventory with staff schedules and an opening day.

Returns

Problems happen. The case of blue widgets that you ordered turns out to be red ones. The #7 widgets are damaged in transit. What can you do?

Two things. First, make a claim. Contact the wholesaler, freight company, or other responsible firm and let them know of the problem, referencing the order or shipping documents as needed. Second, prepare the package for return. If the damage is done by others, it is their responsibility, once notified, to make arrangements for pickup or other disposal. In any case, make sure you keep all paperwork on the damage, claim, and response.

Prepare for Opening Day

It's the day you've been working for: when you get to open the front door and invite your first customers in to shop. At this point, opening day may seem years away, but it isn't. It soon will be here. Your selection and stocking of initial inventory will pay off.

There are many things you can do right now to ensure that opening day is a success, with little stress and big profits. You can make sure the inventory you ordered arrives, that it is prepared and priced, and that it is displayed how and where it has the best chance of selling. Your store has been designed and fixtures installed, so all that's left is preparing the inventory.

Checking Incoming Inventory

Initial inventory has been received and any obvious damage claims were made and recorded. Now it's time to start unpacking the boxes.

First, establish a staging or preshelving area where merchandise can be moved before it is shelved. Depending on the design of your store and the location of fixtures, you may be able to place inventory boxes in the middle of an aisle and work it onto the shelves. Alternately, use a rolling cart or movable table to place inventory boxes. Also, set up an area where empty boxes can be broken down for reuse or recycling. (Some wholesalers ship in their own containers, which must be returned to them for credit.)

Essential

Work safely! Don't ruin opening day because you or a stocker is injured. Don't attempt to move heavy boxes without help; use a two-wheeled freight dolly. Lift with your legs rather than your back. Use a back brace to prevent spinal injury. Don't work when you're tired, and do take breaks every couple of hours. Play favorite music in the background and have some fun.

Preparing and Pricing

Most retail merchandise is prepriced in one way or another. That is, the SRP may be printed on the product, or there may be a universal product code (UPC) that is unique for each product. Each different size or color of the same product has its own unique UPC. The UPC is a 12-digit code. It has variations including UPC-A, UPC-B, UPC-C, UPC-D, and UPC-E. (Your wholesaler or supplier will help you identify the appropriate UPC code for your business.) The European Union has a similar coding system called the European Article Number (EAN).

The price is not included in most UPC coding. Instead, a scanner at the checkout counter reads the UPC code and looks it up in a database that contains product information, including the price established by the store. The default is the suggested retail price from the manufacturer or distributor.

If your store uses UPC codes and scanners (and nearly all retail stores do), you will need to load the product codes and pricing information into your store's computer to interpret and price the inventory. In addition, for each product you will print out a shelf label that will be located in front of the displayed merchandise so shoppers know the product's price.

Fortunately, your wholesalers and other store services can provide you with the UPC and pricing data on CD or online so you don't have to enter it manually. Depending on your business plan and the software you use, you can override the wholesaler's pricing by establishing your own based on target gross margin, markup, or other formulas.

Stocking

Stocking shelves can be an easy job or a difficult one, depending on preplanning. If you're working with a wholesaler with start-up experience, your rep may provide you with display maps, called *planograms*, that show the suggested location for every product you're offering. The map is based on the wholesaler's product placement research, suggested inventory levels, and knowledge of common buying habits.

Alternately, you can develop your own display map. The unknown is determining how many of a specific product to initially put on the shelves. That's where learning how to restock your shelves (Chapter 12) is important. Many small retailers purchase initial stock as recommended by primary suppliers.

Stocking shelves may mean placing boxed products on shelves, loose product in bins, or prepackaged product on pegs. Before you purchased fixtures and inventory you developed an approximate plan of what you needed and where to place it based on start-up inventory. Here is where you find out if you were accurate and where you need to make adjustments. Few small retail stores open up exactly as planned.

CHAPTER 12

Restocking Inventory

Opening day will soon arrive. Merchandise will be flying off the shelves as customers find the things they want in your helpful and friendly store. You're going to be busy. So you'd better plan right now how you're going to easily replenish the inventory you sell. Don't wait until the shelves are bare and your customers are disappointed. Develop an automatic restocking system that will keep your retail store profitable. This chapter shows you how.

Keep Good Inventory Records

The key to restocking is knowing what you've already sold and replacing what sells the best and most profitably. And the key to this knowledge is setting up and using an efficient inventory management system. Whether you already have inventory management software or plan to keep manual records, the following are the basics of inventory management.

Inventory Basics

Inventory is a list. It can be a list of all the assets of your business, the merchandise you have in your store for sale, or even a list of the tools in your garage. Merchandise or goods in your inventory is called *stock*. It is what you sell in your retail store.

Inventory records can be as simple as written lists of stock items or as complex as inventory software that is integrated with data from your wholesalers and incorporated into your record-keeping system (see Chapter 15). For the simplest retail stores, a manual system may be sufficient. However, with the costs of small business software packages relatively low, most owners opt for a computerized system.

Fortunately, there are numerous business software programs that can help you track your inventory. Some are standalone inventory management packages while others, such as QuickBooks (*www.quickbooks.com*), have inventory management modules. Your business plan research (from Chapter 6) should identify the best ones, their requirements, and their pricing.

In addition, primary wholesalers may offer data files that can be imported into your inventory management program. That will save you many hours of data entry and minimize entry errors. Ask your wholesaler what data is available to merchandisers, and which inventory programs are most compatible with it.

Question

Must I have a computerized inventory system?
No laws require that you use computers in your business. But think of a computer as a data bulldozer. It can move more data faster than can be done manually, just as someone can move soil faster with a bulldozer than with a shovel. However, it means that you must learn to operate and maintain the "bulldozer," which often is a frustrating task. Take some classes and use your computer to help you succeed.

Inventory Steps

There are three stages to inventory management. Whether you use a manual or an automated system, you will use these three phases:

- **Starting inventory:** The stock that you start with. It can be the day you open your store, the first day of the year or month, the day you began using the system, or any other period.
- **Inventory adjustments:** The stock that is purchased from wholesalers or returned in salable condition by customers less the stock that is sold.
- **Ending inventory:** The stock that you have at the end of a specified period.

For example, Bob's Widgets had $200,000 in stock at the beginning of the month. During the month the store sold $40,000 in stock, had no customer returns, and purchased $25,000 in new stock. At the end of the month, Bob's Widgets' inventory value was $185,000.

These inventory steps can be applied to the entire store, by department, and even by UPC item for any period. The more detail available, the more accurate the inventory records are.

Inventory Accuracy

Unfortunately, incoming or outgoing stock sometimes is miscounted or inventory walks out of the store, unauthorized. That's why most retailers do a physical count of the stock periodically. The difference between physical and calculated stock is identified and the inventory records are corrected.

Because retailers often work hard for a small profit, inventory accuracy is critical. Entry errors and theft that total 5 percent of sales, for example, can dramatically cut into profits. Inventory losses are an expense, just as if someone took cash from the till or sent you a big bill that you must pay.

Fortunately, computers can reduce the level of inventory errors—if management and employees don't get sloppy. Product and inventory databases supplied by wholesalers are more accurate than what you can provide by entering your own data into the system. The errors can arise in the second step in the preceding list, inventory adjustments. Stock that is manually entered into the system can be misidentified or miscounted. Some wholesalers provide labels on boxes that include coding so you can easily enter the contents into the inventory system. A quick scan of the label enters the UPC, quantity, and other needed data without opening the box. Of course, boxes may be mislabeled. Error is always present. You want to minimize it.

Inventory Knowledge

From your store's inventory data will come knowledge to help you run your retail operation. For example, it can tell you how stock in a specific department is selling, and at what pace. You can then determine when to reorder without filling up your back room.

Your inventory records also may tell you how much lead time you will need for ordering replacement stock. If you are selling 400 widgets a month and it takes two months for replacement stock to arrive, you know you must order at least 800 units more than two months from the day you expect to have an empty hole on the shelves. This is the type of detailed knowledge that retail managers need every day to succeed.

Working with Wholesalers

Most retail stores use their start-up wholesaler (see Chapter 11) to restock the shelves as needed. Others elect to restock the same merchandise using other wholesalers who can provide faster service, lower prices, or other benefits. Alternately, retailers decide to modify their store concept after a few months of operation and select a new wholesaler who better serves their new lines.

Wholesalers are, in many ways, like retailers. Their business is to buy large quantities at one price and sell it in smaller lots at a higher price. In fact, many wholesalers started out as retailers who had difficulty getting adequate stock and identified a common need. The success of wholesalers depends on the success—and the satisfaction—of their customers, the retailers such as you. Some wholesalers understand this and continually attempt to upgrade their product lines and service. Others have developed a comfortable business serving key accounts and are reluctant to expand their business with new retailers.

🔔 Alert

Be aware that "wholesalers" who also sell directly to end users and have no minimum order requirement really aren't wholesalers. They are discounters. Also beware of unlicensed brand-name products that are sold on the black—or gray—market. Know what you are buying and from whom. You want to protect the quality of your merchandise and the reputation of your store.

Restocking Process

As your business is transitioning from a start-up to a running retail store, your processes will change. Your responsibilities will move toward managing inventory: figuring out what is selling profitably as well as deciding what the replacement stock should be. This means you'll be working with your inventory records and your wholesalers' order systems. For some types of stores, the two can be interconnected using computer data lines. Your store sells a #21 widget, it is immediately reflected in your inventory database, an order for a replacement widget is electronically sent to the appropriate wholesaler, and, once shipped, an order tracking number is sent to your system. The shipment received has a packing slip label that can be scanned to quickly enter the contents into inventory records. The restocking process is automated and requires little work beyond checking status and correcting any problems.

Few small retail stores are fully integrated with a single wholesaler. Instead, small retailers develop primary, secondary, and even tertiary wholesalers within various departments and may have to deal with dozens of dissimilar ordering systems. Franchise operations are the exception, getting all or most restocking inventory from their franchisor.

Sales Representative

A major advantage to using the fewest number of wholesalers is that your business is worth more to any single wholesaler. That means you probably will be assigned a specific sales or customer representative. An outside sales rep will visit your store, an inside sales rep will take your orders by phone or data lines, or you may be assigned both.

 **Essential**

Don't expect to get competitive information from your sales rep. He or she will not tell you financial or other sensitive data about specific clients. However, sales reps can give you practical suggestions and recommendations based on their experience without naming names. You can ask for suggestions to help you make decisions, but remember that what is offered is an opinion, not a guarantee.

Outside sales reps are assigned by geographic territory and will know the product line as well as what is going on in the regional marketplace. Inside sales reps more typically are assigned by the size of the retailer's account, the specialty, or other factors. Some wholesalers assign an inside rep to work with a specific outside rep to all clients within a specific region. Relationships can be forged to increase customer satisfaction. A good relationship with a representative can make your job easier and your business more profitable.

Best Pricing

If your store is a multimillion-dollar operation and growing dramatically, wholesalers may be able to offer you pricing they cannot offer to other clients. But they must be careful, as fair-trade laws prohibit them from giving you a deal that another customer may not get on the same order. Discounts and specials are offered to all clients equally and are based on quantity or terms rather than on friendly relationships.

For example, a wholesaler may offer you a deeper discount if you buy a gross (twelve dozen) of the new model widget. Be assured that the offer will be extended to other similar clients as well. However, sometimes terms are discretionary and a rep can offer sixty-day payment instead of thirty-day if the rep deems you a "good customer."

To get the best pricing and terms on restocking inventory, ask. Printed price lists will indicate quantity discounts available, but sometimes the reps are told of specials that can be offered to clients. Keep a good relationship with your wholesale reps and let them know you like to consider all opportunities to save money.

Multiple Wholesalers

One of your jobs as owner/manager of your own retail store is to keep looking for ways of improving profits and your customers' satisfaction. In fact, you will spend many hours each week seeking and developing alternate wholesalers and sources for additional profit lines for your store.

 Fact

Wholesale sources can be found online by searching for "wholesale" and the product line, such as "wholesale rings," "wholesale sewing machines," or "wholesale handbags." Alternately, use wholesale resource sites such as *www.wholesalehub.com*, *www.ibuildstar.com*, and *www.ezgoo.com*.

For example, a customer asks if you have fur-lined widgets. You get the customer's name and phone number, then begin searching your wholesalers' catalogs. None there. So you do some online searching or call your business consultant for resources. Finally, you hit upon a wholesale source for fur-lined widgets in various sizes and colors. A call to your customer gets an order. You now tell other customers (through conversations, signs, and ads) that you have hard-to-find fur-lined widgets. More orders come. You learn that the source also has standard widgets at a price that is comparable to your current source. You now have a secondary source for your basic products.

Even though you plan to continue buying most inventory from your primary wholesaler, you may place some orders for standard widgets with your new source. Why? To keep your options open. At some point you may find that some of wholesaler A's widgets are less expensive than those from wholesaler B. Or your primary wholesaler may drop your lines or even go out of business. Developing multiple wholesalers can keep you profitable and busy.

Clearance Dead Stock

Not all of your purchasing decisions will match the needs of the local marketplace. You may have bought 200 left-handed widgets at wholesale, but, months later, have only sold 10. What can you do?

You have options. If the products aren't returnable to the wholesaler for credit, you can get rid of them in other ways. Following are some suggestions.

Target Customer Needs

The most productive way to sell excess stock is to offer it directly to specific customers. That is, if you have too many left-handed widgets, you can identify customers who will most benefit from these products (left-handers) and suggest the product. You don't have to cut prices; just focus on who the product will benefit and *hand-sell* it.

Hand-selling is the craft of selling specific products to meet the needs of specific customers. It is helping customers, through conversation, to identify their own needs, and then selecting the appropriate product and helping them understand how it meets those needs. This process is time-consuming and requires product knowledge as well as customer psychology. However, it can be very profitable. In addition, it builds solid relationships with your customers and keeps them loyal. It's also a more satisfying way of doing business. Your big-box competitors rarely hand-sell.

Clearance Sales

An easier, though less profitable way to clearance dead stock is to offer it at discount prices. Many retailers try this option first, forgetting that if the need isn't perceived by customers, discounting the product won't change their minds. For products that will sell through your store, but not quickly enough, try clearance sales using markdowns.

A *markdown* is the reduction of a retail price, typically stated as a percentage: "20% Off." Be careful when establishing a product markdown to ensure that you are not selling it at less than you paid for it unless by choice. Many retailers begin with a single discount, followed by a double discount ("take an extra 10% off the markdown price"), and finally a full discount that matches the break-even cost of the product. Note that a double discount is deceptive and may confuse customers—a condition you don't want to encourage. The "extra 10% off the markdown price" after a 20 percent discount is actually only an 8 percent additional discount on the full price. It's less confusing to state an unambiguous markdown, such as 28 percent.

Re-wholesaling

Sometimes you will have stock that you're not going to be able to resell for anything over the wholesale price. Then you can turn to other retailers you know and offer them portions of the stock at wholesale prices or less. They may want 20 left-handed widgets at the 200-widget discount price, or they may take the remaining lot from you at a 10 percent discount on wholesale. You're going to have to beat the wholesaler's price to them to make it attractive.

Optionally, your wholesaler may take the entire batch back and charge you a restocking fee of 5 to 20 percent.

If you're certain that you won't expeditiously sell the stock, bite the bullet, and re-wholesale it. It happens to every retailer. You can make up the loss on the profits from another product. Meantime, you'll learn more about retailing.

Donations

If you just can't get rid of your dead stock in other ways, consider donating it to organizations who need it. That doesn't mean boxing it up and dropping it off at Goodwill. It does mean calling the regional offices of various charities to determine if they have a need for your dead stock and whether they can pick it up. Who could practically use it?

Of course, you will have to write off the wholesale costs of the product, but that can be partially offset by the value of the donation to the charity. Most will give you a receipt based on your estimate of fair market value. A service organization will receive needed merchandise to help in its philanthropic efforts, you will gain some retail education, and your business gets a tax deduction.

Handling Returns

Some of the wholesale merchandise you purchase will be sold to you under a return policy, while other stock will not. It is vital to your inventory management that you know which is which and what limitations you have.

For example, wholesaler A may allow return of all unsold merchandise in salable condition within forty-five days of shipment. Wholesaler B may start the clock once you receive it or charge a restocking fee for returns or be more lenient about what condition it is in when returned. Make sure you are clear on the details of the return policies of your wholesalers and that you conform to their requirements. You don't want to pay the cost and frustration of shipping returns back to the wholesaler and find out that they are rejected because they didn't meet the return conditions, including timelines.

Returning Damaged Merchandise

Merchandise damaged in shipment may or may not be returnable depending on the wholesaler's rules and its contracts with the shipper. Some wholesalers require that all damage claims be handled by the shipper. Others will take damaged goods, but only after a return merchandise authorization (RMA) has been issued by the wholesaler.

It is important that whoever receives and signs for wholesale merchandise at your store understands your guidelines for doing so. And your guidelines must be developed based on your knowledge of each wholesaler's return policies. Set up a receiving book or use a software program at the receiving area to log in received merchandise and to guide receivers on how to accept and prepare incoming stock.

Following Up on Returns

At least once a week you should review the week's inventory to verify that it was accepted following your guidelines. In addition, prepare damaged or returnable goods for return to the appropriate wholesalers.

Too many small retailers get behind on returns and their back room is soon a land of no returns. Piles of unsalable or damaged merchandise stack up and cut into productivity and profits. Decide now to set aside a location and develop guidelines so that your retail store stays on top of merchandise returns.

Special-Order Profits

Most of the merchandise you sell through your retail store will be selected by you with some input from your customers. As your business builds, you probably will get requests from individual customers for specific merchandise: "Can you get me an articulating widget?" Your answer should always be the same: "I'd be most happy to try."

Special orders are single products purchased wholesale for specific retail customers. They typically aren't as profitable as in-stock sales but they help build customer relationships. Here are a few ways to find single units at a price that offers you some profit:

- Ask your primary wholesalers if they have single-unit prices at a reduced discount.
- Find out whether secondary wholesalers will accept special orders at discount prices.
- Try to find the product through a discounter who allows single-unit purchases.
- Contact friendly retailers to see if they have the product and will allow you to purchase it at a discount.
- Buy the item at full retail and resell it at no profit to develop a relationship with your customer.

How can you set up a special-order system for your retail store? Some retail software programs have components for making and tracking special orders. Alternately, use a Special Orders notebook or index cards to manage the process. Make sure you get the customer's name, contact information, requirements, price range, when the item is needed (holiday, anniversary, event), request date, sources contacted, order information, and related data.

It's up to you whether you ask for a deposit on special orders. If you think that you can resell the product to another customer if the requesting customer backs out, not requiring a deposit will improve customer relations. However, if the customer isn't committed to the request, he may not want it when it arrives. If it is a unique and otherwise unsalable product, get a deposit that will cover your costs—or make sure that the source will allow you to return it.

CHAPTER 13

Hiring and Training Great Employees

Employees can make or break your retail business. Survey a hundred independent retailers and most will tell you that the greatest challenge they face is finding, keeping, and motivating good employees. Why is that so hard? Many reasons. This chapter offers proven methods of hiring and training great employees. It also tells you what to watch for and how to know when it's time to let an employee go. Good employees are vital to your business success—and its biggest challenge.

Employees: Assets or Liabilities?

Wouldn't it be great if you could be your one and only employee? You wouldn't have to struggle with hiring and firing. Employee meetings would be short and sweet. You would be available to help every one of your customers.

The downside is that you would have to open and close the store every day it operated. And you'd have other duties— ordering, stocking, recordkeeping, cleaning, and so on—once the store closed for the day. Your life outside the store would be minimal. Optionally, you could dramatically cut back your store's operating hours to give you a more normal life, but your sales and profits would be reduced.

What can you do? You can bite the bullet and hire an employee or two. Fortunately, you're not the first retailer to do so, and the road is well paved. Following are some basics on hiring profitable employees.

The Right Employee

Your retail store will benefit from conscientious, articulate, and helpful employees who are inherently honest and trainable. The problem most employers have is finding that combination in a single person. A candidate may have three of those five traits, but be weak in the other two. More often, it is difficult to fully know how candidates score in these categories based on an application and interview. That's why retailers set up a probationary period to verify the reported and perceived skills of a candidate. Your state's department of employment can assist you in defining what laws cover probationary employment.

In addition to the primary qualities your employees must have, use your retail notebook to list product-specific skills that they need before they can serve customers. Then establish a training system for helping employees master those skills. Candidate trainability is one of the most important factors in hiring. Can this person quickly learn the duties she needs to perform?

Job Description

A small retail store requires that employees have a variety of job skills. Clerks may help customers find products, then handle the transaction. When business is slow, they can go to the back room and bring up inventory to stock or perform other duties appropriate for their position.

Your store should have a job description for every job title in the store. As most small stores hire employees to perform multiple tasks, the list should be comprehensive. As an example, the job tasks for a retail clerk may include these:

- Help customers find widgets
- Help customers purchase widgets
- Replenish store stock from the back room
- Maintain store appearance
- Other tasks, as assigned (change front window, receive freight)

Each of these primary tasks will have a list of components such as the following for "Help customers find widgets":

- Greet each visitor
- Answer telephone "Bob's Widgets"
- As requested, guide customers to appropriate locations in store
- Answer all product questions or ask the manager to respond
- Upon his/her leaving, thank each visitor for stopping by

A job description with task list is a guide to help employees understand their responsibilities. It also guides management in developing appropriate training for each employee. In addition, it can be used to measure job performance and help employees understand what they need to do to continue employment in your store. Make sure that your store has job descriptions for all employee titles, that they are up to date, and that employees have a copy that pertains to their responsibilities. Clear job descriptions also leave no excuses for tasks to be undone.

Finding Valuable Employees

Where can you find competent employees for your new retail store? You might be surprised. In addition to the most common resources—job ads, Help Wanted signs, and walk-ins—retail stores often find potential employees with recommendations from current employees, relatives, friends, customers, other retailers, and merchant associations. Also ask local high schools and colleges about work-study programs.

Advertising for Help

For obvious reasons, many retailers begin by placing a job ad in the local newspaper: they want to reach the broadest candidate pool. However, many small retailers prefer to use state and private employment services to screen potential employees and save time. Employment law is fraught with regulations that you, as a small employer, may not be aware of. That's why it can be a more profitable use of your time to submit your job listing with a state or private employment service. State services are free. Private employment and temp services typically charge a fee, such as 20 percent of the employee's wage or a fee equal to the first month's salary, typically paid by the employer. Depending on the labor market and the skills required, the fees can be higher.

Later in this chapter, you'll learn how many small retailers minimize the hassle of hiring and payroll issues by working with a co-employment service.

 Fact

Before you hire, know how to fire. Employment law has changed dramatically over the past few decades, giving employees more rights and employers more responsibilities in the termination process. Seek professional advice from your state employment office and business advisers on reasons for terminating employees, and how to do so with the fewest hassles.

Help Wanted

Good customers with retail sales experience can make good employees. To attract candidates, you can put a Help Wanted sign in your front window. You may find that one of your best customers currently works for a big-box retailer nearby and is considering a job change. In addition, your sign can attract passersby who regularly shop in your area. One of them might be the right candidate for your store.

The downside of a Help Wanted sign can occur if you're not always in the store. The day you step out for meetings or lunch could be the one when your best candidate asks for more information about the job. Your clerk, especially an insecure one, could drive the candidate away without an application and potentially harm your store's reputation. If you are replacing a current clerk, don't draw candidates with a Help Wanted sign. Also, before putting the sign in the window, discuss the goal and the process with your entire staff before beginning. Assure your staff why the position is opening and, if possible, how it impacts their jobs. You also can limit employees to handing out applications as requested, then referring candidates to you.

Other Retailers

Retailing is retailing. Though you may feel that your specialty shop is one of a kind, it still requires the same basic business and employment practices as most other retail stores in your area. You may find that other retailers can be helpful to you as you gather employment candidates.

First, approach retailers with which you've developed a friendly competitor relationship. Let them know that you are looking for employees and will appreciate their advice. That advice can range from recommending an employment service to recommending a specific person.

Second, look to any merchant associations to which you belong. Some actively assist members in finding qualified retail candidates. Others make referrals to proven employment services. In addition, they often can help you with the sticky issue of background checks. Employment services and merchant associations can direct you to agencies that do background checks on applicants.

Friends and Relatives

There are two schools of thought regarding hiring friends and relatives to work in your retail store: do and don't. You know your friends and relatives better than most other candidates for the position and may be able to match them up to an appropriate job. However, if the job doesn't work out for you or them, you potentially can injure a good relationship. The right answer depends on the people involved and how strong their relationship is versus how beneficial this new component will be to both.

Plan now what your policy will be toward hiring relatives and friends. Think it through thoroughly. Make a decision, and then stick to it. Don't break the policy for one friend and injure another. Many retailers suggest that you consider all applications on merit and not on ongoing relationships.

Hiring Profitable Employees

The candidates are lined up at the door and waiting patiently for you to consider them. Now what? Hopefully, you're ready with needed forms and a process. You're ready to accept their applications, determine which to interview further, verify their credentials, make a decision, and, as appropriate, make a job offer.

Like other retailing tasks, the employment process is relatively well developed. However, you should also seek assistance and advice from your state's department of employment and other professionals. Deal with facts. Minimize opinions. Treat candidates as you wish to be treated. Keep good records. Know your state's employment laws.

The Application

Stationery and office supply stores have employment application forms that conform to generic regulations. Make sure that they apply to your state's employment laws before using them. Alternately, your state's employment website may have sample forms and guidelines for using them. Employment services and counselors may provide the forms and even do the interviewing depending on what you hire them to do.

Question

Should I require or accept candidates' resumes?
Yes. However, you should ask all candidates to also thoroughly complete your standardized application form. It will make your candidate comparison and decisions much easier. If candidates have resumes, attach them to the applications.

The Interview

Not all candidates will get an interview. It is up to you whether you decide to notify candidates who don't get an interview. Many small retailers carefully tell applicants that they will be called within a specified period if selected for an interview.

Make sure you know and understand your state's fair employment practices. There are questions you cannot and should not ask of applicants, especially regarding age, race, religion, political affiliation, and other personal information. Know what they are and be considerate of applicants' personal information.

Decision to Hire

Many retailers say that they either have too many qualified candidates or not enough. Even if your store is desperate for help, don't make the mistake of hiring the wrong employee(s). In fact, if the business is struggling because of the lack of help, the last thing you want is more problems. Make other adjustments in your operations if needed, but don't make the costly mistake of hiring an injurious employee.

Sometimes you will get too many qualified applicants for the positions you have. Your decision is then much easier, but still not easy. Select the best candidate and offer her the job before notifying the other good candidates. By handling it that way, you'll assure yourself of having backup candidates if your first choice has found another job already. What about the others? Tell them of your decision and ask them if they would like to be considered for future openings. Then keep their applications and call them first if you need more or replacement help.

Job Offer

The job offer can actually be a fun event as you bring good news to the candidate and present the terms. Plan the offer in advance, making sure that the new hire understands the job, the pay and benefits package, and what is expected. If you have used a written job description in the hiring process, present the new employee with a copy. Indicate that job performance reviews will be based on this document and subsequent changes. Resolve any problems or conflicts now before employment officially begins.

🔔 Alert

Many experienced retailers refer to the hiring offer as the day the honeymoon ends. Some employees never seem to match up to the way they represented themselves as during the hiring process. Make sure that your store's hiring process draws out any candidate issues and answers all concerns before the official hire. Be honest and fair. You may not always be treated reciprocally, but you will sleep better at night.

Your state employment laws may require a signature or other documentation when an applicant accepts the job. In most states you will have to provide notification of any new hire, along with their Social Security number and other data.

Dealing with Payroll

Payroll comprises the financial records of salaries, wages, benefits, and tax deductions for your employees. If you hire others, you must keep payroll records to document taxes and compliance with employment law. What is involved in paying employees? Following are a few of the major considerations:

- Records must be accurate.
- Payroll must comply with state or federal minimum wage regulations.
- Employees cannot work more hours than state laws allow. Some states limit the number of hours and how late at night employees under eighteen years of age can work.
- Taxes must be withheld from employee payroll based on state tax regulations. In most states, withholding is required for worker's compensation and (un)employment insurance.

In addition, your store should develop a payroll policy regarding benefits and other nonrequired payroll deductions. You may offer health insurance to all employees no matter how many hours they work each week. Or you may decide to offer a bonus or commission on sales levels above a base amount. You can offer health club membership, buyers club membership, a food allowance, or whatever else you want to your employees—as long as you meet the minimum state employment requirements for payroll.

How can you keep track of all of these records? Most small employers hire a payroll service to handle the paperwork and cut the checks. This service may be offered by your accountant or by a payroll professional, which you can find through a local merchant association or business adviser, or in the local telephone book listings.

Alternately, you can use computer software to keep payroll records. For example, QuickBooks has a payroll module that works with its accounting software to manage payroll records. Of course, you'll need to know state employment and taxation laws to set it up. Or you can hire an accountant to set it up for you and show you how to operate it. Other small business accounting software systems have payroll modules as well. In addition, there are stand-alone payroll packages.

Using Co-Employment Services

If you're a small retail store with only one or two employees, setting up a trouble-free payroll system can seem like a lot of trouble. It is. Why not just pay your employees cash under the table? Because it's against the law and will soon get you in trouble. One disgruntled ex-employee can blow the whistle on you and bring down your hard-earned business. You'll have to pay back taxes and penalties, and may even be incarcerated.

 Fact

> An independent contractor is not an employee. However, to be considered an independent contractor by law, the person must truly be independent. If you require him to be in your store every day at 8 A.M., he isn't independent, he is an employee. If he can come and go at will, but has a specific task to do—such as clean the store—without a required time to do it, he is an independent contractor and not subject to employment laws.

All states allow employees to be hired by a professional employer organization (PEO) as the employer of record. Technically, the employees work for the PEO. Practically, you manage the employees as if they were your own. This arrangement often is called *co-employment*. Variations are called employee leasing and staff leasing.

The obvious advantage to co-employment is that your small retail store doesn't have to be burdened by the paperwork of employment, payroll taxes, and worker's compensation insurance. The PEO handles all that. In fact, the PEO typically advises you throughout the hiring process, helping you find candidates and even doing background checks as needed. Some PEOs will actually do the selection and hiring for you, sending you their candidates for final approval. What services you get from a PEO depend on the contract you sign.

The downside can be the cost. Many co-employers will charge you a flat percentage over and above the employee's wage. The rate can vary depending on the PEO and services, typically ranging between 25 and 35 percent. For example, if you hire a clerk at $10 an hour, the PEO will handle all the payroll records plus manage hiring and firing for a rate of $12.50 to $13.50 an hour. For a small retail store that only hires a few people each year and doesn't want the hassle of payroll, it can be a real bargain.

Unfortunately, not all PEOs are reputable, and can end up putting you in a worse mess than if you'd just handled your own payroll. Make sure that the PEO you select is reputable. Your business banker or accountant may be able to recommend such a service to you. Also, look for membership in professional organizations such as the National Association of Professional Employer Organizations (NAPEO). Its website, *www.napeo.org,* offers a list of members by location.

Investing in Employees

Now that the hiring honeymoon is over, how can you keep your employees motivated? It can be a challenge. Employees, like everyone else, soon develop habits. Not all of those habits are good, and a few can be damaging to your newborn business. Your job as owner/manager is to keep employees motivated to provide superior customer service. Your other job is to make sure that this job doesn't take up all of your time and efforts.

The solution is investing in your employees as people and as productive members of your retail team. You must motivate them based on their needs, keep them thinking about the function of your business, keep them honest, and treat them fairly.

Keep Them Motivated

All humans are motivated by the same things. In 1943, Dr. Abraham Maslow wrote a landmark paper called *A Theory of Human Motivation*. It categorized human requirements into basic needs and higher needs. In short, he said that once the basic needs (such as employment for money) are met, the higher needs (love, belonging, esteem, self-actualization) become important to the individual. It is through appealing to these higher needs that managers can help employees enhance their lives.

✦ Essential

Several businesses use titles to build respect and self-esteem for employees. Woolworth's Department Stores built its business by naming one store manager and dozens of assistant managers. Wal-Mart doesn't hire clerks; it hires associates. Of course, the title should accurately reflect the tasks. Otherwise, the titles aren't credible. Motivate your employees with creative and accurate titles, and then give them functional responsibility.

For example, employees want to be known as working for a well-respected business. They want to be recognized as important components of that business. They want the respect of their peers, coworkers, customers, and bosses. They want to see that their contribution is for the greater good.

Managers can help their employees by treating them like customers, educating them and then helping them to feel good about their actions.

Keep Employees Thinking

Good employees need good ongoing training to sharpen their current skills as well as to develop new ones. Using job descriptions, map out a training program that will ensure that all employees meet your store's requirements within a specified period—a kind of probation period. Then encourage them to build additional skills that will help them be more employable. Yes, you may lose well-trained employees to higher-paying jobs. In the meantime, you will be investing in employees who, if paid and treated fairly, will make you many thousands of dollars in profits.

You can find retail employee training materials in a variety of places. Start with your employment service or PEO. Ask your business consultant or a retail mentor. Search online for "retail training" and other terms. Some resources have step-by-step training programs on DVD that your employees can use to build skills. Set up your own training program and invest in your employees' profitability.

Keep Employees Honest

Human nature is situational. A person who would never think of shoplifting may justify taking something from an employer without paying for it. Here are a few ways you can help your employees be honest:

- Make sure that employees know what is expected of them, including honesty.
- Don't make dishonesty easy. Secure cash, negotiables, expensive merchandise, and other valuables so they are not a temptation.
- Watch employees for signs of personal money problems—the primary reason why employees take cash from employers.
- Trust your employees to be honest, but use double-checks to confirm that they are being honest. Recount. Verify.
- Stop by the store when employees don't expect you there, but don't be obvious about checking up on them.
- Reward honesty. If the audit of an employee's actions verifies her honesty, thank her or give her something of appropriate value.

Treat Employees Fairly

Everyone feels unfairly treated by employers, customers, relatives, friends, or strangers at some point. To be *fair* is to be impartial; free of prejudice or self-interest. It may be a perception rather than a reality, but it still seems real to the affected person. No one is free of the feeling or the initiation of unfair actions. Managers can fight unfairness by being more sensitive to the feelings of others and less sensitive to their own.

Business, by nature, seems unfair. Therefore, it requires more diligence on the part of a retailer or manager to treat employees, customers, and others impartially. The result can be better employees, happier customers, and more satisfaction in your role as a retailer.

CHAPTER 14

Smart Store Management

O nce you open the doors of your new retail store, the race begins. You'll be running to the bank, calling suppliers, hustling to meetings, helping customers, meeting with employees, solving problems, and completing the myriad of other tasks that will make up your workday for the foreseeable future. How can you keep it all straight and make sure you are running in the right direction? By applying good management skills. Some you probably already have. Others you can pick up with experience and with the proven tips in this chapter.

Reviewing Your Retail Goals

The adage is correct: When you're up to your neck in alligators, it's difficult to remember that your intent was to drain the pool. So it is in business. As you perform all the tasks required to manage a successful retail store, you may forget why you started it. Or you'll question the wisdom of your decision. That's normal. Retailing is a balancing act that will test your skills and your stamina.

Of course, you're not the first retailer. Nor will you be the last. There are proven methods for keeping on track and even having some fun with your new store. The first step is to remember why you decided to open a retail store in the first place. Remember your dream.

You're the Boss

You're the boss. You have the authority and the responsibility to make your retail store a success. You may share duties and responsibilities with others, but you should have a defined position within the business. Your business needs a well-formed goal and a vision. Like a locomotive engineer, it's your job to keep things moving forward and on track.

Being the boss can seem a meaningless title as you clean the floor, take out the trash, and perform other mundane jobs. Being the boss in a one-person shop means you can't delegate chores. Larger stores have employees and areas of responsibilities. Even in those cases, however, the boss ultimately is responsible for what happens in and to the store.

For many new retailers, being the boss is a new concept. It also may be the reason why some start a store—to be the boss. Get used to it: you're now the boss.

Specify Your Retail Goals

It's a good thing that you developed a business plan for your retail store as you read Chapter 6. It defined and documented your retail goals. It helped you solidify what you want your store to be and what you want from it.

However, as you delve into the numerous daily tasks, you may forget the store's goals and get lost in the details. Many retailers do. The key to smart store management is to keep your store focused on its goals. Profits, certainly, are a primary goal that funds the store. However, most independent retail stores have additional goals that make them unique and rewarding to own. They want to offer specialized products to their community, provide a living wage and a supportive work environment to employees, or build a business to a value that will fund retirement. The problem can be remembering those goals as your business is deluged with opportunities and dilemmas.

Make Plans

A goal is a destination. Plans are the road map. It is how your goals funnel down into your daily activities. For example, the goal of offering merchandise not available at local big-box stores gets funneled down into concrete plans:

- Identify suppliers of imported widgets
- Select best sales floor location for new line of fluorescent widgets
- Train clerks in how to promote widget-buddies
- Make signage for Christmas widgets
- Write press release on a store visit by Mr. Widget

Plans are specific: identify, select, train, make, write. These are the action points that will dictate your daily and weekly duties and those of your staff. Your job as a manager is to develop specific plans from broad business goals.

Stay Focused

How can you stay focused on your retail goals and specific plans? Everyone has a different method of dealing with details, from ignoring them to making long lists. Many multitasking managers use planning tools to manage the minutiae. There are various planner systems and books available at stationery and office supply stores. Some managers prefer electronic planners. The best method is the one that works for you. If you don't have a favorite, try a few of them to see what helps you focus on your planned tasks.

Defining Your Retail Process

Every job has a process. A process is a series of actions toward a specified end result. The process of driving to the grocery store begins with finding the car keys, then going to the car and getting in, starting the car, driving partially out the driveway, remembering that you forgot the grocery list, going back . . . you get the picture. The desired result is grocery shopping, a separate process.

Your retail store has numerous processes. The primary process is the transaction process, helping customers select and purchase merchandise. Other processes include purchasing inventory, stocking shelves, training employees, handling customer complaints, and so on. Each process takes steps toward a desired end result.

✪ Essential

Retailing can be overwhelming unless you look at it as a number of primary and secondary processes, each with an intended result. If you know what those processes are and work out a method of managing them, you'll be more ready to resolve problems that come along through your day.

The results you want for most retail processes are approximately the same as for all other retail stores. It's the steps within those processes that are customized to your operation. Learn how other retailers manage their processes and modify them to fit your needs.

What Does Your Store Do?

Your retail store sells specific products to people who need or want them. To perform this mission, your store implements a variety of processes. For example, your store:

- Helps customers select appropriate merchandise
- Trades money (cash, check, charge) for the merchandise purchased
- Replenishes sold inventory
- Develops additional customers through advertising
- Pays bills
- Trains employees

The list goes on. Each of these responsibilities requires that you take appropriate steps toward a specified result. For example, replenishing sold inventory requires that someone:

- Identify what inventory has been sold
- Decide how many of the item should be reordered
- Place the order with the appropriate supplier
- Track the order through processing and shipment
- Receive the merchandise and inspect it for accuracy and condition
- Stock the merchandise in the store as needed

Each step within the restocking process has its own process. It may seem that all you do is perform tasks within processes toward goals. Correct! In fact, you've been doing that all of your life: going to the grocery store, buying groceries, paying bills, going to a job, and on and on. Even relaxation at the end of a day is a process, culminating in a good night's sleep.

As you build your retail business, consider it as a process with numerous subprocesses. It will give order to seeming chaos and help you sleep better at night.

How Do You Do It?

Some processes are so automatic and understandable that you really don't need to think about the steps. You don't pull out a list titled Going to the Grocery Store and begin checking off the tasks: find the car keys, find the shopping list, go to the car, and so on. You just do it, based on what you remember doing when you last went grocery shopping.

For more complex and less frequent processes, a list helps. The job description developed for employees (see Chapter 13) is simply a list of tasks, each of which has a process. Complex processes, such as computerized transactions, may have numbered steps that trainees can follow to learn the process. Once known, the document can serve as a refresher for experienced employees as well as a training aid for new ones.

Do you need to make lists and document every single process within your retail store operation? If you did, you might not have time to do anything else. Fortunately, the human brain can retain thousands of processes without much conflict. In fact, it can borrow from other processes, applying what is known about grocery shopping to the process of merchandise ordering. Document only those processes that are most critical to your operation and those that seem to be giving you and employees problems. For example, do you forget to check existing inventory before buying new merchandise? Develop a process list that includes this step and make sure everyone follows it until it becomes automatic.

 Fact

Successful retailers often develop an operations manual for their stores. This manual is a collection of documented processes. In fact, there should be two operations manuals: one for management and one for employees, each focused on the processes of their primary responsibilities. If the components of the employee manual changes, make sure that all employees are aware of it.

How Do You Know It's Working?

Not all processes work. Nor are they all carefully followed. Sometimes the defined process doesn't bring the desired result. Redefine it. If a process seems clear to you, but employees are having problems with it, use training. It can help them understand the process better and help you make the process clearer. Training is simply process education.

You'll soon know which of your retail processes work and which don't. How will you know? If the results aren't what you expected, the process doesn't work. If you make a loaf of bread and it turns out as flatbread, the results tell you that something was incorrect in the process. It may have been faulty instructions, or simply failure to follow instructions. If the process isn't working, it will be up to you to figure out why and to correct it.

Keeping Smart Store Hours

The hours that your retail store is open can mean the difference between success and failure. Imagine a baby-clothing store that is only open from midnight to 6 A.M. That may be quite convenient for the owner who also has an evening job, but it doesn't fit customers' needs.

Set your store hours based on your customers' schedules rather than your own. Make sure that you are open when business is most profitable; let customers know when you're open; and carefully make adjustments as needed.

Customer Hours

How can you discover when your customers prefer to shop for your merchandise? The easiest way to learn is to ask them. If you know many of the people who will be buying from you, simply ask them when they prefer to shop for your line. If you are hiring or doing your own comprehensive market research, make sure that it includes questions about preferred shopping times. However, be aware that not all customers consciously remember when they shop. The results of your survey are an indicator, but not the ultimate source of market data regarding shopping times.

🔅 Essential

Observation is a great method of finding out what hours you should open your store. Look to your competitors. Watch their stores carefully. When they open at 10 A.M., for example, are there customers waiting at the door? Does that happen every day, on a specific day, or seasonally? Established businesses already have figured out what store hours are most profitable for them.

As you set your store's hours, think like a customer. If you know that most of your potential customers work in a nearby factory or government complex, find out when they arrive and leave, and when they have lunch. Are they more likely to buy your merchandise before they go in to work, after work, or during their lunch hour? Keep in mind that retail stores should not be closed during the lunch hour, as that's when many people shop.

Profitable Hours

By tracking customer traffic and sales throughout the day and week, you soon will have information to help you determine what hours are most profitable—and which are a loss. For example, if you've determined a break-even point (see Chapter 11) for each day—how much you have to make in sales that day to pay all expenses—you know what your hourly break-even rate is. If the hours that are a loss are at one end of the day or the other, consider dropping those hours from your open schedule.

 Fact

You may find that hours in the middle of the day don't meet your hourly expenses. If that's the case, you can develop promotions that increase traffic during those periods, or you can use the less-busy times to perform other retailing tasks.

If you find that your first or last hours are among your most profitable, consider opening earlier or staying open another half hour or hour later. Then track sales and profitability for at least thirty days before changing your official hours. There will be more on extended-hour tests later in this chapter.

Be sure that you don't change hours on a whim. Customers are creatures of habit. If they expect you to be open when they arrive at 9:30 A.M. and you're not, you will lose a potential sale and you may lose a customer.

Promote Hours

Once you've decided on your store's operating hours and days, let your customers know. There are many ways to do so:

- Post store hours at each entry door.
- Include store hours in all advertisements and announce "new hours."
- Print up small promotional sheets with new hours and place them in shopping bags.
- Post signs on or near your cash wrap about new hours.

Once again, think like a customer. How would you like to be notified that your favorite store's hours have changed? How would you feel if you went to a store and found it closed when others nearby were open?

Adjust Hours

If you are expanding hours, you don't have to announce them initially. You can test the waters. For example, if your store is open until 5 P.M. and the hour is profitable, keep it open until all of your customers have been served. Then note the time. For small retail stores especially, posted store hours should be the minimum.

⊛ Essential

Some retailers are impacted by seasonal shopping more than others. A gift store, for example, will benefit from holiday trade and should consider extended hours seasonally. If a downtown merchant association decides to stay open later during a specified period, it's probably profitable for your store to do so. Make sure your customers know that you will be open during extended hours.

The managers of one successful small retail store decided to have the longest hours on the block. They opened at 9 A.M. and closed at 6 P.M. every day except Sunday, when they closed at 2 P.M. After six months of operation they determined that the first hour and the last rarely covered the expenses incurred, so they cut back to 10 A.M. to 5 P.M., but modified Sunday hours to noon to 4 P.M. to capture better profits from Sunday shoppers. Sales levels were maintained and expenses went down; hence, they profited.

Helping Customers Buy

One of your primary tasks as a smart store manager is to help your customers buy. That doesn't mean high-pressure salesmanship. Most shoppers prefer consultative selling. They may only need help locating what they want (through signs), or they may want help selecting merchandise (with a clerk). In all cases, your store and employees help customers buy. The three steps to consultative selling are need, choice, and commitment. Following are some additional guidelines for helping your customers with consultative selling.

Need

"May I help you?" You've probably heard that question many times as you shop smaller retail stores. (Probably not so much in big stores.) "May I help you?" is a common question, rarely asked with sincerity by clerks. It's more like, "You don't want any help, do you?" And most customers respond as insincerely with "No. Just looking." Which means, "Leave me alone. I'm shopping."

Retailers have found that what works better is *implied* help. The customer *knows* you work at the store by your clothing or nametag. Be within sight of customers so they can ask you any questions they might have. Keep busy straightening shelves, putting up a new sign, or whatever allows you to be nearby without being obvious. Wear a smile. Customers like help to be available rather than intrusive.

Choice

Customers who ask for help are trying to solve a problem. Your merchandise may or may not be able to solve it. If you are asked, your primary task as a representative of the store is to help the customer solve that problem. Sometimes the hardest part of the task is *defining* the problem. The solution is to listen, rephrase the question as a problem, offer a possible solution, and then listen again:

- **Listen:** "I love widgets, but they keep breaking so easily and I don't want to keep buying them."
- **Rephrase as a problem:** "Are you looking for a widget that won't break when handled?"
- **Offer solution:** "Bob's own line of widgets are made to withstand grandchildren and are guaranteed not to break for at least one full year."
- **Listen:** "Do they come in blue?"

You've helped a customer solve a problem. You may have them in blue, leading to a sale, or you may not. If not, you can recommend ordering a blue one or even for the customer to visit your competitors for a blue model. Big Rule of Retailing: Lose a sale, but don't lose a customer!

Commitment

If you've solved the customer's problem, the sale probably is made. If it isn't made, there may be more to the problem, such as "I need it to cost less than $10" or "I need one today." To solve this secondary problem, follow the same steps: listen, rephrase as a problem, offer a possible solution, and listen again.

Getting a commitment to purchase can be as simple as the customer saying, "I'll take it." If you feel the customer wants the product but is reluctant to say so, ask "Would you like to take this home today?" or "Would you like me to set it aside at the front counter for you?"

There is no pressure here. You have used your knowledge of the normal buying process and your communication skills to help a customer solve a problem. You are using consultative selling.

Building Customer Relations

The smartest thing you can do to profitably manage your store is to build customer relations. Obviously, without customers your store will fail. But you want more than just "customers"; you want profitable customers. That means you're going to have to invest time and efforts into building profitable relationships with your core customers.

Who are your core customers? They aren't necessarily the people who visit your store the most, nor those who make the most purchases. They are the ones who bring your store the greatest profits. They may only buy a few items once a week, but the merchandise is highly profitable. You may know who most of your core customers are, but, unless you're always in the store, you may not know *all* of them. Reviewing your sales records may bring to light core customers that you hadn't recognized.

 Fact

To build your business even faster, clone your core customers. Analyze who they are, what they buy, and how and when they buy. Then find others like them. Increase advertising toward target groups of prospects. Ask your core customers to recommend your store to their friends. Offer them one-time discount coupons for themselves or friends.

Like other smart management methods, building customer relations is a process. Set a goal, make a plan, list the tasks, and make it happen. That's the key to running a profitable retail store.

CHAPTER 15

Keeping Good Records

Why do you need to keep good records for your retail store? For the same reason that you take photos of your vacation: to remember where you've been. Instead of views and events, you record income and expenses. Looking back, you can determine whether you had fun—or made a profit—or not. Financial records are snapshots of your business's growth. Good recordkeeping also can keep you from paying too much in taxes. This chapter focuses on how you can develop a good recordkeeping system for your retail store—one that doesn't require an MBA to set up or interpret.

Basic Retail Recordkeeping

The primary function of your retail store is to make a profit. What is a profit? How do you know when you've made one? How can you make more profit? Even if you're blasé about profits, the tax collector isn't. Taxing authorities require that you keep accurate records of income, expenses, and subsequent profits. The more your store makes in profits, the more detail you will need.

More important, *you* want to know where your profits came from and your losses went to. As the owner, manager, and boss, you want to increase profits and reduce losses. That's your primary task. Knowledge is control.

Journals and Ledgers

Journals are the books of original entry, in which you record transactions as they occur. Smaller businesses use a single journal, called a *general journal*, in which all transactions are recorded. Larger businesses also have journals for specific functions: purchase journal, sales journal, cash receipts journal, cash disbursements journal, payroll journal, and others. In larger businesses, the general journal is a catchall document that includes any incidental, start-up, or closing entries needed by the business. Everything else goes into a specialized journal.

As appropriate, journal entries of transactions are transferred or "posted" to *ledgers*. Ledger pages are the gathering place of specific types of accounts. For example, an invoice from a supplier is recorded in the purchase journal, then posted to the accounts payable (an account that needs to be paid) ledger. The five types of ledger accounts are asset (what is owned), liability (what is owed), capital (the difference), income or revenue (money collected), and expenses (money spent). The capital account is also known as the owners' equity account or net worth.

Essential

The concept of debits and credits isn't intuitive. However, it is easy to remember. Debits increase assets and expenses. Credits decrease assets and expenses. Remember: Debits increase assets and expenses. Then you can use logic to correctly record ledger entries.

Debits and Credits

Each ledger account entry is an increase or a decrease to the account balance. An increase to an asset or expense account is called a *debit*, and a decrease is a *credit*. Recording an electric bill is a debit to the utility expense account; paying the bill is a credit. Conversely, an increase to a liability, capital, or income account is a *credit* and a decrease is a *debit*. Buying inventory is a credit to the inventory asset; paying for it is a debit. On the ledger page, debits are always recorded on the left-hand column and credits are on the right. Confused yet? Don't worry. It becomes easier with a little practice.

Single- and Double-Entry Systems

There are two methods of making entries to your recordkeeping system: single-entry and double-entry. Single-entry recordkeeping is obvious: Make an entry into a single account as appropriate. Double-entry recordkeeping adds an extra step, requiring *two* entries to more accurately reflect what happens in a transaction. It also adds a method of verifying record accuracy.

For example, inventory is received. That's an asset. But you're going to have to pay for it, so it's also a liability until you pay the bill. You make a *debit* entry to the inventory account to increase the assets. You also make a *credit* entry to the accounts payable account to increase the liabilities. When you pay the bill, you make a *debit* entry to the cash account to decrease that asset. Then you make a *credit* entry to the inventory expense account to reduce that expense.

Single- and double-entry recordkeeping may seem confusing to retailers who have not used the system before. It can be complex, but if you review and remember the basics you'll become adept at it and soon find it worth the study.

Computers for Retailers

Computers can make retailing easier—if you understand them and aren't intimidated by their power. They are just machines, albeit fast machines. Computers are simply electronic tools or devices. The physical computer is called hardware. The instructions your computer uses is called the program or software. These instructions can be read and used by the computer to do myriad useful tasks such as process words, make calculations, record transactions, and communicate with other computers.

The list of tasks is long—and growing. Tomorrow's computers will be even faster and more versatile, and they will be even more critical to business success.

How Programs Work

Computer programs, called software, are digital instructions for the computer hardware. Without instructions, computers are useless electronic dust collectors. Computers require various layers of software to perform most complex tasks. The types of instructions or software are programming, system, and application. Programmers use programming software to write instructional programs.

System Software

System software includes the operating system (such as Windows Vista or Mac OS), device drivers (like printer drivers), and utilities (such as virus scanners). These are the primary tools that computers use to perform tasks and interact with the user. System software provides instructions to the computer to connect to other computers through a modem, accept commands from the keyboard and mouse, and renders text to a display device.

Application Software

Application software performs tasks. The tasks may be as simple as basic word processing or as complex as industrial automation. Your retail store can benefit from using general and specific business software programs that are purchased to operate with your computer's operating system.

General business software includes programs that all businesses can use. For example, MYOB (acronym for Mind Your Own Business) and QuickBooks are two popular accounting programs widely used in small and medium-size businesses. There is more about accounting software in the next section of this chapter. Other common business programs include office productivity software. The most popular is Microsoft Office, which includes Microsoft Word (word processing), Outlook (personal information manager), Excel (spreadsheet), Access (database), PowerPoint (presentation), and other productivity tools.

The Microsoft Office suite can cost hundreds of dollars, depending on what's included. An alternative is produced by Sun Microsystems—and it's free. It's called OpenOffice (*www.open office.org*), or OO, and includes word processing, spreadsheet, presentation, database, drawing, and math programs. It's an *open source* program, meaning that developers can make additions to the underlying program, called the source code, and offer these additions to others —as long as they, too, are free.

ⓔ❓ Question

How can I find software written for my type of retail store?
The best place to check is on an Internet search engine. Use terms like "retail ___ software" with your type of store in the blank, such as "retail widget software." Remember, however, that the top search results may not be the best programs for your application. With online research, you may find programs that understand your business and fit your budget.

Specialized business software also is available for many retail operations. For example, Visual Anthology (*www.anthology.com*) is a POS (point of sale) and inventory control system that meets the specialized needs of independent booksellers. A more generic (and less expensive) retail POS program is ezPower Retail POS from Denver Research (*www.denverresearch.com*). Versions are available for general retail, bookstores, and restaurants, each customizable to specific store requirements.

Accounting Software for Retailers

Accounting can be complex. Fortunately, computers can take some of the complexities out of keeping your retail financial records. In fact, they can give you calculating and reporting functionality that wasn't previously available to retailers. Want to see a bar graph of daily sales by department? Push a button. Want to make it a pie graph? Push another button. Instantaneously, the information you put in is now helping you make better decisions.

There are dozens of accounting software programs available to retailers. Major players include QuickBooks, Simply Accounting, Peachtree Accounting, and MYOB.

QuickBooks

QuickBooks has the largest market share of business accounting software in North America. First launched in 1992, QuickBooks is international, with separate versions for the United States, Canada, and the United Kingdom. The basic package will give you an integrated place to record all transactions, expenses, and other financial data. Modules can be added to incorporate POS records, manage employees and payroll, manage inventory, and even print invoices and checks.

ⓔ Essential

Don't need all the power—and complexity—of programs like Quick-Books? Many small retailers who only need an electronic check register and basic reports use consumer-level versions, such as Intuit Quicken and Peachtree First Accounting, which are available for less than $100. The learning curve on these products is much smaller, and you can get the basics down in just a few hours.

Because QuickBooks is so widely used and modular, you can have a QuickBooks-trained accountant looking over your shoulder. The version for accountants can pull in your data, make corrections, develop detailed reports, and allow the accountant to audit your financial records via an Internet connection. Of course, these services cost extra. However, they offer retailers a standardized financial recordkeeping system that integrates with an accountant's system for optimum efficiency. If you select QuickBooks, first talk with your accountant to verify compatibility, as not all accountants use QuickBooks. They may have other options for your store.

Other Accounting Software

There are many other accounting software programs available to retailers. Make sure that whichever program you select is recommended and used by reputable accountants—and make sure it does the jobs you want it to do. For small retail stores, some accounting packages can be overkill, offering unnecessary features that become just one more thing to manage.

Fortunately, most accounting software packages offer demonstration versions that are limited in the number of entries or by time. You can get a good sense of what it does, and how well, by investing a few hours in learning and using it.

No matter which accounting program you select, make sure that the data files are not proprietary. That is, they should be easily imported from or exported to other accounting packages. If you select a program and then find out that it isn't sufficient, you should be able to export the data to your new program without loss.

Spreadsheets

Have some experience with spreadsheet programs? Depending on the complexity of your retail operation, you may be able to keep inventory and other records on simple spreadsheets. Many small retailers do this successfully. In fact, there are templates available for the primary spreadsheet programs, such as Microsoft Excel. These templates can be used to enter and track inventory, financial transactions, and other vital business data. Spreadsheet programs aren't as easy to set up as check registers, but are more versatile in financial reports than are most accounting software packages.

Besides Excel, both OpenOffice and Google (*http://docs .google.com*) offer free spreadsheet programs. The OpenOffice version is downloaded; the Google version is used online and can be securely shared with others.

Specialized Software Programs

Depending on your type of retail store, specialized programs are available to take some of the work out of recordkeeping and reporting. They are designed for your type of business and the seemingly unique ways that you do business. In fact, most specialized programs are generic programs that are customized. You may be able to get the same results with a generic program, such as a standard POS package, and some minor customization.

Of course, it's easier to use a program that's set up for your business, but the specialized version may be priced at twice that of the generic. If so, consider whether your retail operation really needs the extra features.

POS Software

You don't need point-of-sale software to operate your retail store. You can use one of the many "smart" cash registers available to retailers at less than $500. You can program them to set up departments, enter product codes and pricing, and give you reports. Some will even export data to popular accounting software so you don't have to re-enter it manually. In addition, some smart cash registers have built-in card readers and modem connections to help you automate credit card approvals.

The advantage to POS software is that transaction data can more easily be integrated into your accounting system. In fact, some major accounting packages offer their own POS module. In addition, a computer's software can be more easily upgraded than that in most cash registers.

The following are questions you should ask about POS software:

- Does the developer have experience developing and installing retailing software?
- Is it compatible with your computer system?
- What types of transactions can it handle?
- What is the data format, and can it easily be exported to other programs?

These are the basics. More specifically, consider whether your store needs the following features and capabilities:

- Receipt printer
- Debit and credit card transactions
- Layaway tracking
- Gift certificates
- Special ordering and tracking
- Split tender (some cash, some check or charge)
- Multiple price levels
- Easy discounting system
- Employee time clock
- Accounts receivable
- Accounts payable
- Read bar codes
- Print bar-code labels
- Import/export inventory
- Import/export customer information
- Track inventory
- Create purchase orders
- Calculate multiple sales taxes
- End-of-day reports

- Promotional pricing
- Automatic backup
- Proven customer service

In addition to POS software, you may need a bar-code scanner or reader, a bar-code printer, a small receipt printer, and a cash drawer (opened by the software). These and related equipment are available through office supply stores and online.

Inventory Tracking

Your largest investment may be in store inventory—what you're selling. You won't know what to reorder or what your most profitable merchandise is if you don't find a good way of tracking it. Previously, businesses tracked inventory manually. They went to the shelves and counted. That's no longer necessary, nor preferred. It's much easier now to closely track inventory and profitability using computer software.

Chapter 11 described the universal product code (UPC) and how it has revolutionized inventory tracking from manufacturer to consumer. Using bar-code scanners (small laser-light tools that read UPCs and other bar codes) and inventory software to interpret the codes, you can track the receipt and sale of virtually all merchandise in your store. In fact, many large stores have special bar codes on every fixture in the store as well—from cash registers to shelving units—to keep track of them. Look around and you'll see bar codes on your car, computer, software disks, and just about everything you buy.

Inventory software can help you track all of your store's inventory from the moment it comes in the door until the time it leaves. Here's what inventory software programs can do:

- Track the amount and location of all merchandise.
- Report when specific merchandise should be ordered.

- Report the age and sales history of all merchandise.
- Create pick lists, packing lists, and invoices if needed.
- Compare reported inventory to actual (counted) inventory and report discrepancies.

Make sure that the inventory system you select is designed for retail stores rather than wholesalers or manufacturers. Also, be sure that it easily integrates with your accounting system so your record-keeping is seamless. If available, request and use a trial version with sample inventory records to see if it fits your store's needs. If you have experience developing databases—or hire someone who has—you may be able to produce a customized inventory tracking system for your store.

Customer Tracking

Many retail stores work primarily with anonymous customers. The owner and clerks recognize them and may even call them by name, but the business doesn't keep any written records of who these customers are, where they live, what they purchase, and other buyer data. Other retailers rely on a customer database to help track the majority of their buyers and their business.

Should your store track its customers? Yes, if tracking is not intrusive and it benefits the customer. For example, if you have customers who like to buy widgets as gifts and have you ship them to friends and relatives, you will want to keep track of the customers and their purchases, previous and possible recipients, and preferred merchandise. How can you do that? Set up a customer tracking system. Even stores with anonymous buyers can benefit from customer tracking.

What to Track

What do you need to know about your customer(s) to make informed business decisions? That's the big question. Your store can benefit from transaction information without names and addresses. You may be able to identify groups of customers and give them descriptive names such as "Saturday morning shoppers" or "suit and tie" or "under twenty" customers.

There are several things you will want to know about each group:

- How to identify them (name, day, dress, and so on)
- What they buy (how much, prices, types)
- How they select (walk directly to merchandise, wander, ask)
- How they pay (cash, check, debit, credit, gift certificate)
- When they shop (early afternoons, Tuesdays, end of the month)

Depending on how your retail store is set up you may be able to track individuals by name or as identified groups. Most small stores will track customers using both types of identification.

How to Track

Once you've identified specific customers or groups and what you want to know about them, you can determine the best methods for tracking them. For example, if all you want to do is get a traffic count—measure how many people come into your store in a specified period—simply purchase a click counter (available at office supply stores) and click it once for every customer who walks in. Alternately, buy an infrared unit that counts each time someone passes it.

Your cash register or POS system also can offer you customer tracking data. It can tell you how much was purchased during specific hours or days, the size of the orders, average price per unit, and other valuable information that can help you make better management decisions.

Using Tracking Information

"Those who don't learn from history are destined to repeat it." But what if you *do* want to learn from history, specifically the history of your customer's purchases? Then you need to study that history, looking at each action, each component that led to the sale. Are suit-and-tie customers making purchases over $100 using credit cards on Thursday afternoons? If so, find out why. Carefully ask them. Study their purchases further. Do they buy mostly from one department? Are they drawn into your store by the window display? Are they focused buyers or wanderers?

You can record your observations in a database program, in a word processor, or a blank book or journal, whichever is easiest for you. The purpose is to analyze and *learn* from the tracking information. How can you make your store better tomorrow based on what you learn today? That's the function of tracking and retail history.

Respecting Privacy

You, as a retailer, must respect the privacy of your customers. However, if you get their approval, you may retain personal information, such as customer name and address. Depending on what is requested, you may need to have the customer sign a permission statement. You *cannot* retain credit card account numbers unless authorized by the customer. Ask your attorney for specifics as needed.

You also will have an obligation to your customers to keep their information confidential unless they authorize you to release it. In addition, national security laws may require you to release customer information to an authorized agency. In any case, it is *your* responsibility to keep specific information confidential and not allow it to be used by others without authorization. Typically, this is information that can identify an individual rather than an anonymous marketing group, such as Saturday shoppers. Treat your customers' information as you would want yours to be treated.

❓ Question

What are privacy rights?
Citizens have limited rights to privacy, defined and protected by law. For U.S. consumers, the laws are managed by the Federal Trade Commission (*www.ftc.gov/privacy*) and cover financial privacy, credit reporting, and children's privacy. Know your rights as a consumer and your responsibilities as a retailer. Check with an attorney or other authority as necessary.

Keeping good records of your income, expenses, transactions, inventory, and customers will help your retail store become more successful. The more you know about who buys, what they buy, product availability, and profitability, the better chance you have of being in business for many years.

CHAPTER 16

Promoting Your Retail Store

There are some great retail stores near you. However, you may only shop at those that promote themselves well. The others might have exactly what you've been looking for inside their store—but you won't know until you are invited in by ads, promotions, signs, or customer referrals. So it is with your own retail store: You must invite customers to visit. Once in, they will find magnificent merchandise and superlative service. This chapter shows you how to tempt customers to shop at your store.

Word-of-Mouth Isn't Enough

"Build it and they will come." Maybe!

As thousands of otherwise successful retailers have learned, having the best store in the area doesn't guarantee success. It takes more. It takes referrals from friends, various media, and other trusted resources. It takes hard work, lots of money, and some time. You can't profitably depend on your first customer to tell ten others, who will then each tell ten more. You can't afford to *wait* for profitable customers.

How Long Does It Take?

Aren't word-of-mouth referrals valuable? Won't quality products and service ultimately be rewarded by drawing customers? The short answer is "Yes." Meantime, your store is paying rent, utilities, salaries, and the inventory is getting older waiting to be purchased. You must pay these ongoing expenses until customers find you. So the more accurate answer is, "Not in time."

How long does it take to build word-of-mouth advertising? There are many factors in spreading "the word" about your store. Even with advertising, many retailers find that local customers will "discover" their store two and even three years or more after opening day. What can help to speed that process is determining who the local authorities are in your field and making sure that they know about your new store. You also can use the proven techniques in this chapter for promoting your store. You can't afford to wait on word-of-mouth advertising to find you more customers.

What Will They Hear?

Another inherent problem with word-of-mouth promotion is that you don't always know what is being said about your store. You are not controlling the conversation. You might have a dynamic and unforgettable mission statement, but few are going to quote it. They will pass along their perceptions, which may be accurate but limited. Or the perceptions may be inaccurate and misrepresent your store entirely. You can't afford to rely exclusively on other people's words.

Will They Hear It Over the Din?

People are bombarded by hundreds and sometimes thousands of consumer messages every day: use this brand; buy from that store; operators are standing by.

Because there are so many messages, most consumers simply turn off their internal message receivers, zoning out during commercials and passing over pages of ads in magazines and newspapers without ever seeing them. What chance, then, does word-of-mouth advertising have? Unless passed along by a trusted authority, it has the survival span of a Saharan snowball.

The Value of Word-of-Mouth

By now you may be asking, So what is word-of-mouth advertising good for? It can, at little or no cost, supplement your primary promotional efforts. If it is offered by a respected authority, it can initiate or support a positive awareness of your retail store in a customer's mind.

However, word-of-mouth promotion cannot supplant smart retail advertising. Your retail store cannot succeed if it must wait idly for customers to discover it. Advertising is a tool that you need to learn to use to grow a successful business.

Retail Advertising 101

Advertising is a paid message calling someone's attention to a product or service. In retail advertising, the message is about a product or a store. It's a one-way message that invites the receiver to take some action.

Promotion is any effort to influence others toward a desired action. It can be advertising, sometimes called above-the-line promotion (because it is obviously a paid message) or below-the-line promotion such as publicity, endorsement, sponsorship, and product placement. Yes, advertisers actually pay film companies to have movie actors hold their brand of soda during a scene.

Publicity is the promotion of a product or service through filtered information, such as a product announcement or press release. Along with promotion and advertising, publicity is a component of marketing. *Marketing* is the task of getting products (and services) from the producer to the consumer. Your retail store is a vital component of the marketing process.

Before you begin advertising your retail store, make sure that you know what your message is, who you want it to reach, and how you can best reach them. Your business' success greatly depends on your ability to promote—advertise, publicize, market—an accurate and needed message about your retail store.

What Is Your Message?

Every product, every retailer, every franchise, has a distinct message that it wants the buying public to hear, understand, and act upon. The message is rarely about a product, but about the *benefits* of a product. Coca-Cola Corporation doesn't sell soda; it sells refreshment.

 Fact

Charles Revson, founder of Revlon Cosmetics, said "In our factory, we make lipstick. In our advertising, we sell hope." What does your retail store sell? Widgets? Or the solution to a customer problem? People really don't buy products; they buy solutions. Make sure you know the answer before spending thousands of dollars in advertising.

What is your store's message? It is different from your mission statement, which probably has to do with customer focus and profitability. The message is what you want your customers to think, to say, to believe, about your store. It can define your customers ("The Readers' Bookstore") or the products and variety you offer ("25,000 Widgets in Stock") or more obvious benefits ("One-Stop Widget Shop"). Make your message memorable. A good place to look for retail messages is in the yellow pages of numerous out-of-area telephone books, available at larger libraries.

To formulate your own store's message, first take a look at your business plan (see Chapter 6). It will offer clues from definitions of your business and your customers. Some business plans outline a unique selling proposition (USP), a list of features and benefits that the store will be designed to provide. However, most USPs are just too long to become a store's message. It may take some creative writing to develop a succinct yet easy-to-remember communication that will be your store's message.

Must your store have only one message? Not necessarily. You may have seasonal messages ("Halloween Headquarters"), verbiage for different market segments ("Bargain Widgets" and "Everything Widget"), and even alternate messages ("Widget Solution Center" and "Widget Help Center") that you alternate and test to find out which draws more customers. However, don't confuse customers by having too many messages. For best results, select one or two and stick with them, building your unique message as you build your store brand. Make your message appropriate.

Who Is Your Audience?

Back in your business plan you developed research and a definition of who your primary customers are. Don't say "everyone," as there are many people within the local marketplace who would never consider buying what you sell. You can't realistically expect to sell something to everyone who walks in your store. You must focus on a specific group of primary buyers who most need what you sell. And you must define them carefully: "Young adults looking for the latest in widget technology at bargain prices," for example.

Of course, you have other customer groups as well, depending on what types of products you sell. However, most of your customers will have commonality. They may primarily be of a specific interest group, economic group, education level, or a geographic area. Your store may attract others, but these are your core customers. That's the audience for your message.

How Can You Reach Them?

Because your core customers have commonality, promoting your business is a matter of getting your defined message to your target audience. Of course, it's not quite that easy. You first must figure out what message paths these people have in common. Do they all live in a defined neighborhood? Are they all readers of a specific newspaper's sports section? Do they drive past your store every day? Mornings or evenings? Do most of them use widgets during the week or on weekends?

Your business plan and market research will help you define the best way of reaching your core audience. The balance of this chapter will help you select the appropriate media and methods.

Which Media?

You've defined your store's message and its audience. How can you reach your audience with your message? Through the media. Media is the plural of medium, which is something in the middle position—such as between you and potential customers. (The term media in business typically refers to news and advertising mediums such as print and broadcast as a whole.)

The primary business goal of the media is to make a profit by delivering advertising messages to prospective buyers. Secondarily, the media does so by offering these buyers something that they want: news, information, data, music, entertainment, or other benefits.

❓ Question

How much should I spend on store advertising?
As much as is profitable to your store. Chapter 6 recommended spending 2 to 3 percent of annual sales on advertising, depending on the type of store you have. Some need more promotion than others. In addition, consider doubling your ad budget for the first year of operation to get the word out about your new store. For example, a new store projecting $200,000 a year in retail sales should consider a budget of $8,000 to $12,000 the first year, then reduce it to half that amount for the second and subsequent years.

What types of media are there? The list is extensive, but many are not appropriate to small retailing, such as skywriting and magazine ads. Small, independent, one-store retailers instead rely on local advertising mediums such as newspapers, shoppers, radio, television, and other resources. Because advertising can be expensive, making smart media decisions can be profitable.

Newspaper Advertising

The task of a newspaper is to make money for its publisher. It does so by developing a relationship of information and trust with its target readers. In fact, it will have numerous target groups, each developed in order to sell advertising to retailers and others who want to reach them. The paper's sports section offers one target group, the classifieds another.

Newspaper advertising is sold by the column inch or other space measurement. Take a look at your local newspaper. Most have between four and eight columns of text to a page. An advertisement that is one column wide and one inch long is one column-inch (1 c.i.).

 Fact

The more space you buy at a time, the lower the advertising rate. That is, the column-inch rate for a quarter-page ad is lower than the rate for a 1 c.i. ad. In addition, buying a specific number of column-inches in advance, for use over a month, a quarter, or a year, earns your store an even lower rate.

Once you've identified the local newspaper *and section of the newspaper* that best reaches your target customers, contact the paper's advertising department and meet with an ad rep to get a rate card and discuss campaigns. Remember that ad reps typically are commissioned salespeople who get paid more when they sell more. Make sure that your ad rep is willing to develop a long-term relationship with you rather than sell whatever is hot this week.

Shopper Advertising

A shopper is primarily an advertising publication. Most don't attempt to be objective news sources. Their function is to bring as many buyers as possible together with sellers. Regionally, shoppers may also be called pennysavers.

One of the big differences between newspapers and shoppers is how they are distributed. Though most newspapers are delivered by carriers, they must limit advertising to qualify for cost-effective U.S. Postal Service second-class postal rates. Shoppers, because they primarily contain ads, don't get this low distribution rate and are distributed either at retail stores or by more expensive third-class postal rates.

Because newspapers are purchased by consumers and shoppers are not, newspapers are considered more desirable media for advertising. People are willing to pay for them. Shoppers simply come in the mail or are handed out free. However, the advertising rate for shoppers (also measured in column-inches) typically is much lower than that of area newspapers. As with newspapers, contact your local shopper publications and ask for a rate card and sales rep to learn more about their market and their advantages. Be aware that, in many markets, newspapers and shoppers may be owned by the same publisher. This may limit your advertising options, but you also may get combined rates that are lower than buying space in them individually.

Broadcast Advertising

Radio and television have revolutionized advertising, bringing sound and moving images to the sales pitch. Each type of broadcast media has its advantage. Radio is more portable, found in cars, stores, homes, and places. Television is more visual, offering additional sensory messages to the advertising process. However, in most markets, television advertising is too expensive for small, independent retail stores. A thirty-second advertisement (called a "spot") can cost thousands of dollars to produce and require thousands more in advertising fees to make a significant impression on viewers. For that reason, most small retailers stick to radio.

The point to remember about radio advertising—and as mentioned earlier, in running your own retail store—is to select what your *customers* want rather than what *you* want. You can be a big fan of PBS, talk shows, or classic rock, but if these local stations don't focus on delivering your message to your prospects, don't advertise on them. Spend your money where it will bring you more money. Advertising must be an investment. Your advertising representative can help you write your store's ads and advise you on whether "talent" (announcers) or you should read them.

Other Media

You've probably already noticed that advertising permeates modern lives. It's everywhere. Why? Because it works. Advertisers wouldn't spend thousands, even millions, of dollars on something that doesn't work.

⚠ Alert

If you are required to join a tenant association, you may not have much say in how and where you advertise your retail store. Some associations require that tenants contribute a significant amount into a common advertising fund. The association also may have limits on what types of additional ads you can run and how you can identify your location within their mall. Make sure you know the rights and limitations that you are agreeing to in a lease.

Once you open the doors, your store will be inundated with media sales reps offering everything from yellow pages advertising to vanity ads. You will hear pitches for placement ads in regional directories, bus bench ads, ads in shopping carts, direct mail campaigns, and many others. Which should you consider? Any that will profitably bring you new customers. How can you know if the medium is profitable for your store? You can't.

The easiest way to determine where you can profitably advertise is to carefully study your best competitors. They know. In their early days they probably spent many thousands of dollars on advertising that didn't return a profit. Now that they obviously have found what works, follow their lead. Eventually, you will discover profitable media that they are missing, but don't try to reinvent retail advertising just yet. Follow the leaders.

Event Planning

Most advertisements focus on products you offer in your retail store. That can get boring. Every once in a while you need to plan an event that will promote your store itself as well as attract replacement customers. That's an event.

There are many types of events your store can host or participate in. They include your grand opening event, holidays, anniversaries, and other local promotions. Find any excuse that you can to celebrate your business—and to draw more customers to it.

Grand Opening

Many retailers don't plan a grand opening event until they have been open a few weeks or even a few months. Why? Because they want to be ready to throw open the doors with a big bang. The store may not be completely ready for such an event when it first opens. Or the initial opening may conflict with other big events that would compete with and draw from the retailer's own event. There is no law that says you must have your grand opening on the day you first open the doors. Have it when you're ready and when it will be most profitable.

What you include in your grand opening event depends on what you are selling, your budget, and other factors. Some proven ideas for retail grand opening events include these:

- Invite a major supplier to offer product demonstrations.
- Offer introductory discount prices on some or all merchandise.
- Ask a local celebrity to appear during the event.
- Offer prize drawings and give away tickets throughout the event.

- Offer live music that will be appreciated by your target audience.
- Consider hiring a local radio station to provide a remote broadcast from your store.
- Offer food, product samples, or instruction to visitors.
- Have all employees wear appropriate costumes for the event.
- Invite the local media to cover the event, or give them a post-event report.

There are dozens of other things that you can do to make your grand opening grand. Ask your local merchant association and other business advisers for more ideas.

Anniversaries

Don't let your store's anniversary go by without reminding your customers of your service to them and telling them of your appreciation for their continued business. An anniversary event doesn't have to be on the exact date that you first opened the doors. It can be held within a week or two either way of the actual date, preferably on a weekend. Make your plans well in advance and plan an appropriate event that will show your appreciation for your customers, the folks who keep you in business.

You can use your retail anniversary to get help from your suppliers toward making it eventful. For example, you can write press releases for the local media. Some media, especially in competitive markets, offer lower-cost anniversary packages to help you promote your business. Your wholesale suppliers, too, may have packages that cut your costs. You are their customer and they may want to thank you for being in business. Let them.

Holidays

It now seems that the sales year is just one big holiday event as Halloween turns to Thanksgiving, then to Christmas, and then to New Year's sales, followed by Presidents' Day, and so on. That's because events offer everyone an excuse to shop. People love to celebrate. Shopping is economic celebration.

Your retail store will have natural holidays as well as ones that stretch logic. It's really your decision whether you participate in them and, if so, how. Just make sure that whatever event you host offers long-term profits to your business so you can celebrate it again next year.

⊛ Essential

Done with your event? Not until the paperwork is complete. Make notes on the event: the number of visitors, prizes given, sales levels, resources, and suggestions for the next time you host this event. A month afterward, you may not remember the details—what worked and what didn't—so you should plan to write thorough notes right after the event in order to learn and profit from it.

Collective Promotions

Merchant associations are notorious for promoting just about anything into a sales event: Groundhog Day, Pumpkin Festival, Second Saturday, whatever. In fact, these events typically are planned for the months that don't already have an accepted event. Or they are set up as politically correct versions of what were holy days—holidays.

Should your retail store participate in collective promotions? Yes, if they are appropriate to your customers. Stores that sell to children should participate in promotions aimed at children, obviously. Remember too that your customers will measure your store by whether you are involved in events that they participate in.

The key to collective promotions is using them to get the lowest advertising rates while developing new customers for your retail store. The event must make sense to your business plan.

CHAPTER 17

Adding Profitable Lines

You know that an important task in retailing is to identify who your profitable customers are, and then clone them. You can do the same with your retail store's profitable merchandise: identify and clone it. You can analyze your store's sales history to learn what is selling, why, and how. That valuable information can guide you toward greater profits—and fewer losses. You also can find risk-free lines to increase profits. This advanced chapter shows you how to build retail profits by adding and promoting proven product lines.

What Do Your Customers Want?

Once your focus transfers from retail start-up to operation, you will spend even more time determining what your customers want. You'll do so by meeting and talking with them. Before opening the doors, customers were your target; now they are your business.

How can you discover what your customers *really* want from you? Watch them. Ask them. Just make sure that the answers you get are measurable and the results can be summarized as action points.

Market Analysis 101

Market analysis is a complex field with a simple goal: find out what customers want. At the professional level, analysts use statistical math and computers to forecast future purchases. You can use them,

209

too. *Statistics* is a mathematical science that collects, analyzes, interprets, and presents data that can help in making decisions. You can apply a simplified version of the statistical market analysis process to your retail store without a PhD or MBA. Here's how:

- **Collect data** (factual information) from observations of and interviews with your customers.
- **Analyze** the nature and the relationship of the data collected; how does it fit?
- **Interpret** or explain the data in clear and useful terms that relate to your store.
- **Present** the data as actionable steps: do this, buy that.
- **Make decisions** based on the data gathered, interpreted, and made actionable.

Want to know more about basic statistics and find a few easy tools? Visit *www.statserv.com*. It lists and describes dozens of statistical software programs, some of them free, that can help in gathering and analyzing all types of data, including retail. One of them, XLStat (*www.xlstat.com*), is an add-on to the popular Microsoft Excel spreadsheet program. StatServ also has a bookstore where you can learn more about statistics.

Asking Your Customers

There are two primary methods of determining what your customers want: ask them and watch them. You'll be gathering customer transaction data from the day you open for business. This includes data on what is purchased, when, which payment method is used, and more. In addition, you may have developed traffic information as well: how many people came into your store, what department they first went to, how long they stayed in the store, and so on. All of this is observable data.

You also may have informally interviewed customers about their choices and wants. Unfortunately, this information is not measurable. To make it so, you must standardize the questions you ask. For example, "What do you like about Bob's Widgets?" is an open-ended opinion question that can take the interview off into a dozen different directions. However, "Do you ever purchase hydraulic widgets?" is a quantifiable question answered with either Yes or No.

The key to getting good market data from customer interviews is to ask a few important and quantifiable questions. Define what you want to know before you write your questions and start asking them. For example, if your survey goal is to determine whether your store should add a line of designer widgets, your interview questions could be:

- What brands of widgets do you prefer?
- Have you seen ads for Yadda Widgets?
- Yadda Widgets are priced between $45 and $75 each. Do you frequently purchase widgets in this price range?
- If Bob's Widgets carried Yadda, would you consider purchasing them?
- What do you think about designer widgets?

That last question, obviously, can't be answered by Yes or No. It's an open-ended question designed to get the interviewee to talk more. Not all survey questions should require closed, multiple-choice responses. Sometimes you can learn more of what the customer wants with an open-ended question than with a dozen closed questions. They're just not as easy to quantify, so most interviewers save them for the last questions.

Quantifying Responses

By standardizing your customer survey and primarily using closed questions, you can soon develop a relatively accurate report on the survey topic. How many customers should you interview? The more you get, the more accurate your survey will be. You don't want to make a $5,000 wholesale purchase based on four survey responses. The larger the required investment, the more surveys you should take. If they are short, uncomplicated surveys, you can give one in less than a minute. If possible, spread the surveys throughout the day and the week to get a better representation of your customers. Surveys will give you the type of actionable data that your retail store can use as you add profitable lines.

Where Are Your Profits Coming From?

Keeping records on everything your store does can be a pain. It's also expensive and time-consuming. Nevertheless, it can pay off big when it's time for you to figure out where your store's profit is coming from.

How you calculate line profitability depends on the type of store you have and how complete your recordkeeping system is. For example, a small retail store that is deep (carries many units of a few products) may have a simple sales tracking system that makes calculating profits on a few primary products relatively easy. A wide retail store (carrying a few units of many products) needs more analysis to determine which of the product lines is most profitable.

At the same time, you should analyze which merchandise gives you the least profits or is being sold at a (gasp!) loss. If sales space is an issue—and it is for most retailers—the more profitable lines will displace the less profitable ones. Retailing is about flexibility, about appropriately responding to evolving data.

When analyzing profitability, factor in all costs. That is, make sure that shipping or freight charges are included in your calculations. Add any prep costs incurred once the merchandise reaches your store. For example, if the widgets come to you unassembled and require twenty minutes each to put together, add the labor and overhead costs for that effort. Another factor is storage. If the products are profitable, but you only sell one a month, add in the storage costs of keeping them on hand until sold. The turnover on some products can be a year or more.

Another factor is determining how locations within your store impact sales and profitability. By changing out merchandise on a shelf that seems popular, you may determine that anything on that shelf sells twice as fast as it does at its typical location. This is good to know, especially when calculating line profitability. This is your store's "sweet spot." Some stores discover that they have a few, each of which increases sales for otherwise slow-moving merchandise.

✅ Fact

Smart retailers use spreadsheets and other business programs to graphically track the profitability of specific merchandise lines and products (Chapter 15). It takes extra effort to produce and prepare the data, but graphs can make analysis much easier. A monthly review of line profitability can help you manage your retail store toward serving your customers—and your investments—better.

Your goal as a retailer is to know where your profits are coming from and making decisions that will increase those profits. You will be rewarded for your efforts by a higher income, greater service to your customers, and better wages for your employees. It's win-win-win.

Encouraging Impulse Buying

An impulse is a force that produces an action. In retailing, an impulse buy is an unplanned purchase triggered by an outside source that touches a need or desire. The best example is the snack foods found at the checkout counters of many types of retail stores.

Selecting Impulse Buys

Your retail store can take advantage of the power of impulse buying, though it doesn't need to be as blatant as jelly beans at the cash wrap. You can select smaller accessories for display near the primary products or at the transaction area. For best results, keep the price low—and the profitability high—for impulse merchandise. Following are some suggested impulse items for Bob's Widgets:

- Widget cases
- Widget replacement parts
- Widget tools
- Mini-widgets
- Widget gift certificate cards
- Widget-shaped candy

You get the idea. Make up your own list of possible impulse items for your retail store. Be sure that the products you add for impulse buys are easily related to the primary products on display—and be sure that they offer you a good markup.

✪ Essential

Selling packaged candy may not be appropriate at all stores, but giving it away can be. One retailer had a candy dish with a FREE, PLEASE TAKE ONE sign near the checkout. Many customers rewarded themselves for purchases by smiling and taking a candy. Others came in to check the candy dish, then browsed. The low-cost candy put out in limited quantities paid for itself many times over in customer appreciation and increased sales.

Promoting Impulse Buys

You can encourage impulse purchases in ways other than product placement. You also can use signage and even conversation to build impulse sales. For example, signs near primary products can direct customers to related merchandise: "AA Batteries, Aisle 14." Additionally, clerks can ask, "Do you need batteries for that?" Of course, you should have handy packs of batteries on or near the checkout counter.

A popular impulse buy is gift certificates. As your store develops a large customer base, you'll hear more people say, "I love your store"—cherished words to the retailer. Make sure that your store has gift certificate forms so that you can suggest this option to satisfied customers (and make sure that clerks understand the process). By asking or pointing to a sign that offers gift certificates for friends, you can both increase sales and get more customers.

Developing Secondary Lines

Your independent retail store will be built around a primary product line: books, gifts, jewelry, clothing, bargain merchandise, or other product groups. In our example, Bob sells widgets. That's his primary product line. However, as Bob's store grows he begins looking for a secondary line or two that can increase profitability. How does he do that? More important, how do you do that?

You can analyze your customers, do some research, and perform some testing. If done on a small scale, developing secondary retail lines can be relatively inexpensive—and may build store profitability.

Analyze Your Customers' Needs

This mantra is repeated throughout this book: know your customers. Now that your store is open and operating, it is even more important to understand your customers' needs because the people who visit your store will change. Some of the people who come in on opening day will be back the following week or month, but others will not, for various reasons. They will be replaced by new customers who are just discovering your store through ads, publicity, and word-of-mouth promotion. The profile of your typical customer will change.

You will use the techniques offered at the beginning of this chapter to find out what your customers want. Initially, you will want to know what additions you should make to your store's primary lines, such as widgets. Designer widgets? Hydraulic widgets? Left-handed widgets? Then you'll ask about related customer needs: What else do you shop for when you buy widgets?

A good starting point is to consider the secondary lines that competitive widget stores are carrying, especially those lines that aren't offered locally. In your research, you may learn that many widget stores in a nearby metro market also sell doohickeys, for example. You then survey your customers and discover that, yes, they do buy doohickeys. Now what?

Find Secondary Lines

Doohickeys aren't widgets. They are marketed differently. They serve a similar, but singular function. Chances are, they are manufactured and distributed by companies that are not your current resources. So you must go back to square one, as you did when you researched your primary product line (see Chapter 11). For this secondary line you must define:

- What you are selling
- Who the wholesale sources are
- How the products are delivered to you
- Line profitability

Once identified, you will contact wholesalers to get more specifics and learn about the ordering process, suggestions for initial inventory, and proven marketing methods. Secondary lines aren't as important as primary lines, obviously, but they can bring additional customers—and added profits—to your store. Finding them will take some work.

Test Secondary Lines

How can you test the sales and profits on secondary lines? By making sure that they are tracked separately. Set up a unique department or group of departments for the new lines. Make sure clerks are knowledgeable about the products and how to sell them. Measure how sales are doing against other products in a control test.

🅔✔ Fact

In marketing, a control is a proven product or sales pitch. If you have an established advertisement that brings in more customers than do other ads, that is your control version. A control test is putting another product or pitch up against the control version. Whichever sells more becomes the control. You can test two ads, two primary or secondary products, and so on to develop a control version.

Be sure to purchase test merchandise wholesale in small quantities or under a liberal return policy.

Upgrading Lines

Another method of increasing store sales and profits is to add a line of more expensive primary products. As with secondary lines, you'll need to do customer research, product research, find wholesalers, test the products, and measure the resulting sales for profitability.

What upgraded products should you consider? Those that have a more recognized brand, are more expensive, or are offered as packages. For example, Bob's Widgets may add a custom line of its own exclusive brand of quality widgets called ThingamaBobs. Or it can offer Yadda designer widgets, as previously discussed. Or Bob's can sell Widget Packs, a package of six popular widgets in a handy carrying case. Each is an extension of the primary product line rather than a secondary line. Each is an opportunity for Bob's Widgets to expand sales and profitability based on the success of the store's primary products. Each offers Bob's customers new opportunities to fulfill their needs for widgets.

Think about your own retail store. Which lines can you upgrade with branded, more expensive, or packaged products? How can you build on your primary product line and help more customers?

Adding Risk-Free Lines

Many small retailers have found risk-free secondary and upgrade lines. The profits typically are smaller, but so is the risk. Your store should consider the three principal types of risk-free product lines: consignment, serviced, and returnable. One might just fit your retail model.

Consignment Lines

A *consignment* is a product that the retailer pays for when the customer purchases it rather than when the store receives it. For example, Bob's Widgets takes a consignment shipment of twenty imported widgets from a supplier. Once a month, Bob counts up how many of the units have been sold at retail and sends the supplier a check for the agreed-upon price. If some of the units were pilfered, Bob still has to pay for the products that walked out the door. The consignment agreement will state that the units must either be paid for or returned.

 Essential

How can you find consignment products for your retail store? As you develop contacts with suppliers, ask them if they offer any product lines on consignment and, if so, what the terms are. Some suppliers have secondary lines that are available on consignment to retailers with proven accounts. Other suppliers use consignment products to develop relationships with target retail accounts.

Consignment sales transfer the risk of winding up with unsold product from the retailer/consignee to the supplier/consignor. In exchange, the supplier will charge more for the product—and the retailer will make less money. However, consignment lines can reduce the risk of testing new product lines.

Fact

Want to try a secondary product line at reduced risk? Ask the sales representative whether the line is available on consignment. Many reps are authorized to ship a limited amount of product on a pay-when-sold basis to established accounts. Make sure that you read the terms and limitations of the agreement before signing, as not all consignors or suppliers are reputable.

Serviced Lines

Related to consignment sales, serviced lines can reduce your store's risks, albeit at the loss of some profitability. Here's how it works: A supplier sets up and stocks display units in your store, typically on consignment. The salesperson visits your store on a regular schedule, counts what is sold (or missing), and gives you a bill to be paid immediately or on account. The salesperson typically works on commission.

Serviced lines are low maintenance for retailers. You don't have to worry about what to buy, unpacking merchandise, or any other tasks. Simply ring up the sale and pay the wholesale price when required. You have no investment other than some floor space. In exchange, you will earn lower profits on serviced lines, typically about 10 to 30 percent. Grocery stores have numerous serviced lines including magazines, greeting cards, bakery items, and related products.

Returnable Lines

Another way of minimizing the risks of adding profitable lines is to purchase from wholesalers who have a liberal return policy.

Many bookstores, for example, operate with wholesalers who offer a forty-five-, sixty-, or ninety-day return policy. If the book doesn't sell and is returned in as-new condition within that period, the wholesaler gives the retailer a credit toward future purchases. Other retail stores have similar returnable product lines.

The two problems with buying returnable lines are that profits are smaller and maintenance is higher. Instead of a wholesale price that's 50 percent of retail, returnable lines are typically wholesaled at 55 to 70 percent of retail. In addition, the retailer must keep track of the age of returnable merchandise. If you are using a variety of wholesalers, each with more than one return policy (depending on the product line), determining what is eligible for return and when you can send it back can be difficult. Some wholesalers will help you keep track, but others would just as soon you didn't meet the deadlines and couldn't return the merchandise for credit.

CHAPTER 18

Expanding Your Retail Store

The day will come when you ask yourself how you can expand your retail store. Your store's success and profitability will encourage you to look around for even greater opportunities. How can you make your sales floor more profitable? How can you expand your physical store? Should you move to a bigger store or open a second one? This chapter will help you answer these and other questions related to growing your retail business. Note that your store should be open at least a few months before you consider expansion, as you will need income, turnover, and other historical data for accurate calculations.

Analyzing Your Sales Floor

Chapter 9 guided you in planning your retail store layout. Subsequent chapters helped you see that your store's sales floor is both expansive and limited. It offers you literally thousands of opportunities to help customers find what they want. Yet it also is restricted in size; you can't buy a truckload of widgets until you figure out where to put them besides the back room.

The first step in analyzing your sales floor for expanded profitability is to make sure you have a current floor map. It should be scaled so that you can measure available space with ease. To map your store, you can use graph paper (available at stationery and office supply stores) or home or retail floor-planning software. If you use departments in your store, as most retailers do, indicate the location of those departments on the sales floor. The more detail you can add, the easier it will be to analyze your options. If you are using graph paper, most of your notes should be in pencil, as they will frequently change.

The next step is to calculate sales floor value by *square foot* and *shelf foot*. You'll look at floor departments, income by department, turnover by department, and profitability by square foot. Get out your calculator; you're going to need it for this important exercise. If possible, use a calculator that makes entries of feet and inches easy as well as allowing basic business calculations.

A *square foot* is a two-dimensional area 1 foot wide by 1 foot deep, or 144 (12 × 12) square inches in size. A *shelf foot* is a linear dimension 1 foot long. The depth depends on the depth of the shelf, most commonly 9 to 12 inches. Shelf foot is a common measurement for merchandise that is linear along the shelf with no product behind it. If your store has a variety of shelving depths, use square feet or inches to calculate available sales space. If your store has wall-hung merchandise, calculate the area of the wall racks but use the racks' footprint—the space they take on the sales floor—when comparing values.

Floor Departments

Your sales floor is now broken into departments on a paper or computerized map. You have located each of those departments, how much of the sales floor each takes up, and maybe you have a calculation for shelf footage. These calculations are vital to figuring out your store's income by department as well as other financial indicators.

Should your calculations be of square feet or of shelf feet? Whatever is most common in your store. For example, if your store is composed only of linear shelves, use shelf feet. Most retailers have a mixture of display fixtures. In that case, use square feet of sales floor space as your primary calculator. You also can figure shelf feet or even shelf inches to help you determine whether racks are more profitable for your store than are bins. However, to compare apples to apples, use a single standard for calculating sales floor income and profitability. It will make your job much easier.

Income by Department

Don't put your calculator away yet. You now must figure out how much income is derived by each department in your store. The more data you have for this exercise, the more reliable your calculations will be. If your store has only been open a month when you calculate this income, the data may not be sufficient to make long-term decisions.

Let's suppose you've determined that $12,000 in merchandise has been sold from Department F in the past six months. That department takes up 100 square feet of sales floor space, meaning that department income is $120 per square foot for the period. Use a spreadsheet or paper to record income by all departments for the period. A spreadsheet program (see Chapter 15) makes the calculations much easier.

Turnover by Department

In retailing, *turnover* is the number of times that a product or line is sold and replenished during a specified period, typically a year. If your store sold 50 chrome widgets during the past six months, annual turnover is calculated as 100 units.

Why is turnover important? Because the location of product on your store's sales floor contributes to turnover. Merchandise that is more often seen is more often sold. As you decide to expand your store, remember that product placement can impact turnover and thus profits.

ⓔ✲ Essential

Don't be too hasty in moving departments around for just a few dollars in profitability. The extra profit may be lost to the confusion factor, especially if customers can't find what they are looking for. Make your moves in logical and orderly fashion, using signage to inform customers of the changes.

Profitability by Square Foot

Profitability is the bottom line. Income and turnover in a department can be good, but if it isn't as profitable as others, the space may be wasted. For that reason, your sales floor analysis should include calculations of profitability. You don't have to get it down to the penny, but accuracy is important to making the best decisions.

For example, Department M's profitability may be high even though it is relegated to a low-traffic area within the store. Knowing these facts invites you to move the department to a higher-traffic location and possibly expand the line for enhanced profits.

Cutting Unprofitable Lines

An important aspect of expanding your retail store's profitability is enhancing the most profitable lines. Once you calculate income by department and by product, analyze turnover, and determine profitability, you can make your decision whether to increase or decrease the sales floor area for specific merchandise. You can fine-tune each department to make it as efficient as possible in serving your customers' needs—and your store's bottom line.

What should you do about the departments, lines, and products that aren't performing well? Maybe the profits are low or even nonexistent. If there is not a compelling reason to retain the merchandise, reduce or remove it.

Cutting Back Merchandise

Cutting back on specific departments or merchandise isn't as easy as pulling them from the shelves, especially if some customers have relied on finding these products in your store. Perhaps your store is the only source for these otherwise hard-to-find products. Maybe your store is the only place some key customers can find left-handed widgets, but you don't sell enough of them to warrant much floor space. Cut them back as needed, but keep them and keep your customers happy. Following are some suggestions on how to minimize unprofitable merchandise in a department.

- Keep a smaller number of each product.
- Reduce the number of individual products in the department, keeping the most popular.
- Post signs that indicate how customers can find discontinued products: "Ask the clerk for left-handed widgets."
- If asked, explain to customers that some products are discontinued to make room for more popular merchandise.

Most customers will understand that slow-moving (or unprofitable) merchandise is discontinued. Just make sure they also know that they can special-order merchandise at your store rather than visit your competitor. Your business goal is to profitably satisfy the needs of your customers.

Removing Departments

Not every product or line purchased by a retailer is sold to customers. Sometimes a "hot product" isn't. Or you discover, too late, that your competitor bought a thousand and is selling them at retail for less than what you paid wholesale. Or you just goofed when ordering. It happens. What can you do when closing out a department or a large group of products?

You can have a closeout sale! A closeout sale serves many purposes. It reduces your inventory of unprofitable or unpopular merchandise, of course. It also offers you an excuse to invite cost-conscious customers back into the store; they may buy what's on sale and/or something else. Closeout sales also notify customers that you are discontinuing a line or department and that they should stock up before everything is gone. Many retailers have annual or semi-annual clearance sales specifically developed to reduce less-profitable stock—and to promote an event.

Why should you discount merchandise that already is unprofitable? Because your sales floor space is valuable. By calculating sales floor value in square feet or linear shelf feet, you have determined what products make you the most money or bring you the best customers. By reducing unprofitable lines, even at a loss, you now have more room for merchandise that you've identified as more profitable. The loss will be small compared to the long-term profit gain.

Expanding Your Sales Floor

Eventually, your store will be operated about as efficiently—and profitably—as possible. All departments will be trimmed to their appropriate and most profitable size for your local market, and your store will take less daily management. You'll find the groove.

About then you'll be tempted to push out the walls to expand your sales floor. More is better, right? It may be. However, before grabbing a sledgehammer, consider whether your fine-tuned store is already at maximum market. Is your marketplace expanding, with new customers coming into the area all the time? Or has your store already drawn most of the potential customers in the marketplace? Do some more market research (see Chapter 17) to better understand whether your customers want and will support an expanded store.

🅐 Alert

Hold it! Don't knock down walls just yet. First try some other, easier methods of increasing sales. Start by expanding your store hours. For the price of an extra employee or two and some utilities, you may be able to dramatically increase store sales without a major remodel. Also consider upgrading fixtures to give you more efficient sales space. You may be able to pay for the investment in just a few months.

If you've decided to expand your store, you have options. You can do so by reducing the back room, moving the back room, adding a mezzanine, or taking over a neighbor. Of course, you also can move to a bigger store or open a second store, which is covered later in this chapter.

Reduce the Back Room

The easiest way to expand your store's sales floor is to reduce the size of the back room. As your store has grown and you've moved all initial inventory to the sales floor, the back room may be less crowded. Or it may just be junky. In either case, turn your efficient mind to how you can reduce the size of the back room. Here are some examples:

- Move replacement stock from the back room to compartments available under, above, or behind sales floor fixtures.
- Restock the sales floor more frequently to minimize stock in the back room.
- Build more efficient shelving for replacement stock that can't go on the sales floor yet.
- Build a more efficient shipping area for returns.
- Get trash and recycling out of the back room as quickly as possible.
- Be more efficient at returning unwanted merchandise quickly rather than storing it in the back room.

Move the Back Room

Do you even *need* an on-site back room? In some retail locations there are nearby spaces that can be used for storage and shipping functions. Maybe there's one in your mall or retail center. Alternately, there may be an easy-to-access storage unit near the property that can securely house secondary stock. Some retailers have even rented portable storage units that they can have parked near the back door and keep locked.

Add a Mezzanine

A *mezzanine* is an intermediate floor between two primary floors or between the main floor and a high ceiling. Not all retail stores have room for a mezzanine or balcony. If yours does, consider installing one following local building codes. The new area can be used as a back room to store inventory.

Alternately, the mezzanine can be a low platform with stairs that becomes a new sales area and offers storage underneath it. The advantage of a low mezzanine is that it can be visible from throughout your store. If this idea works for your store, hire a retail architect to design an efficient one for you. And make sure that you have permissions—and a long-term lease—with your landlord. In fact, if it is a property improvement, your landlord may participate in its design and construction costs.

Take Over a Neighbor

Not all small retail businesses make it past the first year or two. Yours will, of course. But maybe an adjoining store won't. This can give you an opportunity to expand your store, possibly by just removing a wall or installing a doorway. Of course, conditions and timing have to be just right to make this work, but by knowing your neighbors you may be ready and able to expand your store without moving. Some retailers also will rent an empty store within their mall and set up a seasonal-sales shop, such as a Christmas gift annex.

Moving to a Bigger Store

You're on a roll. Your store is expanding, busting at the seams. More customers are coming in every day. Profits are increasing. You're seriously considering moving your established retail store to a location with more room. Should you?

Only you, the owner/manager, can answer that question, based on sales projections and opportunities. However, following are some points to consider as you make that decision:

- Just as when setting up your first store, make sure that the store is located away from potential competitors—including your primary store.
- Be sure that your new location is a more popular shopping site (such as a major mall) than your current location.
- Thoroughly plan the logistics of the move to ensure that you have the fewest days when you are closed. If possible, operate both locations during the transition period.
- Make sure your customers, especially your best customers, know well in advance of your move.
- Work out with your suppliers in advance where inventory will be delivered. You could have a temporary central storage location and distribute it from there to your stores.
- Use the move as an opportunity to rethink the design of your store.
- Expand your advertising budget for a few months to promote your new location.
- If possible, place New Location signs in the windows of your old location for up to six months.
- Get signage up at your new location early with a banner that reads "Coming Soon."
- Work with your new landlord to make the transfer efficient. Some lessors will give you a month or two of "free" rent to help you get moved in.
- Help your employees see the opportunities for personal and career growth as your store expands. Encourage training and possible promotion for employees who will help in the transition.

Opening a Second Store

Success is sweet. Your retail store is profitable and you're even considering opening a second store to double the profits. However, it's not quite that easy. Some retailers suggest that having a second store is like having a second spouse. The benefits can be apparent, but the costs can be immense—especially if you must spread your attention between the two. Under the right conditions, you may someday decide to open a second or even a third retail store—or not. Following are some considerations as you contemplate cloning:

- Make sure that your market research clearly shows that a second store will be profitable.
- Opening a second store means you get a second chance to do it better.
- Hire a trusted manager for at least one of your stores, especially if there is distance between them.
- Standardize how you train your employees and perform primary tasks, as you will be required to do both of these more frequently.
- Consider how you will differentiate between your stores: Bob's Widget Annex, Bob's Widgets at Uptown Mall, Bob's Widgets II, Mary's Widgets.
- Make sure that your recordkeeping system is set up for two distinct entities yet can be consolidated for primary financial reports.
- Be sure that you have the resources—and the energy—to operate two stores before you begin.

You might even consider turning your successful operation into a franchise. However, make sure you fully research and understand what you're getting into. Developing a proven and profitable retail system for yourself is not the same as being able to help others succeed. Franchising is a service business unto itself. If it interests you, start learning requirements from the Federal Trade Commission (*www.ftc.gov*), which regulates franchises. Alternately, you can consider offering a *business opportunity*, similar to a franchise but with less regulation and licensing. Ask your business adviser or regional office of the Small Business Administration for a referral to a franchise developer or attorney.

CHAPTER 19

Selling Merchandise Online

Bob's Widgets may be in trouble. It's losing customers to Widget World, the online retailer that sells millions of widgets. What should Bob do? Ignore them or compete with them? This chapter offers practical tips for both responses, but focuses on how to compete for customers online. You may decide to do the same—or not. You may find, as many small retailers have, that online retailing is complementary to your physical store. It can offer just what you need to increase profitability.

Online Retailing Opportunities

Many small retailers are reluctant to even go into business because they believe that the big fish, Amazon and the like, have gobbled up all of the good customers and left them with nothing. Actually, the opposite is true. Amazon, Yahoo!, and other online behemoths can actually help your small retail operation survive and even thrive. What's that all about?

Initially, Amazon was like a ten-ton gorilla, doing whatever it wanted to satisfy a voracious appetite for new customers. It since has learned that it can actually make more money by helping smaller businesses thrive. Like an anchor store in a shopping mall, it has discovered that it *needs* the traffic drawn by smaller, independent stores. Everybody wins—if they all know how to be friendly competitors.

Online Commerce Basics

The Internet is about fifteen years old and growing quickly. It began as a way for college students and researchers to share information and messages using telephone lines. Rather than spoken words, the Internet uses data, bits of information that can be sent very quickly and interpreted by computer hardware and software at the other end. The software, called browsers, made the data visual.

It wasn't long before people figured out how to buy and sell using the Internet. AOL (previously America Online) and Yahoo! became portals that people used to enter the Internet. Amazon started selling books online, then expanded to other types of merchandise. Online auctions like eBay popped up and grew like wildfire. Money was safely exchanged using bank transfers and a service called PayPal (now owned by eBay). You could find things online using search engines, and Google soon took prominence. Then Google and others began selling advertising online. Today, online shopping is as safe as shopping in a brick-and-mortar (B&M) store—and a whole lot easier. That's why many thousands of dollars are spent *each hour* with online retailers. Some of that money could be yours.

Online Versus Brick-and-Mortar

Physical (brick-and-mortar) stores have been around a long time. Today's online stores are relatively new. What do online stores look like? You might be surprised. Some online-only stores have an office in one city, say Dallas; warehouses in others (Cleveland and Reno); computer servers elsewhere (Toronto); and order takers in foreign lands (India). They are virtual businesses. Unlike B&Ms, they are not confined to a single physical location. The Internet is in operation 24/7 and orders come in from wherever in the world people are awake. Data lines and satellite feeds keep the operation connected so that your order is instantaneously received at the warehouse, where it will soon be packaged and shipped; the delivery service is notified of an impending shipment; and you receive confirmation of your order via e-mail—all within a few minutes!

On the other hand, you can stop by a retail store during your lunch hour and ask the clerk for help selecting a widget, pick it up and try it out, ask about the new line of widgets you've read about, make your purchase, then slip into the café next door for a latte. Which type of shopping is better?

 Essential

> Both online stores and B&Ms know their customers. Online shoppers may want to choose from a thousand widget models, while the local customer is satisfied selecting from a dozen but wants to see all of them before buying. Remember that your online customer will probably be different from those who walk into your local store. Know the difference and satisfy your customers to make a profit.

It all depends on what the customer wants. If the customer doesn't need much help in selecting and would rather have a wide selection, online shopping may work better for them. If the customer needs help in selecting, but doesn't really need a left-handed chrome widget with inlaid pearl handles, the nearby B&M may be the best place to shop.

Supplementing Sales

Chances are that online sales will be supplemental income to your physical store. You may derive just 10 percent of sales from online customers—or you may build it up to 50 percent or more. Or you may opt to pass on online sales; it's not for every retailer.

Online sales work for retailers who find a niche, a specialty within a specialty, that isn't served by the behemoths. Small retailers can offer highly specialized products that they know better than anyone else. Or they can offer products for which they are the manufacturer, importer, or sole source. The key to online sales is *uniqueness*. The rewards are greater income with lower expenses.

Opportunities to Increase Store Sales

Depending on the type of retail store you're building, you may discover numerous opportunities for online sales. Following are some suggestions:

- A brick-and-mortar gift store in a popular destination town can sell souvenirs online.
- Used-book stores can sell hard-to-find books online that have been traded in by local customers.
- A jeweler who imports some products from Bali can offer a wider selection to online customers.
- A clothing store can offer a locally made brand of apparel not otherwise sold online.
- Consignment shops can sell some unique merchandise on eBay or other auctions.

In each example, the key to online sales is uniqueness. The online store offers products that may not sell in quantity to local customers, but can be sold profitably on the Internet. At the same time, the local store is developing an online presence. A website can supplement the B&M store's income without much extra overhead expense.

Finding a Niche

So how can your B&M store find a niche market? In the same way that you developed your initial store concept: by knowing your customers. To do that, you must first become an online customer. In your initial research for a store, you probably spent time and maybe some money searching for products and finding out what is available to your customers. *You* were an online customer. Maybe you saw some opportunities at that time. If not, continue your research, focusing on uniqueness. Building an online store is similar in many ways to building a B&M store. The primary differences are the customers you serve and the way that you serve them.

Problems of Online Sales

Like traditional retailing, online sales aren't always easy. One of the problems is that you don't really know the person you are selling to. If there's a difficulty with the order, you can't just meet with your customer face-to-face and discuss it. You must rely on e-mail and/or the telephone for interaction. That's not always the most efficient or sensitive form of communication.

 Fact

> Have questions about how online transaction security works? Visit the primary transaction resources on the Internet (*www.paypal.com*, *www.verisign.com*, and *www.truste.com*). They offer articles and answer frequently asked questions (FAQs) to help you understand encryption systems and how you can transfer money with confidence. Also ask your banker and your store's merchant account processor or banker about secure online transactions.

In addition, there are fraud issues. What if the credit card used for the transaction is stolen? What if the order isn't legitimate and you'll never see the money or get the merchandise back? What's the solution? Actually, it's similar to how you transact business in the store. If there's a question about possible fraud, make sure that reputable identification is used. In the store, you would ask for ID, such as a driver's license. You would check it over to make sure it was authentic, and possibly get a second piece of ID. Online transactions have authentication processes that can minimize loss and help you—and your customers—feel confident about transaction security.

Building Targeted Online Sales

Once you've identified a niche for your online business, make sure that you fully understand who your customers are. Again, those who buy in your store are different from those who purchase from you online. Their needs will be different. Even their primary language and monetary system may be different. As with your B&M, know who they are, why they buy, and how to develop a successful relationship with them.

Question

Online sales sound complicated and risky. Should I ignore this market?
Maybe—at least until your B&M store is established and you are more comfortable with adding this additional dimension to retailing. However, do your business a favor and periodically revisit this topic, doing a little research into opportunities as well as increasing your comfort level with online transactions. Not being online won't be the end of your business. However, selling online may supplement your sales and bring you new profits.

Finding Your Online Customers

How can you identify your online customers if you can't see them? In the same way that you identified customers for your B&M store: by studying their needs and buying habits. Become one of them. Shop online. Read forums and web logs (blogs) about the merchandise line. Read magazines that your target customers read. Hire or do your own market research to find out as much as you can about prospective customers. Understand their needs—and then sell to them.

Satisfying Your Online Customers

The primary way that you will satisfy your store's online customers is by offering them something that they cannot otherwise easily get. By intimately knowing your online customers' needs, you can learn how to gratify them. As a knowledgeable customer for your line of products, what are you looking for? Is there a niche market or a specialty that isn't being served online? Is there a locally offered product that you can sell through your new online store? Who are your potential online customers, and what do they want?

One problem you must overcome in selling online is helping your new customers trust you. It's not as important with B&M stores that have a physical presence; customers can walk into a store and within a few minutes determine if your store is trustworthy. But your online customers in Australia don't know you from Amsterdam. You could be the answer to their problems—or another problem. You must satisfy their reluctance to buy from you. Use reputable transaction verification systems and secure shopping carts to help them trust you—and buy from you.

Where to Build Your Online Store

Chapter 7 guided you in selecting an appropriate location for your B&M store. Locating your online store can be just as important. Why? Because the location can give you credibility with potential customers. At relatively low cost, you can set up your store next to one or more of the big players—Amazon, eBay, Yahoo!—or as a standalone. Following is a closer look at each of the major online malls.

Amazon

Beginning life as an online bookstore in 1996, Amazon (*www.amazon.com*) is now a humongous online shopping mall. It sells books, movies, electronics, computers and software, home and garden, groceries (yes!), toys, apparel, health and beauty products, sports and outdoor merchandise, tools, automotive, and even industrial products. Who knows what's next? Whatever your store sells, there's a good chance that Amazon sells it, too.

Actually, many of these lines aren't sold directly by Amazon. They are offered through Amazon Marketplace, separate businesses that contract with Amazon to market their wares. Once your account is set up, you list the merchandise you're selling, orders come to you, you ship them to the customer, and then Amazon pays you—less a commission. Customers give feedback on the transaction, helping you build credibility. You also can set up virtual stores, called aStores, through Amazon and link to them from your site to sell products for other merchants—and earn commissions.

One of the advantages of selling online via Amazon is that it handles the transaction and makes payment to you. If there is a problem with the customer, Amazon is good about resolving it.

Amazon also has a referral service, called Associates, that places Amazon products on related websites (like yours) and pays a commission on what is sold through the referral. If you are interested in these opportunities, visit Amazon.com and follow the links on the bottom of the page.

Yahoo!

Yahoo! (*www.yahoo.com*) is one of the most visited sites on the Internet. It offers personalized home pages with news, sports, entertainment, and other information. It also offers shopping opportunities (*http://shopping.yahoo.com*) for clothing, computers, electronics, DVDs, music, books, flowers, gifts, home and garden, jewelry and watches, sports, outdoor, and much more. It's the world's largest shopping mall.

The Yahoo! shopping mall is composed of individual retail businesses that sell a wide variety of merchandise. Some of these businesses also have B&M stores (Target, JC Penney, Nordstrom), but many are online only. To become a Yahoo! business, visit shopping.yahoo.com, go to the bottom of the page, and look for the current links to Build Your Online Store.

eBay

In 1995, eBay began (under another name) as an online auction site. The site (*www.ebay.com*) soon caught on with shoppers around the world and now earns over $6 billion annually in listing fees and other financial fees. It purchased PayPal, an electronic commerce (e-commerce) money transfer service, in 2002. The eBay corporation also owns Shopping.com, StumbleUpon.com, Half.com, ProStores.com, and other online businesses with offices around the world.

Like other big online businesses, eBay partners with small businesses to sell a world of products—for a fee. Not all products sold through eBay are in auctions. Many are offered by affiliate eBay Stores. For a fee, eBay lists and promotes products from other sellers, passing along the orders, and guaranteeing the transaction. Buyers often prefer to purchase online through mega-malls such as eBay, Amazon, and Yahoo! rather than from standalone stores because of their security measures.

Other Shopping Malls

Once you begin shopping online, you'll discover dozens of other virtual malls, some of them more appropriate than others to what you sell. Use search engines to identify and try them out.

The primary advantage of online shopping malls is name value. Online shopping requires a higher level of customer trust than at B&M malls. A trusted online mall can give your new business instant credibility. Remember that setting up stores in more than one mall is relatively inexpensive. In fact, some have little or no start-up costs, and the only expense is a commission paid when you sell something through them. Of course, you must make sure that the online mall that has your store in it isn't keeping your money. Check out any online mall before joining. The big ones discussed in this section are proven; smaller ones may not be.

Your Own Store

Just like B&M businesses, retailers can have standalone online stores that don't depend on surrounding businesses to draw traffic. You can set up your virtual store anywhere on the Internet and customers can access you from anywhere in the world—if they can find you.

The main disadvantage of developing an online store outside of a virtual mall is that you'll have to work harder to develop traffic. There are many methods of doing so, such as search engine optimization and advertising through search engines such as Google and Yahoo! However, it's better to begin your online operation within a large virtual mall, then build your own site later—if ever—once you know more about the intricacies of online commerce.

How Online Stores Operate

Whether you set up your online store in a popular virtual mall or at a standalone site, e-commerce operates similarly. Following is an introduction to e-commerce with lots of the details left out. Once you've decided which route to take, you can do more research and learn how these processes work to help you profit from online sales.

The Website

Your store's website is its virtual location. It may be a part of someone else's site, such as *www.ebay.com*, or it can be your own, like *www.bobswidgets.com*. The site actually is located on a computer, called a server, connected somehow to the Internet. Any connected computer in the world can type in the web address—also known as the uniform resource locator, or URL—and access your website. The files are probably written in a hypertext markup language (HTML) with codes that tell the receiver's browser software how to display it. For example, the <center> code centers the text and <i> italicizes it.

 Fact

Don't worry; you don't have to write all the HTML codes to build a website. You can purchase website design tools that will do the coding for you. However, you should understand basic HTML code, just in case you have problems with your website. Identifying the problem is half of the solution. Alternately, hire someone with website development experience.

Shopping Carts

As a visitor to your website purchases an item, it is placed in a *shopping cart*, a virtual location where item descriptors and pricing are collected prior to purchase. Actually, it's a database that connects the specific customer with one or more products. Once the customer is ready to purchase the items in the shopping cart, she selects Checkout and begins the financial transaction.

Transaction Software

The shopping cart is full, shipping costs and applicable tax have been added, and the customer is ready to pay for the purchase. Transaction software handles this step for your virtual store. If you are an online mall associate, the shopping cart and transaction software are supplied by the mall. If your store is standalone, you may have to provide the cart or transaction software. Alternately, you can use a third party, such as Digital River (*www.digitalriver.com*) or PayPal (*www.paypal.com*), to process the transaction. Or you can work with your merchant account (credit card) vendor to set up a transaction system. In each case, the customer confirms the purchase, the transaction is passed to a secure computer with encryption software for safety, and the banking information (debit, credit card, or other account data) is entered.

Once payment is confirmed, the buyer is notified that the transaction is approved and the seller is notified to ship. Typically, automated e-mails with specific information make the notifications within seconds.

Other Online Business Aids

There are dozens of other programs and services available to online merchants. Many of them are seamless and operated by the online malls rather than by the merchants. They track the orders, advise the buyer of shipment, request transaction feedback, and even suggest future purchases—all automatically.

In addition, online merchants can purchase advertising to help them promote their stores. The current players include Google AdWords, Yahoo! Search Marketing (formerly Overture), and other services. Most are paid by click-throughs. The term *click-through* means that a site visitor has clicked on an advertisement link. You can select the keywords for your business (these are significant words that customers use to search for your products), and search engines will display your ad when those words are searched. As you develop your online store, you should research these opportunities, test them, and determine which best fit your needs and budget.

How to Profitably Compete with Yourself

Yes, once you set up an online store you will be competing with your B&M store. Here are some suggestions:

- Make the products you sell online non-competitive with those you sell in your store.
- If necessary, segregate the online business from the retail store so that inventory and transactions don't overlap.
- Be sure that customer prices are the same for all locations of the *same* business.
- Set up your online store as a separate entity with a different business name (MrWidget.com).

Your online store may be so successful that you consider closing your B&M to concentrate on your online operation. The advantage of operating an exclusively online retail store is that you get to keep your own hours. The disadvantage is that, once the business grows, those hours could be in the middle of the night. Also, people who start a business partially for the social aspect will soon miss interacting with real, live customers. Online store owners rarely speak with customers except through e-mails. That may not be as much fun for you.

CHAPTER 20

Solving Growing Challenges

Retailing is organic. In come customers (and their money) and out goes merchandise (and your profits). That's as it should be. However, sometimes a small retail business can grow in the wrong directions, causing problems and sapping profits. It can get lost in minutiae, the daily details that somehow pull your business in a new and unplanned direction. It can suffer from growing pains. This chapter offers proven methods for managing and controlling the growth of your new retail store.

Growth Isn't Always Good

Growth is good, right? Especially when retailing is the topic. Actually, growth isn't always good. Growth of expenses without improving profits isn't good. An increase in losses certainly isn't good for business. Growth by your competitors isn't necessarily good for your store. It's managed growth toward business goals that benefits your business. Like a living plant, your store must be fed, nurtured, and trimmed as needed to produce fruit. If a plant grows into a tall spindly stalk, or doesn't have sufficient leaves or buds, it won't be as healthy as one that is cared for. Your retail store is similar. Feed it well, keep it trimmed, and watch it grow.

Many otherwise successful retailers don't move their stores to the next level of profitability because they don't recognize what's needed for managed growth. Lost in the details, they don't see the overall changes. More important, they don't control them.

Unmanaged Growth

Your retail store will grow every day it is in operation. Inventory will grow, sales will (ideally) grow, expenses probably will grow, the image that your customers have of your store will develop, and, if these elements are managed well, profits will grow.

At the same time, problems will develop in your store. New opportunities present themselves and must be considered. Customer or employee issues will crop up and require your attention. New laws, new taxes, and other business requirements will attempt to pull your business in new directions. The list is seemingly endless.

There are several ways you can manage growth for your retail store:

- Keep focused on your business objectives.
- Identify problems that keep your store from growing in the selected direction.
- Resolve problems with minimal effort.

These are three important tasks for managing the growth of your retail business. They are vital responsibilities for the owner/manager.

Focus on Your Objectives

Modern retailing is much more complex than it was just twenty years ago. Most of the complexity comes from the new power that computers present to retailers. Yes, they are supposed to make management easier, but they don't. They just give managers a level of detail that was unavailable before.

So a major technique for managing retail growth is to stay focused on your objectives rather than on the details that can overwhelm your days. For the moment, ignore that the printer is keeping you from printing the monthly reports. Fix the problem, yes, but don't take it as an omen of impending doom. Hire a computer consultant or read the reports on screen. Just don't get frustrated and locked into the problem and blow it out of proportion. Instead, focus on your business objectives, as defined in your business plan. Spend your time on identifying and resolving your business's primary problems.

Identify the Problems

In your retail business, sometimes the most difficult task can be to clearly identify the underlying problem. Not having enough customers is a symptom. What's the problem? Are the store hours insufficient? Is advertising reaching your target market? Has a major competitor taken customers from you? Clearly identify the problem and you're halfway to a solution.

Consider the Options

If the business problem is, for example, that a major competitor is taking your customers, your options may include these:

1. Develop an aggressive advertising campaign that targets your competition.
2. Offer your customers more compelling reasons to shop in your store.
3. Build your business to replace lost customers.
4. Hire a consultant to advise you on ways to counter the competition.
5. Sell your retail store.

Option #2 sounds like the best, followed closely by #3 and #4. Option #1 seems too aggressive, and #5 is giving up. Your business always has options. Your job, as the owner/manager, is to determine what they are and make the best decision you can relative to the business's goals.

Growing in the Right Direction

It's increasingly vital to your store's growth that you step back once in a while to take an objective look at your store, its operations, and its results, and to resolve any problems that keep the store from offering its best to your customers, your employees, and to you. It's also vital that you make sure that your business objectives grow as your business does. Over time, what you sell, how you sell it, and to whom, will be modified. Your goal is to control the modification rather than be controlled by it. That is, consciously adjust how you do business rather than allow outside factors to make the adjustments for you. Be a proactive manager.

To adjust your business toward a better business model, you must first identify your initial model. That's what your business plan (see Chapter 6) is all about: defining how you do business. Of course, the business plan is written before you get into the actual operations of your retail store. Once the doors open, you may determine that the business plan isn't fully accurate regarding what your customers need or to how you will manage it. It's okay to revise your business plan as long as the revision brings you a better definition of what works.

ⓔ❗ Alert

A problem for some retailers can be that the business model is revised too often. Selling widgets today is replaced by selling doodads next month. It can be confusing to customers. That's why market research is so important before you open your retail store. Research done after the doors open should help focus your store, but shouldn't take it in a radically new direction. That's an identity crisis.

The key to growing your retail business in the right direction is 1) having a well-defined direction and 2) making only midcourse corrections rather than deciding on new destinations. By planning your business well and making appropriate adjustments you can ensure that it can live long and prosper.

Reducing Operating Costs

Once your retail store gets rolling and profits build, the temptation is to spend more money: "Hey, I can afford that now." Maybe you can. However, remember that profit is what you make minus what you spend. If you want to grow your store you must grow profits, and a proven way of doing so is reducing operating costs.

How can you cut operating costs without cutting profits? You can reduce store overhead, employee costs, and inventory costs. Following are some proven methods.

Reducing Overhead

In retailing, overhead is the ongoing expense of keeping the store open. It includes both fixed and variable costs. Fixed expenses, like rent, go on whether your store is open or closed. Variable expenses, such as electricity, will change if the store is open and lights are on. Employee wages, too, are a variable expense.

The best way to reduce overhead costs is to track and manage them. For example, you can use your recordkeeping system (see Chapter 15) to track electricity usage by month and identify spikes (increases) or drops (decreases), then determine why they occurred. Maybe the spike was due to a billing error that you can report—or maybe a neighboring store is tapping into your electric box. You won't know if you don't track overhead expenses.

Fortunately, computerized accounting systems can make the mundane task of tracking overhead expenses relatively easy. Once reports are set up, you can visually graph various overhead expenses with the click of a mouse. The task of tracking overhead expenses may take just a few hours per month, but can warn you of problems that you can easily manage.

Reducing Employee Costs

Employees can be one of your business' greatest assets or among its biggest liabilities. Tracking overhead expenses is relatively easy because everything is measured in dollars. Measuring employee productivity is more subtle.

The key to managing employee costs is to develop quantifiable measurements for tracking employees individually and as a group. For example, which clerks have the most sales per hour or day? Is the difference the time or the clerks? What are the store averages? Do some employees consistently clock in late? Are their lunch hours accurate?

Your observations should be added to the mix. What attitudes do employees display when dealing with customers, other employees, and managers? What do customers say about your employees?

In many cases, discussing unproductive habits with employees will correct the situation. Be sensitive to the employee, but remember that you are running a business. You cannot take your personal issues out on employees, nor should theirs hurt your business. Be a good listener, but a clear manager.

Reducing Inventory Costs

Another important way to reduce your store's operating costs is to carefully manage inventory. It's easy, especially once your store becomes more profitable, to overbuy stock. Chapter 12 offered proven methods of replacing initial inventory. Use your sales records, sales reps, employee feedback, and good judgment when replenishing stock.

Essential

Make sure that the inventory monitoring system your store uses allows you to easily track sales, inventory levels, history, and profitability. The easier the system is to use, the more frequently it will be used. A major key to retail profitability is saving pennies to make dollars.

Many retailers take a detailed look at inventory once or twice a month, depending on the complexity of inventory and the level of sales. They compare what has been sold to what stock has been ordered. They make adjustments to automated restocking systems as needed to keep inventory at just-in-time (JIT) levels.

Smart retailers also give secondary and new suppliers an opportunity to beat current wholesale prices. Retailers who identify a more cost-effective supplier may use that company for a full line or an entire department, monitoring sales and profitability. The more profitable supplier wins.

Reducing Losses

Another proven way to keep your retail store growing is to cut losses. In any business, losses are inevitable. They are caused by:

- Inaccuracy in counting and tracking incoming inventory
- Inaccuracy in counting cash, checks, and charges collected from transactions
- Spoilage; products that age beyond their usefulness while waiting to be sold
- Theft by employees
- Shoplifting by customers
- Allowing debtors to avoid paying obligations
- Inappropriate buying of replacement inventory

The common element in losses is not verifying records. For example, by not taking a physical inventory once in a while you will never know which losses are due to crime. If you don't double-check the cash drawer, you won't see discrepancies and determine how to stop them. If you don't study store inventory for sales and profitability, you won't know if stock has been purchased that just isn't selling.

Fortunately, by identifying the primary types of losses, your business can manage them without spending most of your valuable time doing so. You can set up systems of checks and balances that quickly let you know when losses occur. You then can take action to stop the loss and to minimize future losses.

Reducing Theft

In an ideal world, theft would be nonexistent. People would not justify taking things that don't belong to them. In the real world, theft happens. Here are several ways you can manage your retail store to minimize theft by customers, employees, and others:

- Make sure that your employees comply with guidelines from credit card processors toward minimizing losses.
- Learn from your banker how to identify counterfeit currency, and make sure that employees are fully trained.
- Ask local law enforcement how you can reduce theft from your store.
- Ask your merchant association about theft prevention education courses.
- Keep valuable merchandise where theft is more difficult.
- Place video cameras (or dummy cameras) and mirrors to view less secure areas.
- If necessary, install a security system and monitoring service.
- Make sure there is always an employee nearby—this deters all but the boldest thieves.
- Reward honesty and reprimand dishonesty in all business dealings.
- In the case of a robbery, *never* challenge the robber. It's not worth the risk. Make sure that your employees know this.

On the other side, don't be paranoid about theft. The vast majority of your customers and employees will not steal from you. In fact, many will not steal even if you leave the cash drawer open and you walk out of the room. Treat your customers with trust, and most will respond accordingly. Just be aware of the methods of the few who do steal, and do what you can to prevent losses from theft.

Fact

Some retailers sell "on account," meaning customers are billed at the end of the month for merchandise purchased during the month. If your store sells on account, here are some suggestions on how to minimize losses: keep good records of all on-account transactions; produce accurate invoices for each customer; send out invoices on time; clearly indicate payment terms on each invoice, such as "payment due by the 15th"; and establish a late fee and indicate it on the invoice.

Beating Your Competition

Another of the challenges to growing your retail store is beating your competition. Especially as your business succeeds, you'll find that competitors will take your store more seriously and take action to keep you from enticing their customers away. Of course, your response will be to entice them anyway. That's the nature of retailing. It's called growth, and customers typically win in the competition.

How can your new retail store beat the competition? By knowing who your competitors are, what they are doing, doing it better, and by letting others know why they should shop with you. Your smarter competitors are doing the same to you.

Who Are Your Competitors?

In the broadest terms, all other retailers are your competitors. However, you can narrow down your direct competitors to those who are competing for the same budgetary dollars as your store. For example, if you sell crafts, your direct competitors are stores that also sell crafts—not stores that sell ethnic groceries or party products.

How can you identify direct competitors for your target customers' dollars? By thinking like your target customers. If you wanted to buy a left-handed widget, for example, where would you, as an informed consumer, shop? Might you go to a nearby metro area or shop online or through a mailed catalog? These sources are your competitors.

Of course, some offer you more competition than others. Mary's Widgets down the block from your store is a primary competitor, while WidgetWorld.com is secondary or even tertiary. So you must consider how much these businesses compete for the dollars of your store's target customer. You probably already know who these competitors are, but it's a good idea to review and add to them periodically—your target customer probably does.

What Are They Doing?

Once your store's competitors are identified and ranked, keep a watch on them. Are they having sales? How often? Who are their primary suppliers? How much do they advertise? What are their operating hours? What lines do they carry in common with your store? What merchandise is different? Why?

Ask lots of questions. The more you know about your competitors' actions, the better you can manage your own store.

Do It Better!

No two retailers operate in exactly the same way. In fact, their target customers may be defined differently. Your primary competitor may be selling widgets to buyers who are more affluent or younger than those who shop at your store. If you're competing for the same target buyer segment, consider the ways that your store can win the competition. Lower prices? More variety? Faster delivery? More helpful clerks? Longer store hours? Don't let your competitors eat your pie!

Let the World Know

It's not enough to win customers from your competitors; your customers must know why you won. If you are winning by offering lower prices or a wider selection, tell them so. In fact, tell the world. In doing so, you also will be telling prospective customers that Bob's Widgets has more doohickeys in stock than does Mary's Widgets. Of course, you'll say it more positively: Bob's Widgets has the largest selection of doohickeys in the area. But you'll say it.

CHAPTER 21

Enjoying Your Retail Store

Remember back in the "old days" when you first began considering a retail store? Now, you may be the owner/manager of a store that brings satisfaction to customers and profits to you. Or you may be wondering why the heck you got into this business. By taking a periodic reality check, remembering your business and personal goals, and learning how to relax, you can enjoy your retail store. Independent retailing is a way of making more than a living. It's also a means of making a life. This chapter will help you take pleasure in your retail store.

Are You Having Fun Yet?

Life is too short to be doing something that isn't enjoyable—at least some of the time. In fact, you probably chose retailing because it sounded like pleasant work. You saw the opportunities to make an income, build equity, and have some fun. But maybe the reality of mundane tasks and the frustration of working with a few ill-tempered customers has taken its toll and you're having serious second thoughts. What can you do?

Many people find that taking a periodic reality check, reviewing your initial goals, and finding things to enjoy can put the fun back into nearly any duty. Retailing is no exception.

Reality Check

The reality of your small retail store is that it provides a valuable service to customers and community, a place for employees to earn an income and grow as people, and a place for you to profit from your skills and efforts. There are problems, of course. Most of them are solvable. In fact, by even starting a retail store you've solved hundreds of problems successfully. You'll solve even more every day—if you don't get lost in the overwhelming feelings of not having control of your life. You do. That's the reality.

Take a deep breath. Find enjoyable activities within and without your retail store. Remember that most problems are solved by time more than effort—and certainly not by worry. Have some fun!

Reviewing Goals

At least once a week, step back from what you are doing and take a look at the wide picture. It will not only help your mental attitude; it can be a productive exercise for any manager. The details and decisions of each day can sometimes result in inadvertent changes to your long-term goals. Do you want them to? Maybe. But don't let those decisions—by you and by others—create big changes without your approval.

Reviewing your business goals can be done in many ways. For example:

- Reread your store's business plan, or at least the executive summary.
- Start a retailer's journal that begins with your business concept. Once a week, add your notes on how reality is stacking up against goals.
- Meet periodically with a trusted business adviser to discuss your business' goals and progress.

Enjoying the Day

Every day as a retailer is a new adventure—or a joyless burden. The facts of the day are often the same, but the attitude is different. Find ways of enjoying your day. Review your days as a retailer to this point and determine what you liked the most. Customer contacts? Employee interactions? Stocking shelves? Counting the till? Then make sure that you give yourself these little pleasures each day that you're at the store. Eventually, you may find that the fun of some jobs will carry over to the not-so-fun jobs that you must do.

Measuring Success

As your retail store grows and begins celebrating anniversaries, you'll wonder whether your business is a success or not. There are many ways to measure success, so the answer is not an easy one. Some suggest that success is a destination, while others see it as a journey. Every day can be a success. Many successful retailers measure their achievements in terms of personal, customer, employee, and community profits and satisfaction.

Personal Profits

Certainly, one of the major reasons for starting a retail store is personal profits. You want to make a living at a rewarding job and, you hope, build equity and goodwill that you can someday trade in for cash.

Your retail store's success can be measured, in part, by personal profits. You want a salary that will fund the other parts of your life: food, shelter, fun. First, it must fund your store: inventory, overhead, taxes. You'd also like to build the assets of your business—stock, fixtures, goodwill, cash in reserve—toward someday passing the business along to a relative or selling it (see Chapter 22). Whatever these personal goals are, your progress toward them is a measurement of success. This doesn't mean that financial setbacks or even losses are failures; it just means that it will take some more management skills to produce success. Profits will return.

Customer Profits

For your customers, success means finding what they want. Their lives are benefited by the successful operation of your store. For some retailers, serving customers is the most important measurement of success. They believe that service to others is the greatest profit. They add to the value of others' lives by serving their needs for specific products.

Customer profits are more difficult to quantify than financial profits. However, they are still measurable. Because the opinions of customers are important to verifying this success, the owner must be in constant touch with them, asking how the store benefits individual customers. The results can be quantified by then looking at sales levels. If one in six customers express their appreciation for your store and it serves sixty customers a day, at least ten customers clearly benefit from what you do. That is customer success.

Employee Profits

It is increasingly difficult to find a job that is both satisfying and pays a living wage. Many retailers take pride in what they can offer their employees. With capital and smart management, retailers can hire the best employees in the area, those who recognize the rewards of offering genuine service to others.

For some retailers, being able to offer employees affordable health care and a safe work environment are vital to their business goals. In any case, offering employees better working and living conditions than the big-box stores provide is a satisfying measurement of retail success. Whether you hire employees now or are building your store in order to hire some later, you can measure success by how you improve the lives of current and future employees.

Community Profits

Your local community benefits from your decision to start and run a successful retail store. In addition to offering customers an excellent place to shop and employees a superior place to work, your store does other things for the community. It pays taxes. It upgrades the merchant community. It makes donations to local charities, as possible. It enhances local pride because your store is helpful and successful.

Question

How can I know that my retail store is perceived by others as successful?
Ask them! Ask customers if they enjoy shopping in your store and what they would change about it. Ask employees similar questions. Ask these questions of community leaders, too. You will derive positive feedback and maybe some ideas on how you can improve your successful retail store. People love to know that their opinions have value.

You should take pride in the services you provide to your local community. Whether your store is located in the downtown area, a strip mall, or a large shopping mall, your community benefits from your efforts—as do you, your customers, and employees. These are very good indications of success.

Avoiding Retailer Burnout

You've probably been in a retail store at some point where the owner is grumpy or angry and not handling the day well. Maybe it was your store. It happens to all retailers at some point: burnout. They are tired, worried, or afraid, and it comes out as anger. Maybe a challenging customer pushes the button, or a slow-to-learn employee does it, or a damaged delivery. Burnout is the problem. What's the solution?

Recognition! Unfortunately, retailers who blow up at a customer, employee, or delivery service haven't yet recognized that they are burned out; they don't see the signs and take action before they become overwhelming. If their boiling point is 212°F, they don't recognize that they're already operating at 211° and are close to producing steam. A common and otherwise minor event—customer request, employee question, or delivery problem—adds a few degrees and everyone gets scalded.

How can you avoid burnout? By recognizing the signs and taking action toward lowering the temperature. Taking a break is a primary step in avoiding burnout. In addition, you can consider what it is that has increased your operating temperature. Is there a conflict at home? Are you frustrated by your lack of control over a business or personal situation? Is there a health or diet issue that is making you volatile? Recognition of the components that can lead to burnout is the first step in minimizing it.

Making Your Store Fun for Others

If you're not really into having fun, get a job at the widget factory. Otherwise, have fun selling widgets (or whatever) in your store—and make sure that others have fun with you. Your customers and employees can be sources and beneficiaries of fun in your store.

Customer Fun

Shopping can be fun. Discovering new products that can solve their problems can be enjoyable for your customers. Make shopping in your store a pleasurable activity. Plan your retail store for efficiency and select inventory of value to your customers.

Of course, your big-box competitors have efficiently planned their stores and stocked them with salable inventory, too. So *your* store needs to take it a step beyond. You need to make it friendly and helpful—something that the big stores rarely do. Following are some suggestions:

- Offer a randomly chosen customer of the day a prize or gift certificate, knowing that these customers will tell their friends what they won at your store.
- Give every person who walks into your store the gift of your (or an employee's) welcoming smile.
- If possible, recognize your customers by name (found on credit cards and checks). If the name is difficult to pronounce, ask for the customer's help. A person's name is a pleasing sound to the person being addressed.
- Post a non-offensive Cartoon of the Day near your cash register. Laughter opens the heart.
- If there is a price discrepancy, *always* decide in favor of the customer. It will build your store's goodwill.

Using these ideas as thought starters, dream up three additional ways to help your store's customers have fun.

Employee Fun

Remember when you were someone else's employee? It probably was the employers who allowed you to have some fun—not at the expense of business, of course. Here are a few ways to make your store more fun for employees:

- Treat employees as individuals and take an interest in their lives.
- Have a monthly or annual reward for employees: a luncheon, tickets to a play or event, a few hours off with pay, or some other gift for their service.
- Provide refreshments or snacks in the break area.
- Honor employees for outstanding service.
- Encourage friendships—and discourage animosity—among employees.

Now come up with three more ways of your own to offer some fun to employees.

Many retailers strive to build their reputation as a "fun place to work." Besides the obvious benefits to employees and to current business, it also helps you develop a backlist of employment applications from which to choose when hiring. Employees—like customers and retailers—want to add some fun to their lives.

CHAPTER 22

Selling Your Retail Store

There comes a time in every retailer's life when thoughts turn to selling the store. It could be family or health reasons, retirement or semi-retirement, better opportunities, low cash flow, or insufficient profits. More often, it is a combination of reasons. Millions of retailers have successfully sold their stores, and so can you. This chapter will guide you in the process for the day that you decide to sell.

Good Reasons to Sell

There are a number of good reasons to sell your retail store. They may be your best option someday after you've started and run your store for a while. How long? Some stores sell within a year of opening, while others will be passed to future generations before being sold to others. Most small independent retailers hold their stores for three to ten years, depending on needs and conditions. Following is a discussion of good reasons why retailers sell.

Not Having Fun

The dream of owning a retail store can soon become the reality of working it every day. Some people discover that the starting-up phase is a real joy, with new and exciting challenges every day.

However, the daily management is boring to them. They get antsy to start up another store or move on to another challenge.

That's okay. There are businesspeople who are more comfortable with starting than running a retail store. And there are people who don't have the skills or desire to start a store, but love the daily details of keeping it on track. In fact, some businesspeople understand this and focus more on starting *or* running a retail store. They do what they know best and then either sell to or buy from businesspeople who have the opposite skills.

Not Growing

Sometimes, conditions outside of your control—or at least outside your field of view—combine to limit the growth opportunities of your retail store. A major employer in the area suddenly lays off or closes up. The national or local economy goes into a recession. A big-bucks competitor sets up across the street and attempts to drive your store out of business. For one or more of a number of reasons, your store's sales aren't growing as planned. It's healthy; just stunted.

If you've done what you can to make the store grow faster, without success, maybe you should consider selling the store while it is growing at least slowly. Don't wait for the store to peak or decline; sell it now. You've done the hard work. Give someone else a chance to take it through the rough times ahead. Granted, you won't get the price you would in a fast-growing market, but as long as your store has potential, it has worth.

Enough Equity

Maybe your plan all along was to sell the store once you developed sufficient equity, meaning lots more assets than liabilities. If the store financials are healthy, start looking for buyers who are willing to trade their cash assets for your fixed assets.

Equity can be converted into a cash payment, a trade for another asset (home, land, equipment), or for an income stream.

For example, you can sell your store with a substantial down payment and short-term monthly payments. Many small retail stores are sold on a promissory note held by the owner, with 25 to 75 percent down and monthly payments paid over two to five years.

An Offer You Can't Refuse

The retailer's dream is that someone—a customer, a retiring executive, a recent lottery winner—will walk into the store one day and make an offer that just can't be refused. Many independent retailers *would* refuse it; they're having too much fun. Others would ponder it for a day or two before answering. A few would shout "Sold!" and reach for a handshake.

 Alert

Be very cautious if someone does walk in and offer to buy your store on the spot. Smart businesspeople don't do things this way. Instead, a business broker or prospective buyer will visit your site, speak with the owner, and ask if the store is possibly for sale. The process of buying and selling business assets can take weeks or months. It's not a handshake deal.

Retailers know approximately what their store is worth at any given point (this will be covered later in this chapter). If other conditions are right and a price is offered at or above perceived value, the store may soon change hands.

Bad Reasons to Sell

There are also bad reasons—the wrong reasons—to sell your store. These are reasons that you can do something about other than selling. Combined with other conditions, you may decide to sell anyway. But, alone, they are not good reasons to put up the For Sale sign.

Not Having Fun

Yes, not having fun can be a *good* reason to sell your store. It also can be a *bad* reason. The difference is figuring out why you're not having fun and what you can do about it. For example, if the reason you're not having fun running your store is that it is too stressful, there are many things you can do first to reduce stress (see Chapter 21) before you consider selling it.

Don't sell your store just because you're not having fun. Find some fun—or at least a better reason to sell.

Loss of Key Employees

Key employees are those that your business requires to function. It could be the manager or an especially popular clerk who sells twice as much as others. Why is the loss of a key a *bad* reason to sell? Because the condition is preventable.

As the owner, you should be the only can't-do-without staffer. All others should be replaceable. In fact, you should be cross-training employees and developing assistant managers who can step in if and when a key employee leaves. Don't hinge the success of your business on anyone other than yourself.

Lack of Profits

The worst reason to sell your store is because you're not making any money. Why? First, there are many other solutions to this problem. Tighten inventory, reduce staffing and do more of the work yourself, cut expenses, advertise better. Second, you're going to lose more money if you try to sell an unprofitable business. Make it profitable, at least marginally, before you sell your store.

If low profits are the problem, review your store's business plan (see Chapter 6) and subsequent chapters for practical ideas on how to increase store profits. You have options.

Tax Problems

Another preventable reason why retailers sell their stores is tax problems. It most often is federal or state income tax; specifically, not making estimated tax payments as required. Retailers also can get into trouble by not turning in collected sales tax when it's due. Cut inventory, reduce staffing, go without other things, but *pay your taxes when due.*

 Fact

Consider hiring a tax attorney who can help you reach a settlement with the taxing agency. In some cases, attorneys can reduce the obligation sufficiently to cover their fees. In other cases, they will just keep you from getting into deeper problems. Check local telephone books and search the Internet for reputable attorneys who specialize in tax law and settlements.

Most retailers who run into tax problems do so because they don't get competent advice or they get too creative with the way they use expense accounts. If you know tax law, follow it; if you don't, hire a tax adviser who will show you how to accurately follow it. Don't make tax problems the reason you must sell your store.

How Much Is It Worth?

The big question for a retailer wanting to sell the store is, How much is it worth? The correct answer is, Whatever a buyer will pay.

Selling a retail store is similar to selling retail merchandise. It's all about selection, pricing, and helping buyers buy. The biggest difference is that most store merchandise is either prepriced ($9.95) or approximated (SRP × 80 percent). How can you identify the approximate price that your retail store is worth?

Valuation

One of the primary indicators of store value is income potential. It can be based on:

- Annual gross sales (AGS)
- Annual net sales (ANS)
- Balance sheet (assets – liabilities = net worth)

For example, a small retail store may be priced at a ratio of annual sales. If the established ratio for your type of store is 1 × AGS and annual gross sales is $200,000, one valuation is $200,000. If the typical ratio is 2 × ANS for a store with net sales of $85,000 annually, the valuation is $170,000. If the store's assets (inventory, fixtures, and so on) total $180,000 with liabilities of $40,000, the net worth valuation is $140,000. Add up the three valuations ($510,000) and divide by three to get an average valuation of $170,000. That's a wide variation—$140,000 to $200,000—but it's defensible. And it's a starting point.

The problem can be coming up with established ratios for your specific type of store and its age. Here's where you need to hire an expert or do some research. Because you're working with lots of dollars, it's best to hire an expert who can give you a justifiable appraisal and valuation. A smart buyer always asks, How did you arrive at your price? Being able to point to an expert's research and opinion can make the negotiations go much more smoothly.

You can do some of your own research. By keeping track of the sale of similar retail stores, you can come up with your own ratios. For example, if stores in your area are currently selling for about 1.2 × AGS, there's your ratio. Of course, there are many other factors that you may not know: Is inventory valued at retail or wholesale? Are the assets included fairly valued? How much of the asking price is goodwill, the worth of the store beyond the tangible assets? Your accountant or business adviser can help you determine the answer to these questions.

Entity Sales

If your retail store is owned by a corporation, even a small S corp, you probably will sell your business as a corporation. That is, what you are selling is the corporation rather than the individual assets (inventory, fixtures, goodwill) that the corporation owns. The buyer will purchase the corporation's stock. If this is the case, you really need a corporate attorney and tax adviser as you prepare to sell your business. The price you establish for your store will depend somewhat on whether the sale is of an entity or its assets.

Asset Sales

An *asset sale* is often preferred by businesses that are owned by individuals (sole proprietors) and partners. In this case, the assets are sold off to a single buyer—an individual, partnership, or a corporation. The assets include the inventory, fixtures, and goodwill rather than corporate stock.

GOOB Sale

Some businesses, especially retail stores that haven't been around long enough to develop goodwill or a large following, will profit more by holding a going-out-of-business (GOOB) sale. The store's "buyer" is its customers and suppliers. Following is a scenario for a typical GOOB or liquidation sale:

- Owner sets a closing date, such as six months hence, based on lease and other factors.
- A discount calendar is developed, such as reducing storewide prices by 10 percent every month.
- Inventory suppliers are contacted to determine whether they will buy back undamaged stock, when, and for how much.
- Fixture suppliers are contacted to learn whether they will purchase used fixtures, and approximately how much they will pay.
- Competitors are contacted, when appropriate, to find out if they will purchase remainder stock, and for how much.

- Creditors are contacted, as appropriate, to work out financial arrangements.

GOOB or liquidation sales aren't for every retailer. However, they are a viable option for retailers who, for whatever reason, may not be able to draw an entity or asset buyer.

Finding a Buyer

Once you've decided to sell your store, have an approximate value, and have decided whether it's probably going to be an equity or asset sale, you're ready to go looking for potential buyers. Where should you look?

Buyers for big-box stores are found on Wall Street. Independent retail stores are sold on Main Street. There are four primary sources of store buyers: customers, suppliers, competitors, and entrepreneurs. Following is a description of each and methods for approaching them.

Sell to a Customer

You might be surprised at how many of your customers have considered someday owning a store just like yours—especially if it is unique and successful. After all, you probably were a good customer at similar stores before you became a retailer.

The question is, How can you offer your store to customers without undermining your strong customer base? The answer is—Carefully! Here's how to go about it:

- Estimate the approximate value of your business and the terms under which you would sell.
- Choose your pitch carefully, such as this: I'm retiring next year and looking for a candidate to take over the store. Do you have any interest?

- Choose your customers carefully. From your observations, do they have the qualities that would make a good retailer?
- Consider what you should and should not tell customers before they sign a non-disclosure agreement (see the next section).
- Keep track of your discussions with customers in a log book or calendar.
- Follow up with customers who show some interest, especially if price or terms change.

One retailer was planning a six-month liquidation sale when a customer asked if the store was for sale. The answer was, Possibly. Conversations began, financial information shared, and the customer soon owned the store. The customer was saved the arduous start-up, and the seller was saved the laborious liquidation. Good customers can be good shopkeepers.

Sell Through a Supplier

Your primary suppliers may be a good source for finding a buyer. In fact, they may be looking for a retail outlet themselves. Alternately, they know the owners of similar stores who may be interested in either adding a new store, exchanging stores, or purchasing large inventories.

The best way to approach a supplier about your store is through your sales rep. If you don't have an assigned rep, contact the supplier and ask for the manager of sales or marketing, or an executive. It's their job to know what is going on in the business and who the players are. They may be able to help you sell your store.

Sell to a Competitor

Most small retailers eventually develop good relationships with their competitors, even those who own local franchises. These contacts may turn into prospects for selling your store. A competitor may want to expand, the store manager may want to go out on her own and buy your store, or the competitor may prefer to simply buy you out and thus reduce the competition.

Approaching a competitor about offering your store can be difficult, depending on your relationship. The best way to start is with a feeler: I'm considering retiring in the next year or two. Do you have any interest in purchasing my store? It's smart to get at least a verbal agreement of confidentiality, but the better indicator is whether or not you trust the competitor. If you have concerns about confidentiality, use a business broker to approach your competitors.

Sell to an Entrepreneur

You may sell your store to someone who is considering retailing, but isn't a customer, supplier, or competitor. The entrepreneur may not even care much what type of small retail store it is, as long as it is established, healthy, and profitable.

You can find entrepreneurs by hiring a business broker to represent your store or by offering it yourself through business-paper ads or online brokers.

Offering your store online presents it to a wide audience of entrepreneurs. With carefully worded ads you can present your store without identifying it. The largest online business ad services include *www.bizbuysell.com*, *www.businessbroker.net*, and *www.sunbeltnetwork.com*. Ad rates vary, and some services allow photos of the business. Alternately, you can set up your own website and advertise the URL address in business papers.

The Paperwork

The job isn't done until the paperwork is finished. In selling your store, the paperwork can be simple or complex. In fact, if there is no real estate involved, a handshake can seal the transaction. However, most retailers selling a property worth $50,000 to $250,000 or more will want a non-disclosure agreement, offering a memorandum, sales agreement with a non-competition clause, and maybe a promissory note. Corporate sales will require more paperwork and should involve an attorney.

Non-Disclosure Agreement

The first document that potential buyers should sign for you is a non-disclosure agreement. It says that they will not disclose or use the proprietary information that you supply them in a way that will harm your business. Otherwise, a potential buyer could learn the valuable information you've developed about the local market and your store operations, then open a store nearby and take your business.

Generic non-disclosure agreements are available at office supply stores and in books that focus on selling your business. Unless you're knowledgeable in business law, you should have an attorney draw up the non-disclosure agreement or at least review the form you will use.

Offering Memorandum

Your store's offering memorandum outlines what your business is, what it does, how it does it, and the results: profits. It is a summary of how your store works. It's a valuable document that has cost you thousands of dollars in efforts to develop. It represents the results of your business plan. Don't let anyone see it without their first signing a non-disclosure agreement.

A typical offering memorandum for a retail store will include:

- Executive summary
- Store description
- Store history
- Product lines
- Sales and marketing procedures
- Competition
- Operations
- Facilities

- Personnel
- Goodwill
- Growth potential
- Industry overview
- Financial information (specifics available)
- Reasons for selling
- Price and terms
- Contact information

Additional documents, including profit-and-loss statement and balance sheet, can be provided when the prospective buyer is ready to move to the next level. Most buyers will want an independent audit or verification of the facts before proceeding.

Sales Agreement

The sales agreement outlines how the sale is structured. This can be important not only to the buyer and seller, but also to the tax collector. Yes, you probably will have to pay income tax on the sale of your business. Whether the tax is based on ordinary income or capital gains, (lower) tax rates depends on how the sale is structured and reported. You'll need a tax adviser to help you set up the sale to benefit the seller while meeting the requirements of the buyer.

The typical asset sale agreement will include:

- Names of seller(s) and buyer(s)
- List of assets being sold by seller
- List of liabilities being accepted by buyer
- Sale price, typically broken down by type of assets
- Price of inventory and how it is determined
- How accounts payable will be paid
- Terms of sale: deposit, payment at closing, promissory note (if any)
- How seller's debts and obligations will be handled

- Seller's representations
- Buyer's representations
- Covenant not to compete
- How disputes will be handled
- Governing law

The covenant not to compete typically says that the seller will not start or work for a similar store within a specific geographic area for a specified time. This covenant is not easily enforceable in many jurisdictions if the seller must find employment after the sale.

Promissory Note

In many sales, the buyer has all cash or has obtained financing. In others, the seller agrees to finance a portion of the sale under a promissory note and security agreement. The security agreement says that the business assets—and any buyer assets that are agreed upon—serve as security for the note. If not paid as agreed, the security can be sold to collect the balance.

The promissory note outlines the terms of payments. Commonly, equal monthly payments are made over a three- to five-year period at a specified interest rate, often from 8 to 12 percent, until paid off. A large payment at the end of the note, called a balloon payment, may be required.

If selling your business on a promissory note, it is especially important to have legally binding documents. Use an attorney to draw up all the documents or, at the least, to review form documents.

Retailing Resources

Books

Dion, James E., and Ted Topping. *Start & Run a Retail Business* (Bellingham, WA: Self-Counsel Press, 2007).

Ennico, Cliff. *Small Business Survival Guide* (Avon, MA: Adams Media, 2005).

Harrington, Judith B. *The Everything Start Your Own Business Book, 2nd ed.* (Avon, MA: Adams Media, 2006).

Kingaard, Jan. *Start Your Own Successful Retail Business* (Irvine, CA: Entrepreneur Press, 2002).

Schroeder, Carol L. *Specialty Shop Retailing* (New York: John Wiley & Sons, 2002).

Segel, Rick. *Retail Business Kit for Dummies* (Hoboken, NJ: Wiley Publishing, 2001)

Steingold, Fred. *The Complete Guide to Selling a Business* (Berkeley, CA: Nolo Press, 2005).

Trade Magazines

Franchise Times
www.franchisetimes.com
Magazine offering news and opportunities on retail franchises.

Gift Shop Magazine
www.giftshopmag.com
Magazine focusing on retail gift stores.

Retail Merchandiser
www.retail-merchandiser.com
Free monthly publication for larger retailers.

TD Monthly
www.toydirectory.com
Magazine for toy, hobby, gift, and game retailers.

Government Agencies and Business Organizations

American Franchisee Association
www.franchisee.org
Trade association for those who own or are considering franchise retail opportunities.

Federal Trade Commission
www.ftc.gov
Government body responsible for regulating many retail and other businesses.

Internal Revenue Service
www.irs.gov
Provides extensive information on business tax structure with downloadable tax forms and other online information.

International Franchise Association
www.franchise.org
Major trade association for franchise opportunities.

National Association of Professional Employer Organizations
www.napeo.org
Trade association for professional employment and co-employment services.

Service Corps of Retired Executives (SCORE)
www.score.org
Nonprofit organization of experienced entrepreneurs who offer advice to small businesses in all stages of development.

Small Business Administration
www.sba.gov
Sponsors programs assisting small businesses with various issues, including financing, site location, start-up, and management

U.S. Department of Commerce
www.commerce.gov
Provides statistics about specific industry sectors and regional economic developments.

U.S. Department of Labor
www.dol.gov
Provides important information regarding labor laws and practices, including minimum wage, benefits, and unemployment insurance.

Other Useful Resources
AllBusiness.com
www.allbusiness.com
Provides small business owners with advice, business directories and products, forums, news, and downloadable business forms and plans.

Annual Credit Report
www.annualcreditreport.com
Free credit reports are available from each of the major credit reporting services: Equifax,

TransUnion, and Experian, per
the Fair Credit Reporting Act.

Bplans.com
www.bplans.com
Provides guidance on writing business
plans with feature articles, tips and
advice, and sample business plans.

Business Plan Pro
www.businessplanpro.com
Computer program for developing a business plan.

Display Warehouse
www.displaywarehouse.com
Resource for new retail store
displays and fixtures.

Entrepreneur.com
www.entrepreneur.com
Resources for building and running a wide variety of small businesses, including retail stores.

Fixture Depot
www.fixturedepot.com
Resource for new retail store fixtures.

International Franchise Expo
www.ifeinfo.com
Information on one of the largest
single-franchise trade shows.

Living Wage Data
www.livingwage.geog.psu.edu
Calculations of living wage
by geographic locations.

Microsoft Small Business Financials
www.microsoft.com/smallbusiness
Financial planning software.

MYOB
www.myob.com
Financial planning software.

QuickBooks Accounting System
www.quickbooks.com
Computer software for accounting and financial planning.

Specialty Store Services
www.specialtystoreservices.com
Resource for new retail store fixtures.

Retailing Glossary

Accounts payable: Money that you or your business owes to others.

Accounts receivable: Money owed to you or your business.

Acid-test ratio: A measurement of how well a business can meet its short-term financial obligations without selling any inventory.

Accrual: An accounting term for the increase over time of expenses incurred by your business. They are accrued up until the time they are paid.

Acquisition: The takeover of a retail operation by another company.

Anchor store: A major retailer chosen for its ability to drive traffic to the mall or shopping center in which it's located.

Asset: Things of value. Tangible assets include cash, receivables, inventory, and buildings. Intangible assets include goodwill.

Atmosphere: The physical characteristics and surrounding influence of a retail store, which are used to create an image in order to attract customers.

Automatic reordering system: Program that reorders merchandise when in-store supplies fall below a predetermined level.

Average inventory cost: Found by adding the beginning cost inventory for each month plus the ending cost inventory for the last month in the period. If calculating for a season, divide by 7. If calculating for a year, divide by 13.

Big-box store: Large standalone store specializing in one category of merchandise.

Bill of lading: A contract between a freight company and a shipper regarding transportation, which includes the exact contents of the delivery.

Blue law: Rules created to prohibit particular activities on certain days or during certain hours. Many blue laws have been rescinded or are no longer enforced.

Brand: A name, symbol, or other identifying mark for a seller's goods or services. It is distinct from other sellers.

Brand awareness: A gauge of marketing effectiveness measured by the ability of a customer to recognize and/or recall a name, image, or other mark associated with a particular brand.

Break-even point: The point in business at which the sales equal the expenses. In other words, there is no profit and no loss.

Brick-and-mortar: Refers to retail shops that are located in a building as opposed to an online shopping destination, door-to-door sales, kiosk, or other similar site not housed within a structure.

Business plan: A detailed document describing the past, present, and future financial and operational objectives of a company.

Button ticket: A pricing ticket with a hook at the top that can be attached to a button.

Buying office: A central office where buyers purchase merchandise for all stores in a department store chain.

Capital assets: Long-term assets used to produce income, such as buildings and equipment.

Cash discount: A percentage reduction in price for payment within a specified period of time.

Cash flow: The movement of money in and out of a business and the resulting availability of cash.

Category killer: A large retail chain store that is dominant in its product category. This type of store generally offers an extensive selection of merchandise at prices so low smaller stores cannot compete.

Centralized buying organization: Company in which all buying decisions for all the stores in the company are made by one central office.

Chain store: One of a number of retail stores under the same owner-

ship and dealing in the same merchandise.

Classic: A product or style that does not lose popularity over time.

Comp sales: A measurement of productivity in revenue used to compare sales of retail stores that have been open for a year or more. Historical sales data allows retailers to compare this year's sales in their store to the same period last year.

Contribution margin: The difference between total sales revenue and total variable costs. The term is applied to a product line and is generally expressed as a percentage.

Convenience products: Merchandise that is purchased frequently, without advance planning, including staples, impulse items, and emergency items.

Cooperative: A group in which several retailers pool their resources to buy products at a discount from manufacturers; also called group buying.

Corporation: A legal entity that can buy, sell, and enter into contracts as if it were a person.

Cost of goods sold (COGS): The price paid for the product, plus any additional costs necessary to get the merchandise into inventory and ready for sale, including shipping and handling.

Coupon: A promotional tool in the form of a document that can be redeemed for a discount when purchasing goods or services.

Customer relationship management (CRM): A business strategy designed to reduce costs and increase profitability by strengthening customer loyalty.

Delivery receipt: A receipt from a delivery driver that indicates a delivery was made to a store.

Demographics: Characteristics of a specific group of people, such as potential customers.

Department store: A large retail store that sells a variety of merchandise, organized into departments.

Destination retailer: Retailer to which customers will make a special trip, even if it entails going out of their way.

Differentiation: The process of distinguishing services or products through design.

Digital signage: Refers to a variety of technologies used to replace traditional retail signs. Instead of static print signs and billboards, digital signage is composed of electronic signs dispersing content and messages in the most targeted, interactive way.

Directory: A list of the departments of a department store and their locations.

Discount store: A self-service retail store with low markups.

Dollar control: A buying method that depends on the amount of purchases, rather than the number of items purchased.

Double entry: An accounting system that requires two balancing entries, a debit and a credit, to be made for each transaction.

Durable goods: Products that can be used frequently and have a long life expectancy, such as furniture, jewelry, and major appliances.

Electronic shopping: Shopping over the Internet or through a TV cable channel.

Employer identification number: Also known as a Federal Tax Identification Number, and is used to identify a business entity. Most businesses need an EIN. You may apply for an EIN in various ways, including online.

Facing: The number of identical products (or same SKU) facing out toward the customer. Facings are used in planograms and when zoning a retail store.

Fad: A fashion that gains and loses popularity very quickly.

Fashion: The popularity of a certain product, style, or appearance.

First in, first out (FIFO): A method of stock rotation in which goods that are received first are sold first. Newly received product is stocked behind the older merchandise.

Free on board (FOB): Shipping term used to indicate who is responsible for paying transportation charges. FOB factory means the buyer must pay shipping from the factory.

Forward reserve stock: Reserve stock that is kept in a stock room near the selling floor.

Forward stock: Merchandise that is kept on the selling floor.

Freestanding store: Store that's not part of a shopping center or a mall.

Full background: The rear of a window display that completely covers the display, closing it off from the store.

Full line: Department stores that carry a full line of merchandise.

Goods: Tangible products for sale.

Grade labeling: Product labeling that includes a quality rating for the product.

Gross income: Total income derived from a business.

Gross leasable area (GLA): Total floor space available for retail sales.

Gross margin: The difference between wholesale cost and the retail price.

Gross profit: Profit calculated after deducting all costs of merchandise, labor, and overhead.

Group buying: A group in which several retailers pool their resources to buy products at a discount from manufacturers; also called a cooperative.

Gummed label: A pricing ticket with adhesive on the back, used on cloth, leather, and unpainted wood.

Hard goods: Non-textile products.

Hard lines: A store department or product line primarily consisting of merchandise such as hardware, housewares, automotive, electronics, sporting goods, health and beauty aids, or toys.

Heterogeneous products: Durable products that are

different in quality, appearance, and other features.

Hole pin ticket: A pricing ticket used on paired items such as gloves.

Homogeneous products: Durable products that are similar in quality, but are different in price and require comparisons.

Hypermarket: A huge retail store that is a combination of a drugstore, supermarket, and discount store.

Image: The impression customers have of a company or service.

Impulse items: Products that people purchase without planning for it, such as magazines or candy bars.

Informative labeling: Product labeling that includes the product's performance in tests.

Inventory turnover: The number of times during a given period that the average inventory on hand is sold and replaced.

Keystone pricing: A method of pricing merchandise for resell to an amount that is double the wholesale price.

Layaway: Taking a deposit to set aside merchandise for a customer to purchase at a later date.

Leased department: A part of a department store that is actually leased out to another company and operated as an independent store within the department store; common with cosmetics companies.

Liabilities: Amounts that a business owes to suppliers and other creditors.

Limited line: Describes a department store that carries a limited amount of merchandise, usually concentrating on clothing, accessories, and beauty supplies.

Loss leader: Merchandise sold below cost by a retailer in an effort to attract new custom-

ers or stimulate other profitable sales.

Loss prevention: Loss prevention is the act of reducing the amount of theft and shrinkage within a business.

Margin: The amount of gross profit made when an item is sold.

Markdown: Planned reduction in the selling price of an item, usually to take effect either within a certain number of days after seasonal merchandise is received or at a specific date.

Market area: Geographic area from which a store draws its customers.

Marketing calendar: A tool used by retailers to show what marketing events, media campaigns, and merchandising efforts are happening when and where, as well as the results.

Markup: A percentage added to the wholesale cost to get the retail selling price.

Merchandise mix: The breadth and depth of the products carried by retailers.

Merchandising plan: A strategy for actual and projected sales for a specific period of time.

Merger: The combining of two or more retail organizations into one company.

Minimum advertised price: A supplier's pricing policy that does not permit its resellers to advertise prices below a specified amount. It can include the resellers' retail price as well.

Multiline drugstore: A store that sells a variety of health and beauty products, plus some small appliances and household items, in addition to prescription drugs.

Net lease: Lease in which the tenant pays the base rent plus property taxes. Also known as a single net lease.

Net-net lease: Lease in which the tenant pays the base rent plus property taxes and building insurance. Also known as a double-net lease.

Net-net-net lease: Lease in which the tenant pays the base rent plus property taxes, building insurance, and maintenance. Also known as a triple-net lease.

Nondurable goods: Products that are purchased frequently and used in a short period of time, such as beauty supplies and cosmetics.

Nonmarking: A pricing system in which individual items do not have price tags; instead, a price is labeled on a bin or a shelf.

Odd-even pricing: A form of psychological pricing that suggests buyers are more sensitive to certain ending digits.

Open background: Describes a window display with a completely unobstructed view of the interior of the store.

Open-to-buy: Merchandise budgeted for purchase during a certain time period that has not yet been ordered.

Operating expenses: The sum of all expenses associated with the normal course of running a business.

Overerr: A mistake made when an employee enters an amount into the register that is more than the sale price.

Partial background: The rear of a window display that is partially covered, but allows customers to see through the display into the store.

Partnership: An entity wherein two or more people own a business.

Patronage buying motive: A reason customers will shop at one store instead of another; can be rational or emotional.

Pin ticket: The sort of price ticket used on towels and washcloths that is attached with a pin.

Planogram: Visual description, diagram, or drawing of a store's layout to include placement of particular products and product categories.

Point-of-purchase display: Marketing materials or advertising placed next to the merchandise they are promoting. These items are generally located at the checkout area or other location where the purchase decision is made.

Point-of-sale (POS) system: Combination of hardware and software that records customers' purchases, accepts payments, and adjusts inventory levels.

Point-of-sale terminal: An electronic machine at a checkout station that feeds information from product tags directly into a computer.

Premarking: A system in which the manufacturer, rather than the retailer, marks merchandise with the retail price.

Preretailing: A system in which a duplicate purchase order is sent to the receiving department when merchandise is ordered so that as soon as the merchandise is received, it can be marked with the correct prices.

Price: A price is the monetary value placed on a product or service.

Private label: Generally, products that are manufactured or provided by one company under another company's brand.

Product breadth: The product breadth is the variety of product lines offered by a retailer.

Product depth: Product depth is the number of each item or particular style of a product on the shelves. Product depth

is also known as product assortment or merchandise depth.

Product life cycle: The stages that a new product is believed to go through from the beginning to the end: introduction, growth, maturity, and decline.

Product/service mix: The number and kind of products and services a general merchandise retailer will offer.

Profit center: A section of a store that earns money for the retailer.

Profit margin: A ratio of profitability calculated as earnings divided by revenues. It measures how much out of every dollar of sales a retail business actually keeps in earnings.

Proxemics: The nonverbal communication suggested by the space between two people.

Pull policy: A promotional policy aimed at

building strong consumer demand for a product.

Purchase order: A (PO) is a written sales contract between buyer and seller detailing the exact merchandise ordered or services to be rendered from a single vendor.

Push policy: A promotional policy aimed at markets with the intention of getting retailers to stock a product in order to build supply in the marketplace.

Quantity discount: A reduction in price based on the amount purchased. May be offered in addition to any trade discount.

Reserve stock: Merchandise that is kept somewhere other than the selling floor.

Retail: The sale of small quantities of goods directly to the user.

Retailers: Businesses that buy goods from wholesalers or manufacturers and resell them to customers.

Retailing: The sale of goods or commodities in small quantities directly to consumers.

Retailing strategy: A strategic plan to adapt to changing technology and markets and meet company goals and objectives through retailing.

Returns percentage: The relationship between returns and allowances and sales, calculated by dividing returns and allowances by gross sales.

Ringseal ticket: A pricing ticket shaped like a butterfly bandage, used on jewelry and lampshades.

Run of paper (ROP): An advertising term used by newspapers referring to an advertisement that may be placed anywhere within the paper.

Run of schedule (ROS): An advertising term used by broadcasting stations referring to an advertisement that may be placed

anywhere within the broadcast schedule.

Sales floor: The location of a retail store where goods are displayed and sales transactions take place.

Sales transaction: A sales transaction occurs when a seller and a buyer agree to trade ownership of a product (or service) for money.

Service business: A business that offers only a service, with no accompanying product needed or wanted; for example, an insurance policy.

Shoplifting: Theft of property that is worth less than $500 and occurs with the intent to deprive the owner of that piece of property. The crime of shoplifting is the taking of merchandise offered for sale without paying.

Shoplifting detection wafer: A small device attached to goods, especially clothing, that sets off an alarm if it is taken through the doors of the store.

Shopping items: Durable goods that require a great deal of comparison before purchase, such as appliances and furniture.

Shrinkage: Retail shrinkage is a reduction or loss in inventory due to shoplifting, employee theft, paperwork errors, and supplier fraud.

Sliding: A loss prevention term referring to the act of a cashier passing merchandise around the cash register bar-code scanner without actually scanning the item.

Soft goods: Textile products.

Soft lines: A store department or product line primarily consisting of merchandise such as clothing, footwear, jewelry, linens, and towels.

Sole proprietor: One person who owns a business; also can be a married couple.

Specialty products: Products that solve a specific want or need for specific customers. These products offer special characteristics or brand identity, and often are expensive.

Specialty store: A store that specializes in selling a specific kind of product.

Specification buying: Demands made by retailers and wholesalers to manufacturers of the products they sponsor and sell.

Standard industrial classification code (SIC code): A coding system using four digits to identify specific industrial sectors within the federal government. The first two digits identify the broad industrial sector, and the last two digits represent a facility's specialty within this broad sector.

Staple goods: Products purchased regularly and out of necessity. While price shifts may raise or lower demand for certain kinds of products, the demand for staple goods rarely changes when prices change.

Stock keeping unit (SKU): A number assigned to a product by a retail store to identify price, product options, and manufacturer.

Store operations: Includes all functions of operating a store except merchandising, such as customer service, protection, maintenance, and distribution.

String ticket: A pricing ticket attached with a piece of string.

Supportive services: Free services offered to customers to increase convenience, make shopping easier, and entice customers to buy more.

Textile merchandise: Products made from natural or manmade fibers, including clothing, curtains, and bedding.

Trade credit: An open account with suppliers of goods and services.

Trade discount: A discount on the list price given by a manufacturer or wholesaler to a retailer.

Traffic driver: Marketing material that isn't a direct-response vehicle but rather serves to draw customers to a store.

Turnover: The number of times during a given period that the average inventory on hand is sold and replaced.

Undererr: A mistake that occurs when an employee enters an amount into the cash register that is less than the sales price.

Under-the-counter stock: Merchandise that is kept under the counter or in drawers rather than on open display, usually because the items are easily shoplifted.

Unit control: A buying method in which the buyer makes buying decisions based on inventory and sales records, rather than the cost of items purchased.

Universal product code (UPC): Bar code used for electronic entry.

Universal vendor marketing (UVM): Product code that appears as a series of numbers across the top of a price tag.

Unsought products: Products that consumers don't know about and aren't asking for.

Variety store: Focuses on low-cost stock merchandise, with a limited selection of low-cost furniture and appliances.

Visual merchandising: The art of implementing effective design ideas to increase store traffic and sales volume.

Warehouse club: A giant store that sells merchandise in bulk at low prices, and in which customers must buy a membership.

Warehouse reserve stock: Reserve stock that is stored in a warehouse, with only one example item on display in the store.

Wholesale: The sale of large quantities of goods to a retailer who will resell to the end-user.

Widget: An unnamed article or gadget used as a hypothetical example.

Word-of-mouth: It is the verbal recommendation and positive approval by a satisfied customer.

Index